THE ECONOMICS OF ORGANIZATION

ADVANCED TEXTBOOKS IN ECONOMICS

VOLUME 21

NORTH-HOLLAND PUBLISHING COMPANY
AMSTERDAM · NEW YORK · OXFORD

THE ECONOMICS OF ORGANIZATION

JAMES D. HESS
Claremont McKenna College, Claremont, California

1983

NORTH-HOLLAND PUBLISHING COMPANY
AMSTERDAM · NEW YORK · OXFORD

ISBN: 0444 86589 6

Publishers

NORTH-HOLLAND PUBLISHING COMPANY
AMSTERDAM · NEW YORK · OXFORD

Sole distributors for the U.S.A. and Canada

ELSEVIER SCIENCE PUBLISHING COMPANY, INC.
52 VANDERBILT AVENUE
NEW YORK, N.Y. 10017

PRINTED IN THE NETHERLANDS

INTRODUCTION TO THE SERIES

The aim of the series is to cover topics in economics, mathematical economics and econometrics, at a level suitable for graduate students or final year undergraduates specializing in economics. There is at any time much material that has become well established in journal papers and discussion series which still awaits a clear, self-contained treatment that can easily be mastered by students without considerable preparation or extra reading. Leading specialists will be invited to contribute volumes to fill such gaps. Primary emphasis will be placed on clarity, comprehensive coverage of sensibly defined areas, and insight into fundamentals, but original ideas will not be excluded. Certain volumes will therefore add to existing knowledge, while others will serve as a means of communicating both known and new ideas in a way that will inspire and attract students not already familiar with the subject matter concerned.

The Editors

ACKNOWLEDGEMENTS

I am deeply indebted to Kenneth Arrow. As the ideas for this book developed, it was his ear that was bent and his encouragement which pushed the project ahead. For several years we considered making this a collaborative effort, but since the initial draft came off my pen, it seemed appropriate that I go ahead and complete the manuscript. Ken may have difficulty recognizing the final product, for my selection of topics has changed dramatically over the last two years. Naturally all errors and stylistic difficulties are mine alone.

Jacob Marschak was an enthusiastic supporter of my work on organizations and his death was a deep loss to me. Many ideas found here can be traced to him. Roy Radner shaped my thinking on so many topics that it is hard to conceive of this book without his creative work. Ted Groves' exciting contributions on incentives was a major reason that I found the economics of organization so interesting. My colleague during my years at USC, Bob Kalaba, was a tremendous resource and I owe him more than I can ever repay.

Finally, the process of completing a significant project like this necessitates sensitive, considerate personal support which was provided in abundance by Frances and Courtney.

CONTENTS

CHAPTER 1

INTRODUCTION

Seldom does a day pass when we do not make a purchase in a market, whether it be at the corner newspaper stand, the cafeteria, or the gasoline service station. Much of our working lives are spent in organizations, such as business firms, government agencies, or non-profit institutions, carrying out the responsibilities associated with our positions, responding to our supervisor's requests to perform new tasks, and directing the activities of our subordinates. For many years economists have concentrated their investigations on the behavior of buyers and sellers in markets, leaving it to social psychologists and management scholars to investigate the internal functioning of organizations. It is the thesis of this book that economics' dedication to the market allocation of resources is an artificial and unsound view of social activity. The proper view should be that markets and organizations are alternative social inventions which can both guide economic decision-making. A study of either institution without comparison with its alternative leads to a biased judgement of that institution's merits. This point is often made by political economists who feel that reliance upon governmental organizations ignores the advantages of markets in dealing with many economic problems. The objective of this book is to study the strengths and weaknesses of organizations as private resource allocation institutions.

Markets and organizations are substitutes and the replacement of one by the other is a common event. A market displaces an organization when a travel agency replaces its ticket delivery person with a messenger service. An organization supplants a market when a firm begins photocopying its own circulars rather than paying for the services of a printer. Given the ease with which the economic system can flow from market to organization and back, it should be clear that there is a need for a framework for comparing the two institutions. Comparative economic systems is a branch of economic analysis but it traditionally investigates public changes in the form of the economic system, capitalism versus socialism, and leaves the private micro choice of institutions unexplored. This textbook examines a range of recent economic models which juxtapose market and organization and which consider their qualities as private institutions for allocating resources.

Comparison must be preceded by discrimination. A *market* is an assemblage of persons who want to arrange the exchange of property. An *organization* is a group of persons deliberately united to advance the interests of the group. The distinction between these institutions hangs on the term "united", for people use the market to further their own goals of rearranging the ownership of property and the members of an organization provide services and receive rewards, a form of property exchange. To unite, the persons must exchange promises to act in concert, but for such mutual promises to have value the promisors must anticipate sanctions for reneging. An organization might be thought of as a system of complicated "social" if not "legal" contracts between the participating parties. Since contracts are an integral feature of market exchange, the distinction between market and organization must lie in the form of the contract.

Consider the following situation. An individual, referred to as a coordinator, believes that there are desires for hand sewn leather slippers which are not currently being satisfied. Although the coordinator knows little about leather working he decides to enter this industry. He advertises that he would like artisans who can tan leather to process hides at a given payment per hide. The coordinator also contacts artisans who can cut and sew slippers to produce a finished slipper from leather he supplies. To minimize transportation the coordinator rents a building which the artisans can use. Finally, he arranges to sell the hand-sewn leather slippers to door-to-door salespersons for a specified number of dollars per slipper. The coordinator matches the number of hides with the number of slippers and buys hides to be delivered to his building. Production begins. The coordinator's only role at this point is as an accountant to keep track of the payment due to the workers.

Has the coordinator created an organization or a market? Is he an organizer or marketeer? The coordinator has constructed a slipper "factory", but he has only provided the workers with the plant, equipment, and materials and made no attempt to instruct, supervise, manage, or administer. His final role was only to verify that contracts were executed properly. The artisans and salespersons have acted as "independent contractors" who have agreed to transform one commodity into another but have not subordinated themselves to the coordinator, any more than he subordinated himself to the suppliers of hides and buildings. It will be argued below that there is no "united" organization in this example, yet this is the picture of the firm that corresponds to the standard economic model. Inputs of various kinds are hired, including different types of labor, and once contracts are struck the firm's only role is as a contract monitor.

The crux of the illustration is that the coordinator has not purchased the right to tell any person what actions should or should not be taken. All the actions are predetermined in the market. There has been no grant of *authority* by the artisans or salespersons. The leather tanners have used hides owned by the coordinator but they may work in their own fashion without interruption or guidance from anyone. The coordinator may be a capitalist employer but he is not a commander. The essence of an organization is presence of contracts where persons are "united" by an authoritarian relation. Some members of the group have been authorized to direct the activities of other members in order to further the goals of the group. Simon (1951) made the case that the employment relation between worker and boss is different from the relation between the seller and buyer of most property since the employer has purchased the right to change the worker's tasks ex post. The worker has not relinquished all rights to use his labor capability, but within broad limits he has authorized the employer to decide his activities for him.

This distinction is not universally recognized. Alchian and Demsetz (1972) argue that the relationship between a consumer and his grocer is not significantly different than that between employer and employee. They feel that authority is a deceptive concept because the employee always has the option of quitting if the management requires labor which is unacceptable. In this respect they have a point since courts generally will not enforce specific performance of a personal service contract, feeling that this conflicts with constitutional safeguards against involuntary servitude. However, they push the argument too far when they deny the existence of voluntarily granted authority. The worker often accepts legitimate orders from the employer to perform tasks which are unpleasant but still within the definition of the job requirements. The construction worker responds to his foreman's order to unload the truck even though he would rather measure and cut lumber. One of the aims of this textbook is to develop those reasons why workers choose to accept employment in authoritarian organizations.

Authority exists when a subordinate has agreed to an open-ended employment contract allowing the superior to adjust the tasks performed to best suit the evolving circumstances. The authoritarian contract is not the only possible form of an employment contract. Alternatively, the parties could enumerate all the possible circumstances beforehand and negotiate an acceptable work assignment for each contingency. If the worker does not like performing one particular task, he may refuse to accept such a contractual clause or accept it only for additional compensation. Such a "contingency" contract eliminates authority. The employer's role changes from a director to a monitor, because he has no right to ask the worker to perform a task which is not already specifically assigned to the observed circumstance.

Detailed contingency contracts are not generally used to arrange employment. Contrary to Alchian and Demsetz's view, neither are contracts which call for a renegotiation of the work assignment as new circumstances develop. Coase (1937) observed that this replacement of market exchanges by organization is economical because there are significant costs involved in negotiating and enforcing such contracts. The nature of the firm, in Coase's view, is the replacement of markets by organizations due to significant *transaction costs* associated with the markets. A large portion of this book is an extended analysis of those factors which make the market a relatively costly institution for arranging work compared with authoritarian organizations.

The major sources of labor market transaction difficulties are uncertainty and informational asymmetries. If the world was certain to evolve in only one pattern, the coordination of activities would easily be standardized. However, the environment is a whirlwind of unpredictable events – rain falls out of season, machine parts break without warning, and flu epidemics incapacitate the work force. These uncertainties create a multitude of contingencies and therefore the negotiation of complicated contractual plans for handling each possibility becomes very costly. Even if such contracts were economical to construct, natural informational asymmetries make the enforcement of the planned responses difficult. The worker might for example find it very hard to verify if a machine on the far side of the plant has malfunctioned and would be unable to assure that the employer has stated the true situation.

Authority is not always placed in the hands of the employer. Workers are given the responsibility of making decisions on behalf of the employer when information availability and experience dictate that the worker can make more effective choices. The salesperson in the field is in a better position to evaluate what discounts and service commitments are opportune to guarantee a sale. The relationship between employer and worker in such circumstances is called the principal–agent relationship. The design of reward systems to guide the agent toward choices in the interest of the principal are discussed in a separate chapter.

While organizations have a comparative advantage in situations where uncertainty is large and informational difficulties exist, the construction and operation of organizations is costly. In a group of individuals with differing needs and desires the goals of the group which provide direction for individual activities do not spontaneously appear. The amalgamation of individual beliefs and tastes into a coherent pattern of goals requires a governance system within the organization. Arrow's (1951) study of the relationship between individual and social choice provides a framework for investigating the difficulties which organizations may face in choosing a formal governance system.

Once a governance system for the organization is in place the effectiveness of the system may be undermined by participants who want to manipulate the groups goals and activities to suit their personal desires. The detection and elimination of deception and malfeasance is particularly difficult because of the uncertainties and informational asymmetries which give the organization its advantage over markets. The design of incentive and control systems is perhaps the most challenging aspect of organization.

The design of economic organizations faces other difficulties in addition to governance and control. The organization has the ability to capture returns to specialization in informational acquisition but this requires that many individuals resolve small uncertainties in their particular work areas. The elimination of uncertainty can be very valuable by improving the organization's response to variations in its environment, but the efficient use of information in coordinating activities often demands complicated communication systems within the group. The evaluation of communication systems is a central topic of several chapters in this book.

CHAPTER 2

THE GENERAL RESOURCE ALLOCATION PROBLEM

A theory of resource allocation is built in two stages. In the first the conscious, deliberate, purposeful choices of individuals is studied to provide a model for human behavior in the economic realm. In the second a theory of exchange, coordination, and equilibrium must be developed to explain social interlinkages. Economics has found it most useful to examine these aspects in the context of a competitive market system where all property is bought and sold at a price. It is clear that markets are not the only organizations which help arrange the allocation of resources. The internal workings of corporations, families, recreational clubs, government bureaus, judicial systems, and legislative bodies provide examples of non-market systems of resource allocation. Some goods and services are not available for purchase but may be obtained by participation in organizations. Examples might be bargaining services which are obtained only by membership in a union or job skills which can only be obtained by working for a particular firm. Other goods and services may be obtained in both markets and organizations. Automobile repairs might be available from other members of an antique car club as well as from a mechanic-for-hire. Since the system used to allocate resources is the object of investigation, the problem of allocation will be presented here with as few assumptions as possible so as to provide an unbiased frame of reference.

Our definition of the resource allocation problem begins by describing the environment facing the economy. The environment will include the list of commodities, the names of all individuals in the society, the tastes, technology, and endowment of each individual, and the physical or legal restrictions on individual choices.

It is important to be specific about the commodities that are involved in the economic problem. A commodity is any distinguishable service or object of desire or necessity. The list of commodities may be much more extensive than commonly understood because commodities can be distinguished by their physical characteristics: quality, date of availability, location of availability, the natural circumstances of availability, or even the property rights associated with it. An example of an "object" commodity is a pair of size five, women's white tennis shoes, available in Miami, in the sixteenth week of the year, if there is no hurricane, and with the right to use, alter, or sell at will. A change in any one or more of these features will mean that a different commodity is defined. If the shoes are in St. Louis, or available a week later or when there is a hurricane or without the right to alter or sell, the shoes are viewed just as different from the original object as if they were black, size ten, men's sandals. An example of a "service" commodity is the labor of a Ph.D. chemical engineer in redesigning an ammonia production plant, available in Houston next month if the chemical factory is malfunctioning, with the right to use but not to alter or transfer to another individual. As above any distinguishing characteristic is just as important as any other. Changing this job description to include writing a report on the old production system if the employer so desires is just as significant as changing the location to Frankfurt. Similarly, giving the employer the right to transfer the engineer to a different employer may be an important modification in the specification of the service, making it more desirable to the employer and less so to the engineer.

The list of commodities is assumed to be extensive. Every conceivable commodity is included in the list, so there may be many thousands of different types of human labor as well as numerous machines, tools, food items, and other types of commodities. The catalog of commodities may include many objects and services which typically are not available for sale in the markets we commonly observe. Workers, for example, may view bagging groceries as much less desirable than operating a cash register, yet there may not be separate markets for two such labor services. The existence of a market is not to be taken as a sine qua non for commodities. The existence of markets should be derived from the characteristics of the economy rather than required ex ante.

The commodities will be numbered from 1 to ℓ and indexed by an integer $h \in L = \{1, 2, ..., \ell\}$. The quantity of each commodity h is given by a real number, x_h. A *commodity plan* is a sequence of ℓ real numbers, $x = (x_1, ..., x_h, ..., x_\ell)$, written as a column vector, where x_h is the quantity of the hth commodity. It is assumed that each commodity is measurable and infinitesimally divisible, an element of the Euclidian space $\mathbb{R}$. A commodity plan may involve both inputs and outputs. The distinction is handled by a sign convention; commodities acquired and used by an economic actor are given positive quantities while those relinquished and not used are given negative signs.

The economic actors are human beings. It is traditional to add fictitious legal individuals called firms to the list of economic actors, but since these are in fact just complicated contractual arrangements of human beings, the existence of a firm should be endogenous just as the existence of a market. The human actors in our economy are assumed to be identifiable by a numerical index i which takes on values in the list of names of economic actors N. For simplicity it will be assumed that $N = \{1, 2, ..., n\}$.

The economic activity of the society is specified by listing the flow of commodities from one actor to another. The commodity plan $a^{ij} \in \mathbb{R}^{\ell}$ denotes the flow of commodities to individual i from individual j, where $i \in N$, $j \in N$, $i \neq j$. (Superscripts denote names; subscripts denote commodities.) The commodity plan $a^{ii} \in \mathbb{R}^{\ell}$ will denote the production activity of the individual $i \in N$. To conveniently summarize the economic activity these flows are placed in a *commodity-flow matrix*:

$$a = \begin{bmatrix} a^{11} & a^{12} & \dots & a^{1n} \\ a^{21} & a^{22} & \dots & a^{2n} \\ \cdot & & & , \\ \cdot & & & \cdot \\ \cdot & & & \cdot \\ a^{n1} & a^{n2} & \dots & a^{nn} \end{bmatrix},$$

where $a \in \mathbb{R}^{\ell \cdot n^2}$. (Hurwicz, 1960, puts production in a separate row-column, whereas it is put on the diagonal of a here.) For example, an economy with two goods, corn and wheat, $h = 1, 2$, respectively, and labor, $h = 3$, with two individuals, John and Wendy, $i = 1, 2$, respectively, in which John produces one bushel of corn from a unit of labor and trades half of this to Wendy for a third of the two bushels of wheat produced by Wendy with a unit of labor, has a commodity flow matrix:

$$a = \begin{bmatrix} \begin{bmatrix} 1 \\ 0 \\ -1 \end{bmatrix} & \begin{bmatrix} 0 \\ \frac{2}{3} \\ 0 \end{bmatrix} \\ \\ \begin{bmatrix} \frac{1}{2} \\ 0 \\ 0 \end{bmatrix} & \begin{bmatrix} 0 \\ 2 \\ -1 \end{bmatrix} \end{bmatrix}.$$

Not all commodity flow matrices are sufficient to supply the biological necessities of the individuals in N. Moreover, not all commodity flows are permissible within the legal context of the society. For example, Wendy may require at least one bushel of corn or wheat to provide nutrition for her survival. In the above matrix her net consumption of wheat is 4/3, enough for her survival. If corn were a forbidden crop, then the above commodity-flow matrix would be illegal since John has produced corn. A matrix which is sufficient for her survival and which is legal is called an *admissible resource flow.* The collection of all admissible commodity flow matrices is denoted $\mathscr{A}$.

It is assumed that each individual naturally possesses an *endowment* of commodities, denoted by a commodity flow matrix with the endowment of individual placed in the ith row and ith column and zero vectors elsewhere:

$$\omega = \begin{bmatrix} \omega^1 & 0 & \dots & 0 \\ 0 & \omega^2 & \dots & 0 \\ \vdots & & & \\ 0 & 0 \dots \omega^i \dots 0 & & \\ \vdots & & & \\ 0 & 0 & \dots & \omega^n \end{bmatrix}.$$

The ith individual possesses the endowment ω^i but this does not imply that he has the legal right to use these resources as he sees fit. The property rights may not allow him to use, destroy, or transfer these commodities. Although individuals come into possession of their own labor power, they may be obligated to donate some of this to the military (or some other organization) in a time of emergency.

Individuals are presumed to have preferences which rank the aggregate commodity-flow matrices, $a + \omega$, in terms of their relative desirability. When $a + \omega$ is at least as desirable as $a' + \omega$, this is denoted

$$a + \omega \succsim_i a' + \omega.$$

The preferences are taken as given; it may be true that the consumption of a television advertisement influences the ranking of other commodities, but such interdependencies are assumed to be captured by the extensive list of commodities, including advertisements. The preferences of actor i provide a binary relation on the set of commodity-flow matrices $\mathscr{A}$. Notice that individuals may care about the source and destination of commodities which they handle: preferences may not be anonymous. Moreover, individuals may be selfish or altruistic: the relative desirability of a commodity-flow matrix may depend on elements which do not directly impact an individual. The sequence of preferences $(\succsim_1, \succsim_2, \ldots, \succsim_n)$ is the economy's preference profile.

Economic actors possess knowledge about the productive transformation of some commodities into different commodities. The technological know-how of individual i consists of a collection Z^i of commodity plans, negative elements corresponding to inputs and positive elements to outputs. The possession of technological knowledge should conceptually be divorced from the access to resources needed to carry out the productive activities. The above specification implicitly assumes that the production capabilities of an individual is independent of the consumption and production of other agents. Such external effects could be incorporated by assuming that the technology set depends on the resource flow matrix (except the ith diagonal element). That is, $Z^i = Z^i(a)$, where $Z^i(a) = Z^i(a')$ if $a^{jk} = a'^{jk}$, except for $j = k = i$. This dependence is interpreted as follows. The ith individual can produce any consumption plan in $Z^i(a)$ if the other actors' activities are those given in the commodity-flow matrix.

The *economic environment* with which society is confronted consists of the following components:

$$e = (L, N, (Z^i, \succsim_i, \omega^i)_{i \in N}, \mathscr{A}),$$

the list of commodities, the names of the individuals, for each individual their technological knowledge, preferences and endowment, the set of admissible commodity-flow matrices. The economic activity of the society is given by the commodity-flow matrix a. The economic system by which a commodity-flow matrix is determined from a particular economic environment is a *choice system* which maps the set of all possible environments into the collection of all subsets of $\mathbb{R}^{\ell \cdot n^2}$:

$$\beta(e) = A \subseteq \mathbb{R}^{\ell \cdot n^2}.$$

The set of commodity-flow matrices A is all the economic activities that the choice system might produce if the economic environment is e. This leaves open for the time being the question of the uniqueness of the outcome of the choice system.

There are many examples of economic systems which have been or are used to arrange the allocation of resources. It would be a task well beyond the scope of this study to describe and model any moderate menu of such choice mechanisms. Rather, there will be an attempt to compare a competitive market mechanism, modelled in the traditional microeconomic fashion, with mechanisms which involve authority and command control. The emphasis will not be on global systems of resource allocation but on private localized modifications of the market including hierarchical business enterprise, agency relations, partnerships, employment contracts, and participatory labor-managed enterprises.

While there will not be an attempt at cataloguing many choice systems, it might be useful to describe in a simplified manner several choice systems which might provide alternative procedures to choose allocation of resources. The market mechanism will be discussed at length in the following chapter, so let us consider some alternatives. The simplest choice system is a dictatorship. The dictator may face some legal restrictions on his choices but is otherwise free to choose that commodity-flow matrix, including the activities of all individuals, according to his tastes alone:

$$\beta^1(e) = \Big\{ a \in \mathscr{A} \mid \text{ for all } i \in N, a^{ii} \in Z^i,$$
$$\sum_{i \in N} \Big(\sum_{j \in N} (a^{ij} - a^{ji}) + a^{ij} + \omega^i \Big) = 0,$$
$$\text{and for all } a^* \in \mathscr{A} \text{ which satisfy the above,}$$
$$\text{it is true that } a \succsim_1 a^* \Big\}.$$

Moving to the other extreme, one might contrast the dictatorship with a consensus mechanism which requires approval by all individuals before a commodity-flow matrix is chosen:

$$\beta^2(e) = \Big\{ a \in \mathscr{A} \mid \text{ for all } i \in N, a^{ii} \in Z^i,$$
$$\sum_{i \in N} \Big(\sum_{j \in N} (a^{ij} - a^{ji}) + a^{ii} + \omega^i \Big) = 0,$$
$$\text{and for all } a^* \in \mathscr{A} \text{ which satisfy the above,}$$
$$\text{it is true that } a \succsim_i a^*, \text{ for all } i \in N \Big\}.$$

Naturally one might expect that a consensus is almost impossible to find, and an intermediate system such as majority voting might be more decisive:

$$\beta^3(e) = \Big\{ a \in \mathscr{A} \mid \text{ for all } i \in N, a^{ii} \in Z^i,$$
$$\sum_{i \in N} \Big(\sum_{j \in N} (a^{ij} - a^{ji}) + a^{ii} + \omega^i \Big) = 0,$$

$$\text{and for all } a^* \in \mathscr{A} \text{ which satisfy the above,}$$

$$\left.\text{it is true that } \sum_{i \in \{i \mid a \succsim_i a^*\}} 1 \geqslant \sum_{i \in \{i \mid a^* \succsim_i a\}} 1 \right\}.$$

A commodity flow is chosen according to β^3 if a majority of individuals prefer it to all other possible commodity flows.

Communal production and distribution forms the basis of the following more complicated choice system. Suppose that there exist m communes which organize production and allocation of goods among members. The members must contribute inputs in a prorated basis according to their share of participation and will receive the fruits of the production in a similar share. For simplicity it will be assumed that no trade takes place between individuals. The participation share of individual i in commune k is denoted θ_{ik}, these shares being non-negative numbers which sum to one for each commune. It is convenient to consider the commune as a person, a legal fiction, so that there are $n + m$ persons in the economy, the first n names corresponding to individuals and the remaining m names corresponding to communes:

$$\beta^4(e) = \Big\{ a \in \mathscr{A} \mid \ (1)\ a^{ij} = 0 \text{ if}[i \leqslant n \text{ and } j \leqslant n] \text{ or } [i > n \text{ and } j > n], i \neq j;$$

$$(2) \text{ for each } k > n,$$

$$a^{kk} \in Z^k \equiv \bigcup_{\{i \mid \theta_{ik} > 0\}} Z^i;$$

$$(3)\ a^{ik} = \theta_{ik} a^{kk\oplus}, a^{ki} = \theta_{ik}\, \omega^i \Big/ \Big(\sum_j \theta_{ij}\Big), i \leqslant n, k > n;$$

$$(4)\ a^{kk\ominus} + \sum_{i=1}^{n} a^{ki} = 0, k > n;$$

$$(5) \text{ for all } a^* \in \mathscr{A} \text{ satisfying (1) -- (4), for each } k > n,$$

$$\left.\sum_{i \in \{i \mid a \succsim_i a^*\}} \theta_{ik} \geqslant \sum_{i \in \{i \mid a^* \succsim_i a\}} \theta_{ik} \right\},$$

where $a^{kk\oplus} \equiv (\max\,[a_1^{kk}, 0], ..., \max\,[a_\ell^{kk}, 0])$ and $a^{kk\ominus} \equiv (\min[a_1^{kk}, 0], ..., \min[a_\ell^{kk}, 0])$. Condition (1) states that individuals do not exchange commodities with other individuals and communes do not trade with communes. Condition (2) implies that the technological knowledge of the commune comes from active participants. According to condition (3) the output produced is sent to participants in proportion to their share in the commune, but the commune members are responsible for dividing their endowment among communes in proportion to relative shares for use as input. Condition (4) guarantees that the commune believes there are enough resources to stoke the production process.

Finally, the voting on alternative commodity flows is based on participation shares and each commune must approve the final matrix according to condition (5).

The study of choice mechanisms requires a set of criteria by which we can judge the mechanisms themselves. The following list provides some of the criteria which economists have used. Naturally some limitation on the domain of economic environment should be included in the criteria. In the following we will take the set of potential economic environments to be an arbitrary set E.

A. A choice mechanism *preserves feasibility* on E if for all $a \in \beta(e)$, $e \in E$, the production activity is technologically feasible for each individual. That is,

$$a^{ii} \in Z^i, \qquad i \in N.$$

B. A choice mechanism *preserves admissibility* on E if for all $a \in \beta\,(e)$, $e \in E$, the commodity flow permits the survival of all agents and is within the legal realm of activities. That is,

$$a \in \mathscr{A}.$$

C. A choice mechanism is *consistent* on E if for all $a \in \beta(\mathrm{e})$, $e \in E$, this commodity flow provides material balance. That is,

$$\sum_{i \in N} \left(a^{ii} + \sum_{j \in N} (a^{ij} - a^{ji}) \right) + \sum_{i \in N} \omega^i = 0.$$

D. A choice mechanism is *non-wasteful* on E if all commodity-flow matrices $a \in \beta(e)$, $e \in E$, are efficient in e. That is, a is feasible, admissible and consistent on e and there is no other feasible, admissible, and consistent matrix a' on e such that

$$a' \succsim_i a, \qquad i \in N \text{ and } a' \succsim_k a \text{ for some } k \in N.$$

E. A choice mechanism is *decisive* on E if for all $e \in E$ there is an efficient commodity-flow matrix in e, then $\beta(e)$ is not empty.

F. A choice mechanism is *essentially single valued* on E if for all $e \in E$, $a \in \beta(e)$, $a' \in \beta(e)$, $a \neq a'$, then a is viewed as indifferent to a' by all actors. That is,

$$a \sim_i a', \quad \text{for all } i \in N.$$

G. A choice mechanism is *unbiased* on E when for each $e \in E$ if a is efficient in e, then by changing only the endowment a can be achieved by the mechanism. That is, there exists some $(\omega^{i*})_{i \in N}$ such that $\Sigma_{i \in N} \omega^{i*} = \Sigma_{i \in N} \omega^{i}$, and such that

$$a \in \beta((L, N, (Z^i, \succsim_i, \omega^{i*})_{i \in N}, \mathscr{A})).$$

H. A choice mechanism is *core-selecting* on E when for each $e \in E$ if $a \in \beta(e)$, then there is no coalition $C \subseteq N$ and commodity flow a' such that $a^{ii'} \in Z^i$, $i \in C$, $a' \in \mathscr{A}$, $\Sigma_{i \in C}(a^{ii} + \Sigma_{j \in C}(a^{ij} - a^{ii}) + \omega^i) = 0$, $a' \succsim_i a$ for all $i \in C$ and $a' \succsim_i a$ for some $i \in C$. That is, if a is an outcome, no coalition could form, isolate itself from the rest of society, and improve upon the commodity flow a.

I. A choice mechanism is *individually-incentive compatible* on E when for all $e \in E$, $a \in \beta(e)$ there is no individual $k \in N$ such that the environment appears to be

$$e^* = (L, N, (Z^i, \succsim_i, \omega^i)_{\substack{i \in N,\\ i \neq k}}, (Z^{k*}, \succsim_k^*, \omega^{k*}_*), \mathscr{A}),$$

where $Z^{k*} \subset Z^k$, $\succsim_{k*}$ is a complete, reflexive, transitive ordering on $\mathscr{A}$ and $\omega^{k*} \leqslant \omega^k$, then for all $a^* \in \beta(e^*)$, $a^* \succ_k a$. That is, no individual can misrepresent his technology by understating his capabilities, or misrepresent his tastes or underreport his endowment so that the outcome is preferred to the outcome with honest representation.

J. A choice mechanism is *anonymous* in E if the labels of the ith and jth individuals are switched in the environment, then the ith row and column of the new commodity-flow matrix equals the jth row and column of the original matrix and vice versa. That is, if $a \in \beta(e)$, then there exists an $a' \in \beta((L, N, (Z^k, \succsim_k, \omega^k)_{k \in N, k \neq i,j}, (Z^i, \succsim_i, \omega^i)_{k=j}, (Z^i, \succsim_j, \omega^j)_{k=i}, \mathscr{A}))$, such that $a^{kt} = a^{kt'}$ if $k, t \notin \{i, j\}$ and $a^{ik} = a^{jk\langle}$, $a^{jk} = a^{ik'}$, $k \notin \{i, j\}$.

K. A choice mechanism is *independent of irrelevant alternatives* in E if when $e \in E$ and $e' \in E$ differ only on the relative desirability of a commodity flow matrix a which is not feasible, admissible, and consistent, then $\beta(e) = \beta(e')$.

L. A choice mechanism is *non-dictatorial* in E if there is no actor $i \in N$ such that if a and a' are feasible, admissible, and consistent commodity flows and

$a \succ_i a'$, then $a' \notin \beta(e)$. That is, there is no individual who has dictatorial powers over the commodity flow.

This list is not meant to be complete. There are many additional properties of the mechanism which pertain to the international workings of the mechanism which cannot be expressed via the mapping β. For example, if a choice mechanism involves internal communication prior to determination of the final allocation one might want to evaluate the difficulty of the language used by the mechanism or how much information an individual must reveal about himself in the communication.

CHAPTER 3

MARKET ALLOCATION

When economists speak of the allocation of resources what they mean is the distribution of property among economic participants. The common usage of the word "property" to refer to the good itself has sometimes led to misunderstandings of the concept, for property is the exclusive right to control a thing. Property is a right, which implies that property is fundamentally a relationship between humans, not a relationship between human and thing. In order to understand the economic relations of individuals and groups one must know the conditions which define property in the society. Clearly the exact specification of the rights to control things have varied with different things, different cultures, and different times. For example, only in recent centuries has the right to own other human beings disappeared in Western cultures. In many countries a person has the right to own certain types of drugs, such as distilled alcoholic beverages, but no rights to control other types of drugs, such as opium, cocaine, or marijuana. In some primitive societies individuals cannot control major resources used in production, such as hunting grounds or machinery.

Property may exist even when the state and its legal system are not available to define and enforce the rights. When individuals recognize certain privileges of one human to control a particular object then property is defined. In the early part of the nineteenth century western adventurers trapped beaver in the Rocky Mountains of the United States, outside the range of government and the legal system, yet property rights to traps and locations were respected by other men. Nonetheless, the ability to control commodities and enforce rights often is only effective when the sanctions which the legal system provides are manifest. For property to be valuable it must be relatively inexpensive to protect.

Property rights are exclusive, meaning that no two individuals simultaneously have the right to control the same article. This does not imply that the rights are unlimited, for when it gives its members rights, society also restricts the range of activity. One individual may own an automobile and another may own a grassy yard, but the right of control of the automobile does not include the privilege of leaving tread marks across the neighbor's yard, since this violates the right of the neighbor to have a well-manicured, grassy yard. Property is a reciprocal relationship between individuals.

Complete ownership rights to an object allow an individual to (1) use the object in any manner within the boundary of the rights of others, (2) enjoy all the advantages which can be obtained from the object without damaging it (usufruct), (3) change the object in form or substance, (4) transfer usufruct to others by rental, and (5) sell all the ownership to another human.

Some objects cannot be completely owned by this definition. Modern law prevents a person from selling himself to another, even if this is a fully rational action for that person. Although a mother's children are starving and the only offer of employment is lifetime servitude, she cannot purchase life for the children by alienating herself. Real property is subject to the states' right of imminent domain and the owner may be forced to sell the property for the benefit to the whole society.

Usufruct is an incomplete property right. A person who owns the rights to use a piece of land during his lifetime, does not own the right to abuse the land; the law of real property places many limitations on such waste of real property. If an individual has borrowed or leased a machine from the owner, the borrower may use the machine anyway he desires as long as the machine is not damaged. An employer may have the right to determine the details of a laborer's daily tasks as long as he does not put the laborer in a hazardous situation.

Exchange is the transfer of property from one individual to another. This is a statement about rights of control not about objects, so perhaps it would be clearer if we defined exchange as the transfer of the right to control a good or service. If a buyer does not gain the socially or legally sanctioned right to use, change, or transfer the object as he deems desirable, what value does the commodity have? When a buyer is given control of a piece of land by another, control implies that he can prevent other people from trespassing on the land. Land is valueless to a new owner who wants to farm the land but cannot prevent theft of the crop or collect suitable compensation for damages caused by trespass.

A great deal of economic activity involves the turnover or transfer of physical possession from on individual to another. When a moving van delivers an object from one loading dock to another, a transfer takes place. This is a production activity, not an exchange activity, since the rights to the object may have been transferred months or years earlier by a mutual agreement. That is, exchange may have occurred long before turnover.

Many exchanges take place with the aid of a contract: a promise made by one person to another which is enforceable by law. Some exchanges involve a simultaneous turnover of commodities between two people and do not involve a contract. Whenever the turnover by one or the other person is not instantaneous, so that there may be future difficulties of an individual controlling his new commodity, exchange involves only a promise to relinquish property. A contract naturally requires the mutual assent of the two or more parties participating in the exchange but a contract involves more than mutual assent; the mutual promise must be legally enforceable. The law of contracts is a collection of rules which specifies for a particular culture the exact conditions defining the existence of contracts, what the promises actually mean in terms of performance, what constitutes a breach of the contract, and what compensation is due to the party which has been injured by such a breach of contract. Enforcement of a contract does not literally mean that agreement must be carried out, but only that compensation must be paid for broken promises.

A market is an institution which specializes in the arrangement of contractual exchanges of standardized property. A crucial postulate in the theory of markets is that every commodity can be bought or sold at a price. For this reason the price system is a dual concept of the commodity space. To each commodity h corresponds a real number called the price; the collection of all prices is the *price vector*:

$$P = (p_1, p_2, p_3, \ldots, p_\ell).$$

The inner product of a commodity plan and a price vector defines the market value of the commodity plan:

$$\text{value}(x) = Px = \sum_{h=1}^{\ell} p_h x_h .$$

The assumption that each commodity has its price is not a trivial one. In fact many commodities do not have a price, an obvious example being air free of nitrous oxide. There is no single price which agents may use to evaluate the quantity of nitrous oxide-free air they use or produce, so the market for pollution-free air fails to exist. Certain skills of organization which are commonly referred to as entrepreneurial activities are not marketed. One can hire managers who can administer a given enterprise but this is not the same type of service provided by the individual who organizes the enterprise itself. Many distinct labor services are not marketed even though individuals find them to be distinctly different. Teachers are paid a salary for a collection of services, from verbal exposition to examination construction or curriculum development. There is no separate market for exam preparation. It is not always possible to exchange money today for the right of ownership of some object many time periods in the future. There is no market in which you can buy a loaf of bread to be delivered in five months. While the assumption of complete markets is unrealistic, in this chapter we will summarize the competitive market choice mechanism in a complete general market system. In this and succeeding chapters reasons will be introduced for a less complete market system.

The competitive market system is based on the private ownership of property. Individuals own all commodities. Production may take place in enterprises which are treated legally as persons but such firms are completely owned by the human actors. A firm which produces valuable commodities sells these to generate profit to be distributed among the owners as dividends. From these dividends and from the sale of endowments, the individuals derive income which is used to finance the purchase of final consumption goods. The prices determined in the markets play a role as balancing instruments, adjusting until the supply of commodities forthcoming from sellers exactly matches the demand for commodities of the buyers.

For simplicity the role of an individual as a consumer is separated from his role as fount of technological knowledge. It would be realistic to assume that a person can not only consume the cooling services of a refrigerator, he can transform a refrigerator today into a refrigerator tommorow. To focus on one problem at a time, such an individual is thought to have two roles. In one role he is a (proprietary) firm interested in profit, while in the other the individual is a consumer of goods and services. All production will be assumed to take place in a firm, although this may just be a formal way of treating such activities as the simultaneous use and storage of a refrigerator.

Let $M = \{1, 2 \ldots, m\}$ be a list of firms. Firms are characterized by the collection of commodity plans which they believe to be technologically feasible and their ownership profile. Let $Y \subseteq \mathbb{R}^{\ell \cdot m}$ be the collection of all technologically possible commodity plans for the group of firms, M. The projection of Y onto the jth m-tuple is denoted Y^j and called the jth firm's technology set. The ownership profile of firm j is an n-vector of ownership shares $(\theta_{1j}, \theta_{2j}, \ldots, \theta_{nj})$, where θ_{ij} is the fractional share of firm j owned by human i. Each individual can own at most 100 percent of a firm and at least 0 percent, and all shares are owned by the group of consumers:

$$0 \leqslant \theta_{ij} \leqslant 1, \quad i \in N, \; j \in M$$

and

$$\sum_{i \in N} \theta_{ij} = 1, \quad j \in M.$$

The source of firms' technological knowledge is usually unspecified in the competitive market mechanism. However, if firms are recognized as fictitious actors, then one might presume that the firm's knowledge is derived from the knowledge of owners. One possibility is

$$Y^j = \bigcup_{\substack{i \in N \\ \theta_{ij} > 0}} Z^i .$$

This says that all individuals who own a part of an enterprise contribute all their technological knowledge to that firm.

Individual consumers are characterized by their tastes, endowments, consumption possibilities, and ownership shares of firms. Some restrictions on these characteristics are traditionally made in the theory of markets. A classical assumption about preferences is that individuals care only about the final net commodity plan that they consume and are indifferent to the source of this consumption plans of others. If a is a commodity-flow matrix (see Chapter 2 for a definition) then the corresponding net consumption plan of actor i is

$$x^i = \sum_{j \in N} (a^{ij} - a^{ji}) + a^{ii} + \omega^i ,$$

where $a^{ij} - a^{ji}$ is the net flow of commodities to i from j and a^{ij} is the commodity plan obtained from production and ω^i is the endowment. A consumer i has a binary preference ordering, $\succsim_i^*$, defined on final consumption plans. The classical ordering over net consumption plans implies an ordering on commodity flows as follows:

$$a + \omega \succsim_i a' + \omega, \quad \text{if and only if } x^i \succsim_i^* x^{i'} .$$

It is sometimes useful to represent tastes by an ordinal utility function, $U^i(x^i)$, which numerically ranks consumption plans. Changing an element of a commodity-flow matrix outside the ith row or ith column leaves actor i unaffected. Similarly, adding a consumption plan x to element a^{ij} and subtracting it from a^{ik} does not change the net flow and, under the classical assumption, does not influence the ith consumer.

The set of commodity flows which permits the individual consumer to survive also is restricted in the classical environment. To each actor i is associated a survival set $X^i \subseteq \mathbb{R}^\ell$ which is independent of the tastes, endowments, or activities of any actor, including himself. If actor i has a net commodity plan x^i which belongs to X^i then he can survive. This implies that the admissible commodity-flow matrices are of the form:

$$\mathscr{A} = \left\{ a \in \mathbb{R}^{\ell n^2} \,\middle|\, \left(\sum_{j\in N} (a^{ij} - a^{ji}) + a^{ii} + \omega^1, \ldots, \sum_{j\in N} (a^{nj} - a^{jn}) + a^{nn} + \omega^n \right) \in X^1 \times \ldots \times X^n \right\}.$$

The consumer has complete ownership rights to his endowment, ω^i, as discussed above. The firms are also owned by consumers, which means that consumers are given a fractional share of the profits of firms which they own, but not the right to select the activity of the firm. The firm is chartered to select outputs to maximize the aggregate market value of its production activity. When markets are complete, as is assumed here, this objective is the unanimous objective of the owners.

A competitive equilibrium is defined to be a price vector, P^*, a commodity plan for each consumer, $(x^{i*})_{i\in N}$, and a commodity plan for each firm, $(y^{j*})_{j\in M}$, such that

(1) profit is maximized for each firm at those prices: $P^*y^{j*} \geqslant P^*y^j$ for all $y^j \in Y^j, j \in N$;

(2) happiness is maximized for each individual subject to budget and survival restrictions: x^{i*} is optimal with respect to $\succsim_i^*$ on the set of x^i such that $x^i \in X^i$ and

$$P^*x^i \leqslant \sum_{j\in M} \theta_{ij} P^*y^{j*} + P^*\omega^i;$$

(3) supply equals demand:

$$\sum_{i\in N} x^i = \sum_{i\in N} \omega^i + \sum_{j\in M} y^j.$$

In competitive markets all persons take the price as a given parameter but the price in fact will adjust to equalize supply and demand.

The competitive market system can be formulated as a choice system in the framework of the previous chapter. The outcome of an economy in a classical environment e is:

$$\beta(e) = \Big\{ a \in \mathbb{R}^{\ell n^2} \mid \text{for some price vector } P \in \mathbb{R}^{\ell}_{\oplus} \text{ there exists}$$

$(y^1, \ldots, y^m) \in Y^1 \times \ldots \times Y^m$ such that:

(a) $Py^j \geqslant Py^j$ for all $y^i \in Y^i$, $\quad j \in M$;

(b) $a^{ii} = \sum_{j\in M} \theta_{ij} y^j$, $\quad i \in N$;

(c) (1) $\sum_{k \in N} (a^{ik} - a^{ki}) + a^{ii} + \omega^i \in X^i, \quad i \in N;$

(2) $P\left(\sum_{k \in N} (a^{ik} - a^{ki})\right) \leqslant 0, \quad i \in N;$

(3) $a \succsim_i a^*$ for all $a \in \mathbb{R}^{\ell n^2}$ such that:

$a^{ii*} = a^{ii}, \quad i \in N,$

$a^{jk*} = a^{jk}$, for $j \neq i$ and $k \neq i$, and which satisfy (c1) and (c2) with a replaced by a^*, $\quad i \in N;$

(d) $\sum_{i \in N} \left(\sum_{k \in N} (a^{ik} - a^{ki}) + a^{ii} + \omega^i\right) = 0 \Big\}.$

Condition (a) is profit-maximization criteria. Condition (b) states that the diagonal element a^{ii} is given by the shares of firms' productive activity which is assigned to actor i. Condition (c1) says that the net consumption of each actor permits survival. The budget constraint of each actor is given by (c2) in the form that the value of goods acquired cannot exceed the value of goods given up. Condition (c3) is the preference optimization subject to fixed production-endowment demand and constraints (c1) and (c2). Finally, condition (d) states that material balance occurs for each commodity. The set $\beta(e)$ is generated by collecting all flow matrices which produce a competitive market equilibrium in this economic environment for some price vector.

The competitive market mechanism has many desirable characteristics. We will outline below the environments which guarantee that the market mechanism has those properties discussed in Chapter 2, beginning with the condition of decisiveness. What conditions on tastes, technology, and survival assure that there always exists a competitive market equilibrium? First, it is assumed that there are no external effects. The commodity plans which are technologically feasible for a firm must be independent of the production activities of the other firms or consumption activities of the human actors. The consumption plans which permit a human actor to survive should be independent of the activities of firms or other human actors. Formally, this says that the set of possible productions for the firms and consumptions for the individuals can be written as

$$Y^1 \times Y^2 \times \ldots \times Y^m \times X^1 \times X^2 \times \ldots \times X^n.$$

Such an economy is decomposable into the independent sets Y^j and X^i.

Second, it is assumed that the consumers are selfish and not interested in the source of their consumption plan. As noted above, this implies that the only aspect of a commodity-flow matrix which influences a consumer's well-being is

$\Sigma_{j\in N}(a^{ij} - a^{ji}) + a^{ii}$. The preference is complete, reflexive, and transitive on X^i.

Third, specific assumptions must be made about the technology of the economy. Inaction is possible for each firm: $0 \in Y^j, j \in M$. Production requires inputs in aggregate $\Sigma_{j\in M} Y^j \cap \mathbb{R}^{\ell}_{\oplus} = \{0\}$. Extremely subtle distinctions between aggregate possibilities and impossibilities do not occur: $\Sigma_{j\in M} Y^j$ contains its boundary. Aggregate production is irreversible: $\Sigma_{j\in M} Y^j \cap \Sigma_{j\in M}(-Y^j) = \{0\}$. Free disposal is possible in aggregate: $\Sigma_{j\in M} Y^j \supseteq \mathbb{R}^{\ell}_{\ominus}$.

Fourth, suppositions must be made about consumption possibilities and tastes. Extremely subtle distinctions should not be important for survival: X^i contains its boundary. There is an admissible consumption which can be obtained by using only the endowment: there is a $x^i \in X^i$ such that $x^i << \omega_{ii}$. The admissible consumptions are bounded below: there is an $\overline{x}^i$ such that $\overline{x}^i \leqslant x^i$ for all $x^i \in X^i$. Preferences are continuous in the sense that as a sequence of commodity plans moves from worse to better than some alternative, it passes through indifference: $\{x \in X^i \,|\, x \succsim_i \hat{x}^i\}$ and $\{x \in X^i \,|\, x \precsim_i \hat{x}^i\}$ contain their boundaries for all $\hat{x}^i \in X^i$. Consumers are not satiated in their admissible set: for all $x^i \in X^i$ there exists an $\tilde{x}^i$ such that $\tilde{x}^i \succ_i x^i$.

Fifth, diversity must be desirable in consumption and possible in production and consumption, and returns to scale in production are non-increasing. Thus, Y^j, X^i, and $\{x \in X^i \,|\, x \succsim_i x^i\}$ are convex sets for all $j \in M, i \in M, x^i \in X^i$.

Sixth, ownership rights are exclusive so that one and only one person holds property rights to each commodity. This eliminates the possibility of jointly consumed "public goods". All agents obey legal property rights. Theft is non-existent and financial budget constraints are respected.

Seventh, everyone is well informed in the sense that the full price vector is known and there is no confusion over what index to apply to any commodity. However, everyone is naive in that they do not know how others will respond to prices, and as a result firms and consumers are price takers.

Eighth, the competitive price mechanism itself uses no real resources to arrange for the allocation of property rights. The discovery of equilibrium prices, the drawing of contracts, and the enforcement of exchanges of property rights are costless activities.

With assumptions one through eight, it has been verified that there will exist at least one price vector such that profit maximization by firms and preference optimization of human actors leads to a feasible allocation of resources. This is one of the major results of modern general competitive market theory to be found in Debreu (1959), Arrow and Hahn (1972), or McKenzie (1981).

Proposition 3.1. In economic environments which satisfy assumptions one through eight, the competitive market mechanism is decisive.

These eight assumptions are sufficient conditions for the decisiveness of markets. When some of the conditions are dropped this does not imply that the mechanism is indecisive, but there would be a possibility that the markets cannot produce an equilibrium.

Roughly, the decisiveness of the competitive market mechanism means that supply and demand curves intersect each other. Assumptions one and two help assure that the supply and demand curves are well defined. The technological restrictions are used to bound the economy from above and make sure the response of the firms is suitable continuous. Assumption four bounds the economy from below and assures that the response of consumers is well defined. Convexity assumtion five guarantees that if there are points of discontinuous behavior these are not too serious because gaps in supply and demand are filled. The sixth restriction assures us that all commodities can be legally owned and traded. Knowledge of the mechanism is complete but not very sophisticated by assumption seven. Finally, the price-making market process does not use up society's scarce resources and hence all costs are private. With these suppositions one can show that supply curves must cross demand curves, thus generating the equilibrium prices and the quantities of traded commodities.

When the competitive market system is decisive it is also consistent and preserves feasibility and admissibility.

Proposition 3.2. In economic environments which satisfy assumptions one through eight the competitive market mechanism preserves feasibility, admissibility, and is consistent.

Feasibility is a consequence of conditions (a) and (b) of the competitive market choice system $\beta(e)$. Condition (c1) assures the admissibility of consumption plans. The mechanism is consistent because of the material balance condition (a).

When the competitive market mechanism produces an allocation of resources the allocation is efficient under conditions which are less restrictive than is necessary to prove decisiveness.

Proposition 3.3. In economic environments which satisfy assumptions one, two, six, seven, and eight, which have preferences that are locally non-satiated (there is always a neighboring consumption plan which is an improvement on any consumption) and which have an equilibrium, the competitive market mechanism is non-wasteful.

Assumptions one and two are needed so that individuals care only about things that they are financially responsible for. Restrictions six through eight imply that there is no cheating. Local non-satiation replaces convexity and all the conditions which generate nice supply and demand curves. This single restriction implies that at equilibrium if a consumer is to improve on his allocation he must spend more monetary units, but this is impossible for everyone to do simultaneously because of the material balance equation.

The competitive market mechanism can support an efficient allocation of resources if prices can be found to make the allocation most profitable for all firms and most desirable subject to budget restrictions for all consumers. To assure this, the economic environment must be convex.

Proposition 3.4. In economic environments which satisfy assumptions one, two, and five through eight, and such that for each equilibrium x^{i*}, P^* there is an $x^i \in X^i$ such that $P^*x^i < P^*x^{i*}$ and preferences are continuous, the competitive market mechnism is unbiased.

The additional restrictions in proposition 3.4 are needed to eliminate some difficulties which can occur if an efficient point is on the boundary of a survival set. (See Arrow, 1951b; Koopmans, 1957, p. 34.)

Edgeworth (1881) demonstrated that the market system determines an allocation which is stable against cooperative attempts of coalitions to improve upon their allocation. This has recently been shown to hold in a wide class of environments. (See Hildenbrand, 1974; Aumann, 1964; Debreu and Scarf, 1963; and Nikaido, 1968.) A core allocation is one such that any alternative allocation which is feasible, admissible, and consistent from the perspective of some coalition of individuals is detrimental to the welfare of at least one coalition member.

Proposition 3.5. In economic environments which satisfy assumptions one, two, six through eight, and local non-satiation of preferences, the competitive market mechanism is core-selecting.

The local non-satiation assumption again allows us to infer that more desirable allocations are more expensive, which would lead to a contradiction of the coalition's material balance condition.

While the competitive market allocation is in the core this does not mean that this allocation is the most desirable allocation in the core for each individual. Hurwicz (1972) has shown that the competitive market mechanism is not individually incentive compatible in economic environments in which some individuals understand the behavior of others (see Chapter 17). By misrepresentation of preferences or endowment, a sophisticated individual can influence the outcome of the market system toward an outcome which improves on the competitive equilibrium from his viewpoint. However, if the individuals do not know the behavior of others or if they are just too small to influence the final outcome, the competitive market mechanism is individually incentive compatible.

Proposition 3.6. In economic environments where assumptions one, two, and five through eight hold, or where assumption 7 is modified so that naive behavior is replaced by the assumption that the number of participants (m, n) is very large, the competitive market mechanism is individually incentive compatiable.

Postlewaite and Roberts (1976) show that as the number of participants increases, the payoff to manipulative behavior shrinks to zero. For example, in a pure exchange model with two commodities and two actors, let preferences, endowments, and admissible consumptions be

$$U^1 = \sqrt{x_1 x_2}, \quad \omega_{11} = (1, 0), \quad X^1 = \mathbb{R}^2_{\oplus},$$

$$U^2 = \sqrt{x_1 x_2}, \quad \omega_{22} = (0, 1), \quad X^2 \in \mathbb{R}^2_{\oplus}.$$

The competitive market equilibrium E is in the middle of the Edgeworth–Bowley box in fig. 3.1. The offer curve of actor 1 is given implicitly by his optimal choice as a function of relative prices $\hat{P} = p_2/p_1$:

$$(x_1^1, x_2^1) = (\tfrac{1}{2}\hat{P}, \tfrac{1}{2}).$$

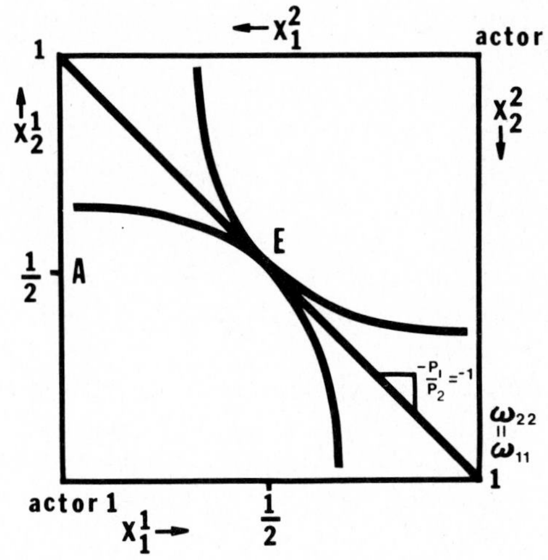

Figure 3.1

If actor 2 knows this offer curve of actor 1, he will find it in his self-interest to misrepresent his tastes so that the equilibrium relative price is $\hat{P} = 0$. In this case the first actor gives up half a unit of commodity 2 with nothing in exchange. The point A in fig. 3.1 is the most desirable point where actor 2 can manipulate the outcome, knowing the first actor's offer curve. This manipulation would be undetectable if actor 2 pretends to have preference

$$U^2 = \min (x_1, 2x_2).$$

Now suppose that this economy is enlarged by cloning N copies of type 1 actors and N copies of type 2 actors. Let us presume that just one of the type 2 actors is knowledgeable enough to manipulate prices. This actor of type 2 knows the offer curves of actors of type 1 and knows that type 2 actors have offer curves

$$(x_1^2, x_2^2) = (\tfrac{1}{2}, \tfrac{1}{2}(1/\hat{P}).$$

For any relative price $\hat{P}$, the excess demand for commodities by the N type 1 actors and $(N - 1)$ other type 2 actors is:

$$ED_1 = N\tfrac{1}{2}\hat{P} + (N - 1)\tfrac{1}{2} - (N - 1),$$
$$ED_2 = N\tfrac{1}{2} + (N - 1)\tfrac{1}{2}\hat{P}^{-1} - N.$$

The manipulating type 2 actor must be able to supply this excess demand from his endowment, therefore he must restrict the price range so that

$$ED_1 \leqslant 1; \qquad ED_2 \leqslant 0.$$

The first inequality implies that $\hat{P} \leqslant 1 + 1/N$ and the second implies that $\hat{P} \geqslant 1 - 1/N$. The strategic behavior of the individual is limited to a range of prices near 1:

$$1 - \frac{1}{N} \leqslant \hat{P} \leqslant 1 + \frac{1}{N}.$$

As the size of the economy increases, this range shrinks to the competitive market equilibrium price $\hat{P}^* = 1$. If there is any cost to discovering the others' tastes or to manipulating the economy to the most desirable P, we would expect this agent to give up price-making behavior as N gets very large.

Ledyard (1971) and Osana (1972) extended the basic theorems of welfare economics to a class of economic environments which includes externalities.

Suppose that the jth producer's technological capabilities depend on the production of other firms. If we denote the production plan of the other producers $y_{-j} = (y^1, ..., y^{j-1}, y^{j+1}, ..., y^m)$, then the jth firm's technology with external effects is given by the correspondence

$$Y^j(y_{-j}).$$

When these technological correspondences are continuous, Arrow and Hahn (1972) have shown that the price system must have an equilibrium under conditions similar to those of proposition 3.1. One would normally expect, however, that the external effects make the equilibrium inefficient, since the producer only looks at his personal costs and benefits when considering a change in his production plan and ignores the impact his choice has on the technological capabilities of others. Ledyard (1971) and Osana (1972) demonstrate that this is not necessarily true if the producers mistakenly believe that their production capabilities exceed their true limits.

Suppose that firm j conjectures that its production technology is influenced by the external actions of others according to the correspondence

$$Y_0^j(y_{-j}).$$

These beliefs are fairly extensive at $y^1, ..., y^m$ if every allocation $\bar{x}^1, ..., \bar{x}^n$, $\bar{y}^1, ..., \bar{y}^m$, which is admissible, consistent, and truly feasible is conjectured to be feasible by each firm:

$$\bar{x}^i \in X^i, \quad \bar{y}^j \in Y^j(y_{-j}), \quad \sum_{i \in N} \bar{x}^i = \sum_{j \in M} \bar{y}^j + \sum_{i \in N} \omega^i, \quad i \in N, \; j \in M,$$

$$\text{implies } \bar{y}^j \in Y_0^j(y_{-j}), \quad j \in M.$$

Fairly extensive conjectures about the effect of externalities exaggerate how little it will cost to avoid pollution damage or how much a neighboring farm's pest control activities will improve crop yields. Because the conjectures exaggerate this way, a competitive equilibrium will be efficient with respect to the true capabilities.

Proposition 3.7. Let $x^{1*}, ..., x^{n*}, y^{1*}, ..., y^{m*}$ be an allocation of resources such that for prices P^*:

(a) y^{j*} maximizes P^*y^j subject to $y^j \in Y_0^j(y^*_{-j})$,

(b) x^{i*} is optimal with respect to $\succsim_i^*$ on the set X^i such that $P^*x^i \leqslant P^*\omega^i$ + $+ \Sigma_{j\in M}\theta_{ij}P^*y^{i*}$,

(c) $\Sigma_{i\in N}X^{i*} = \Sigma_{j\in M}y^{j*} + \Sigma_{i\in N}\omega^i$.

If

(d) $y^{j*} \in Y^j(y_{-j}^*)$,

(e) producer information is fairly extensive, and

(f) consumers are locally non-satiated,

then $x^{1*}, ..., x^{n*}, y^{1*}, ..., y^{m*}$ is efficient.

Ledyard (1971) and Osana (1972) show that this result can be expanded to include external effects in consumption. Conditions (a), (b), and (c) state that the prices P^* produce a competitive equilibrium given the conjectures about the external effects. Such an equilibrium in the market may not lead to an implementable allocation because the firms may find it impossible to deliver what they have contracted to produce. If, however, this problem does not arise – condition (d) – then no efficient activities will go unconsidered by the fairly extensive firms.

While the optimistic view of the fairly extensive firm guarantees the non-wastefulness of the competitive equilibrium, it does not assure decisiveness. In fact, the exaggerated conjectures needed for efficiency are quite likely to lead to contractual promises which cannot be executed when reality sets in. In order to guarantee the feasibility of a competitive equilibrium with production externalities, the conjectures would have to pessimistically exaggerate the damage from external effects.

An alternative approach suggested by Arrow (1970) and Starrett (1972) is to internalize the external effects by defining new commodities which include the identity of the user and observer as a characteristic. If y_h^{jk} is the quantity of commodity h used by firm j as observed by firm k, firm k can purchase at a price p_h^{jk} the reduction of any diseconomy. The price system for these personalized commodities must adjust to bring equilibrium in the following sense:

$$y_h^{j1} = ... = y_h^{jj} = ... = y_h^{jn}.$$

That is to say, the amount of commodity h produced by firm j, y_h^{jj}, exactly equals the amount which all other firms would like the jth firm to produce.

The desirable properties of the competitive market mechanism are often robust with respect to isolated violations of classical assumptions. One illustration is the convexity requirement. Convexity is not necessary for decisiveness of the competitive market mechanism. Obviously, if non-convexities occur in regions of the technology or preferences which are not really relevant for the optimal behavior of participants, they will not prevent equilibrium, but even when the non-convexities are relevant, the wrinkles in aggregate behavior may be smoothed out by the sheer numbers of participants. For example, in a pure exchange economy let there be two actors with preferences given by utility functions

$$U^1 = \min(x_1, x_2),$$

$$U^2 = \begin{cases} x_1, & \text{if } x_1 + \dfrac{1}{I} \leqslant x_2, \\ x_2, & \text{if } x_1 \leqslant x_2 \leqslant x_1 + \dfrac{1}{I}, \\ x_1, & \text{if } x_1 - \dfrac{1}{I} \leqslant x_2 \leqslant x_1, \\ x_2, & \text{if } x_2 \leqslant x_1 - \dfrac{1}{I}, \end{cases}$$

where I is an integer. Suppose the endowments are

$$\omega^1 = (1,0), \qquad \omega^2 = (0,1).$$

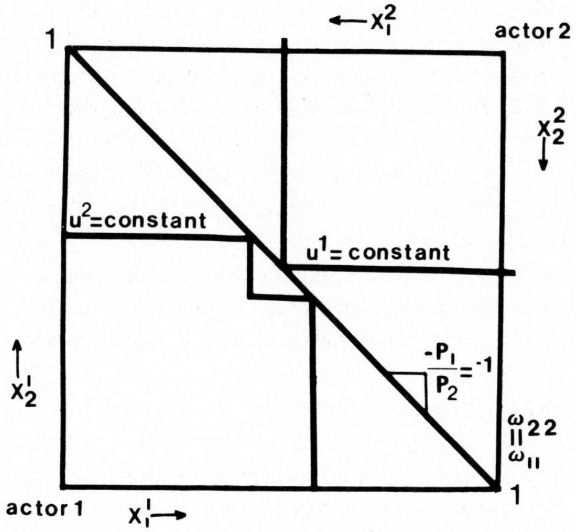

Figure 3.2

The closest the market mechanism can come to an equilibrium is when prices are equal. The demand by actor 1 is:

$$x_1^1 = \tfrac{1}{2}, \quad x_2^1 = \tfrac{1}{2},$$

and the demand by actor 2 is:

$$x_1^2 = \tfrac{1}{2} + \frac{1}{2I}, \quad x_2^2 = \tfrac{1}{2} + \frac{1}{2I}$$

or

$$x_1^2 = \tfrac{1}{2} - \frac{1}{2I}, \quad x_2^2 = \tfrac{1}{2} + \frac{1}{2I}.$$

The minimum absolute value of excess demand for each good is $1/2I$. However, if the economy were enlarged to create I identical clones of type 1 and 2 actors, an equilibrium can be achieved. If $P_1^* = P_2^*$ and if half the type 2 actors are given $(\tfrac{1}{2} + 1/2I, \tfrac{1}{2} - 1/2I)$ and the other half $(\tfrac{1}{2} - 1/2I, \tfrac{1}{2} + 1/2I)$ (which are viewed indifferently) then total demand vector is:

$$\begin{aligned} & I \cdot (\tfrac{1}{2}, \tfrac{1}{2}) + \tfrac{1}{2}I(\tfrac{1}{2} + 1/2I, \tfrac{1}{2} - 1/2I) + \tfrac{1}{2}I(\tfrac{1}{2} - 1/2I, \tfrac{1}{2} + 1/2I) \\ &= (\tfrac{1}{2}I + \tfrac{1}{4}I + \tfrac{1}{4} + \tfrac{1}{4}I - \tfrac{1}{4}, \tfrac{1}{2}I + \tfrac{1}{4}I - \tfrac{1}{4} + \tfrac{1}{4}I + \tfrac{1}{4}) \\ &= (I, I). \end{aligned}$$

The total endowment vector of this I-replicated economy is $I \cdot (1{,}0) + I \cdot (0{,}1) = (I{,}I)$, so this allocation is a competitive market equilibrium even though the non-convexities occur near the equilibrium allocation. This convexifying effect was first pointed out by Farrell (1959) and was formalized by Starr (1969); also see Arrow and Hahn (1972, ch. 7).

While isolated discrepancies in the classical assumptions do not destroy the properties of the market system, there are combinations of violations of classical conditions which build on each other rather than ameliorating the difficulties. The competitive mechanism may be indecisive or wasteful in environments which are interesting and realistic, and the thesis of this book is that other varieties of organizations are created to attenuate such problems. The large diversity of non-market organizations which presently allocate scarce resources – partnerships, government agencies, corporations, cooperatives, communes, universities, hospitals, legislatures, courts – provide indirect evidence of the impracticality of markets in many environments.

An illustration of the confluence of violations of classical conditions is the markets for "named" commodities needed to deal with externalities. The market for y_h^{jk} contains but one buyer and one seller, making it difficult to justify the traditional assumptions of price-taking behavior. Such an economy is not made more "competitive" by adding participants. There is an incentive problem which markets may not be able to overcome. When externalities are present, the assumption of costless transaction is more difficult to justify. The number of commodities has expanded dramatically and the personalized nature of these new commodities introduces difficulties pertaining to standardization of contracts and enforcement of the equilibrium contracts. If a participant must contract with a large number of neighbors on a one-to-one basis and in each situation negotiate a complex contract, the costs of exchange cannot reasonably be assumed to be negligible. In conclusion, externalities are compounded by opportunistic behavior and transaction costs and may prevent an efficient allocation of resources via the price system.

In the following chapters the cost of negotiating and enforcing contracts in economic environments which include uncertainty and informational asymmetries will be viewed as the primary impediment to using markets to organize the employment of workers. On the surface it would appear that markets are commonly used for those commodities called labor, but this is not correct. The employment of a worker is not done by purchasing separately each of the types of labor which will be needed. The employment contract is less precise and involves the payment for general labor capability, the exact nature to be determined as needs arise. The incompleteness of the market system is the object of investigation.

CHAPTER 4

TRANSACTION COSTS

Coase's (1937) insightful explanation of the existence of business firms simply points out that prices are costly to establish and use for allocating resources. Where there are no costs to the price system, the theory of the invisible hand (Smith, 1776, or Arrow, 1951b) would imply that prices should be attached to every possible commodity and that the final allocation of society's resources should be determined by the combined effects of self-interested optimization and balancing of supply and demand. The authoritative, quantity-guided business firm would provide no additional benefit to society, but the price system does not itself meet the market test. Authority has replaced (or has not been replaced by) prices in many situation requiring the allocation of scarce resources: in the business firm, government bureaucracy, household, or legislature. The presence of "islands of conscious power in this ocean of unconscious cooperation like lumps of butter coagulating in a pail of buttermilk" (Robertson, 1935) must be explained and Coase uses the tools of economic analysis to provide a rationale.

When two agents sign a contract specifying some time and location that particular commodities will be exchanged, a transaction has taken place. At the particular time that the possession of the commodities is physically transferred, turnover takes place. The cost of turnover may involve storage or transportation resources but this is to be considered part of the productive activity of changing the commodities. As long as the exchange of commodities is to take place, little can be done to eliminate these productive turnover costs.

The resources that are used up in the design and enforcement of the contract are resources associated with the method of exchanging ownership rights and are called *transaction costs*. Transaction costs may involve bringing agents together physically or by some communication system, acquiring and disseminating information about the terms of exchange (prices and characteristics of the commodities), drawing legally binding contracts, and the enforcement of such contracts. Some common types of resources used in transaction are labor used to find equilibrium rates of exchange, the loss of commodities due to spoilage while transactions are arranged, effort used in standardizing and certifying the quality of commodities, legal fees for assurance that transactions meet legal restrictions, and socially determined taxes on the exchange of certain types of commodities. Unlike turnover costs, transaction costs are intimately tied to the method used for allocating resources.

Transaction costs vary from society to society due to differences in the attitudes of individuals toward property. In a one-member society there are no transaction costs because exchange involves at least two parties, and in a society without property rights exchanges are valueless and thus no resources are used in transactions. We categorize the sources of transaction cost as either *negotiation* or *enforcement* costs. Negotiation costs are those resources used up in the process of arranging mutual satisfactory exchanges of property, while enforcement costs are resources used up with the aim of preventing breach of contractual stipulations.

Consider the impact of transaction costs on the market for used cars. The used-car dealer guarantees the immediate exchange of used cars of a given quality and money and by providing this intermediation earns income. In any particular month the desires of the economy to sell or buy used cars are represented by the supply and demand curves, *SS* and *DD*, fig. 4.1. However, on any particular day the seller of a used car may not find a buyer at the equilibrium price P^* and may be forced to wait several days to exchange the car for cash. The used-car

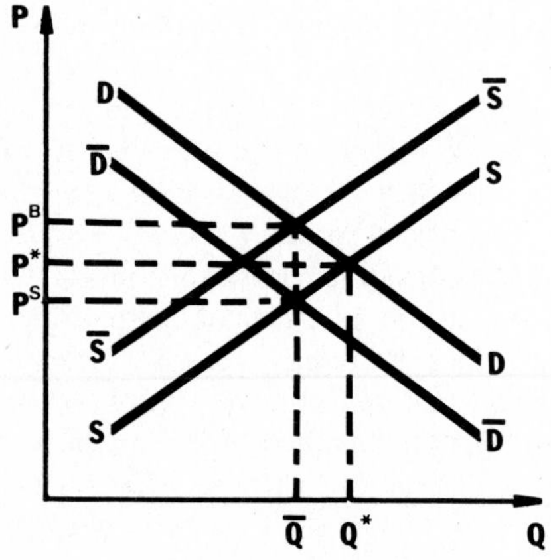

Figure 4.1

dealer provides an instantaneous buyer; since he must incur inventory costs and costs of advertising before he can resell the car, he will demand a slightly lower price for any given quantity of cars (represented by the curve $\bar{D}\bar{D}$.) The market for instantaneous sales clears at a lower price P^S. On the other side of the market, used-car buyers may not want to wait for its appearance at the equilibrium price. The used-car dealer provides an inventory of cars from which the buyer can satisfy his immmediate needs. Since the dealer incurs the transaction costs of providing standardized commodities and, in part, guaranteeing the quality of the cars, he will charge a slightly higher price at each quantity, $\bar{S}\bar{S}$. The clearing of this market occurs at the price P^B. At equilibrium the margin, $P^B - P^S$, adjusts so that the monthly flow of cars into and out of the used car lot equilibrates at $\bar{Q}$. This margin or markup covers the transaction costs incurred by the used-car dealer and competition among used-car dealers will keep the margin at socially optimal levels, in line with the actual costs of transaction. It should be noted that the introduction of transaction costs causes the equilibrium number of exchanges to decline from Q^* to $\bar{Q}$.

In general, the presence of transaction costs will make it more costly to buy than it is profitable to sell. An agent with an endowment of two goods, (ω_1, ω_2), has a budget

$$B(P^B, P^S, \omega) = \{ (x_1, x_2) \mid p_1^B x_1 + p_2^S x_2 \leqslant p_1^B \omega_1 + p_2^S \omega_2 \text{ if } x_1 \geqslant \omega_1 \text{ and } x_2 \leqslant \omega_2, \text{ and } p_1^S x_1 + p_2^B x_2 \leqslant p_1^S \omega_1 + p_2^B \omega_2 \text{ if } x_1 \leqslant \omega_1 \text{ and } x_2 > \omega_2 \}$$

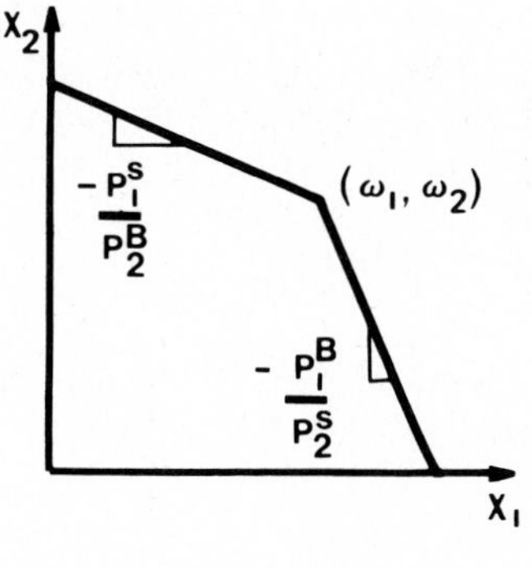

Figure 4.2

(see fig. 4.2), where P^{B} are the buying prices and P^{S} are the selling prices, $P^{\mathrm{B}} \geqslant P^{\mathrm{S}}$.

Foley (1970) has shown how transaction costs may be introduced to models determining the general price equilibrium. He assumes two sets of prices: a buying price, P^{B}, and a selling price P^{S}. If consumer i selects a consumption plan, x^i, then his purchases are represented by

$$x_h^{i\mathrm{B}} = \max\,[x_h^i, 0]$$

and his sales are represented by

$$x_h^{i\mathrm{S}} = \min\,[x_h^i, 0]$$

(where h is a commodity index). The value of a purchase plan $X^{i\mathrm{B}}$ and sales plan $x^{i\mathrm{S}}$ is $P^{\mathrm{B}}x^{i\mathrm{B}} + P^{\mathrm{S}}x^{i\mathrm{S}}$. The consumer with a fixed wealth, w_i, looks at consumption plans belonging to the budget set

$$B^i(P^{\mathrm{S}}, P^{\mathrm{B}}, w_i) = \{x^i \in X^i \mid x^i = x^{i\mathrm{B}} + x^{i\mathrm{S}} \text{ where } P^{\mathrm{B}}x^{i\mathrm{B}} + P^{\mathrm{S}}x^{i\mathrm{S}} \leqslant w_i\}.$$

Another way to express these constraints is to define the activities of a household in an enlarged commodity space. The budget constraint may be written as

$$P^{\mathrm{B}}x^{i\mathrm{B}} + P^{\mathrm{S}}x^{i\mathrm{S}} = P^{\mathrm{S}}x^i + (P^{\mathrm{B}} - P^{\mathrm{S}})x^{i\mathrm{B}} = P^{\mathrm{S}}x^i + \pi z^i \leqslant w_i,$$

where $\pi = P^{\mathrm{B}} - P^{\mathrm{S}}$ is the margin or markup premium on commodities and $z^i = X^{i\mathrm{B}}$ is the purchasing activity of the consumer. The consumer evaluates his consumption plan x^i at the prices P^{S} but must also pay πz^i for the marketing activities associated with buying commodities. An extended admissible set may be defined

$$\bar{X}^i = \{(x, z) \mid x \in X^i, z_n \geqslant \max\,[x_h, 0], h = 1, \ldots, \ell\}.$$

Preferences may also be extended to this larger admissible set by assuming that purchasing activities are neither goods nor bads:

$$\text{if } (x, z) \text{ and } (\bar{x}, \bar{z}) \in \bar{X}^i \text{ then } (x, z) \succsim_i^1 (\bar{x}, \bar{z}) \text{ when } x \succsim_i \bar{x} \text{ in } X^i.$$

This reformulation does not take any economic changes since a consumer would have chosen x^{i*} at prices P^{S*}, P^{B*} if he would have chosen (x^{i*}, z^*) at price and margin P^{S*}, $P^{B*} - P^{S*} = \pi^*$.

Theorem. Suppose $(x^{i*}, z^*) \in \bar{X}^i$ satisfies (for $(P^{S*}, P^{B*}) \geqslant 0, \pi^* \geqslant 0$):

(a) $P^{S*} x^{i*} + \pi^* z^* \leqslant w_i$,

(b) $(x^{i*}, z^*) \succsim_i^1 (x^i, z)$ for all $(x^i, z) \in X^i$ such that

$P^{S*} x^i + \pi^* z \leqslant w_i$, and

(c) $x^{i*} \in X^i$,

then $x^{i*} \in X^i$ will satisfy

(d) $P^{S*} x^{iS*} + P^{B*} x^{iB*} \leqslant w_i$, and

(e) $x^{i*} \succsim_i x^i$ for all $x^i \in B^i(P^{S*}, P^{B*}, w_i)$.

The Foley model assumes that consumers perform none of the intermediary roles themselves. They always buy at the higher price and sell at the lower price. The marketing activities, like the used-car dealing described above, are carried out by profit-maximizing producing agents. (See Kurz, 1974, for a model where consumers are also marketeers.)

Firms may buy commodities at the low selling prices and sell them at the higher prices but they must incur a loss of resources for arranging the exchange of property rights. In addition, the producers may transform commodities (produce). Some firms combine marketing and producing activities; used-car dealers may buy low-priced cars and repair them for later sale. Moreover, firms may buy at the high price and sell at the low if they do not have efficient transaction technologies; a car repair firm may buy used cars from a dealer, repair them, and sell back reconditioned automobiles. Foley models the transaction technology by working in an extended commodity space; a production activity of the firm j is written as (y^j, y^{jB}), where y^j is the total net transaction and y^{jB} is the vector of purchases and sales at the premium buying price. The technology of the firm is a subset Y^j of $\mathbb{R}^{2\ell}$ representing the feasible production and marketing activities.

Example. A firm produces a good from labor according to a production function $x = f(L)$. Labor may be hired from an employment agency which charges a premium due to its transaction costs. Labor may also be hired directly, but this entails using some labor for interviewing prospective workers; thus the "effective" labor is smaller than L due to the staff of the personnel department. The technology is the set

$$Y = \{ (y, y^{\mathrm{B}}) \mid y = (f(L^{\mathrm{B}} + \delta L^{\mathrm{S}}), -(L^{\mathrm{B}} + L^{\mathrm{S}})), y^{\mathrm{B}} = (0, -L^{\mathrm{B}}),$$
$$\text{where } L^{\mathrm{B}} \text{ and } L^{\mathrm{S}} \text{ are non-negative and } 0 < \delta < 1 \text{ is a fixed parameter} \}.$$

The firm j will pay or receive the low price P^{S} for the y^j component of its production activity and will purchase or sell $y^{j\mathrm{B}}$ only by paying a premium π. The profit associated with a production activity is

$$\pi^j(P^{\mathrm{S}}, \pi) = P^{\mathrm{S}} y^j + \pi y^{j\mathrm{B}}.$$

In the above example, profits are

$$P^{\mathrm{S}} f(L^{\mathrm{B}} + \delta L^{\mathrm{S}}) - P^{\mathrm{S}} L^{\mathrm{S}} - (P^{\mathrm{S}} + \pi) L^{\mathrm{B}}.$$

If the staff requirement per worker, $(1 - \delta)$, is relatively small in comparison to the premium paid to the employment agency, then this firm will hire all of its own labor directly. If the opposite is true, it will hire through an agency.

An equilibrium of an economy which has transaction costs may be defined in a fashion exactly like that of the standard competitive model.

Definition. A *competitive price equilibrium with transaction costs* is a vector of prices $(P^{\mathrm{S}*}, \pi^*)$, a consumption-marketing vector (x^{i*}, z^{i*}) for each consumer $i = 1, \ldots, m$, and a vector of production-marketing activities $(y^{j*}, y^{i\mathrm{B}})$ for each producer $j = 1, \ldots, n$, such that

(a) $(x^{i*}, z^{i*}) \in \bar{X}^i$ is optimal with respect to $\succsim_i'$ in the set

$$(x^i, z^i) \in \bar{X}^i \mid P^{\mathrm{S}*} x^i + \pi^* z^i \leqslant \sum_j \theta_{ij} (P^{\mathrm{S}*} y^j + \pi^* y^{j\mathrm{B}}) \quad ,$$

(b) $(y^{j*}, y^{j\mathrm{B}*})$ maximizes profit $\pi^j(P^{\mathrm{S}*}, \pi^*)$ on Y^j,

(c) $\Sigma_i (x^{i*}, z^{i*}) = \Sigma_j (y^{j*}, y^{j\mathrm{B}*})$,

(d) $P^{\mathrm{S}*} \neq 0, \pi^* \geqslant 0$.

The standard assumptions on $\bar{X}^i$, $\succsim_i'$, and Y^j are also sufficient to show that a competitive price equilibrium with transaction costs exists. Foley points out that the assumption that transaction technologies are free from indivisibilities is a vulnerable assumption, so this will be discussed at length below.

Foley quite correctly points out that care must be taken in analyzing the efficiency of price-determined allocations with transaction costs. It follows in a trivial fashion that classical conditions guarantee that such an allocation is efficient in the class of economies which must face these transaction technologies. But autarky is an efficient allocation in the set of economies where trade is prohibited. The transaction technology is highly dependent on the institution used for resource allocation (in this case, the price system). There may be other allocation mechanisms which attenuate the costs of exchanging property rights and hence expand the set of possible allocations. The obvious example is the hierarchical, authoritative approach to resource allocation taken by most business firms.

There is another way in which the price system may fail to provide efficient allocations. As noted in the used-car dealer example, transaction costs tend to lower the number of exchanges which take place in the market. Foley analyzes this by assuming that consumers have differentiable utility functions and that the marginal transaction cost of expanding trade at equilibrium is C. If

$$C \geqslant \max_i \left[\frac{1}{\mu^i} \frac{\partial U^i}{\partial x_h} \right] - \min_i \left[\frac{1}{\mu^i} \frac{\partial U^i}{\partial x_h} \right],$$

then the market for commodity h will involve no transactions; that is, if μ^i is the marginal utility of wealth, the difference between the highest price a consumer is willing to pay is still too low to cover the sum of the lowest price at which a seller is willing to sell and the cost of arranging the trade. Essentially the demand curve lies everywhere below the supply curve, including the cost of transactions.

In Kurz (1974) the transaction costs in a pure exchange world are modelled so that the consumers must supply the resources from their endowments. Suppose that in a two-good–two-consumer economy if a consumer plans on any purchases or sales he must expend $\bar{g}^i = (\bar{g}_1^i, \bar{g}_2^i)$ units of the two goods. This cost might reflect the opportunities forgone while the exchange is arranged. If $P = (P_1 - P_2)$ is the price vector the consumer choice problem is to maximize by choice of x^{iB}, x^{iS}, g^i

$$U^i(\omega^i + x^{iB} + x^{iS})$$

s.t.

$$Px^{iB} + Px^{iS} + Pg^i \leqslant 0,$$

$$\omega^i + x^{iB} + x^{iS} \in X^i,$$

and

$$g^i = \begin{cases} 0 & \text{if } x^{iB} = 0 = x^{iS}, \\ g^i & \text{otherwise.} \end{cases}$$

The budget constraint given above is equivalent to $Px^i \leqslant P(\omega^i - g^i)$, where x^i is the final consumption, $\omega^i + x^{iB} + x^{iS}$.

Geometrically, this example can be represented in a Edgeworth box whose dimensions are $\omega^1 + \omega^2 - g^1 - g^2$ (see fig. 4.3). There are three endowment points in the box, A, B, and C. Point C is the endowment of individual 1 while point A is his endowment if he incurs the transaction cost $\bar{g}^1$ by entering the

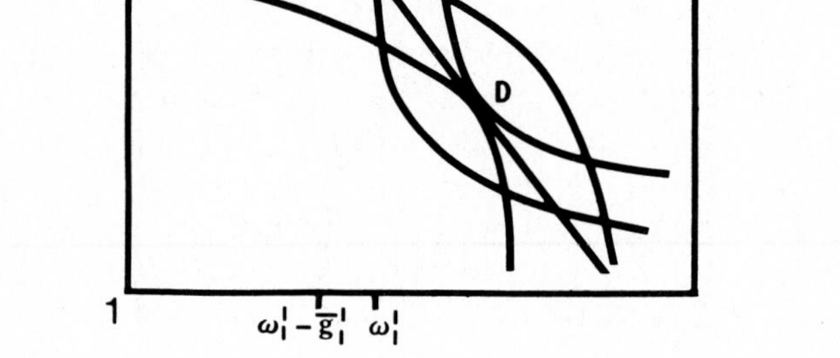

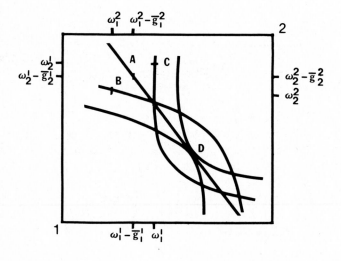

Figure 4.3

market. Point B is person 2's endowment as viewed from the northeastern corner of the box and A is his endowment minus transaction costs as viewed from his corner. In order for trade to be mutually beneficial the indifference curve of person 1 which passes through endowment point C must intersect the indifference curve of person 2 which passes through endowment point B. The further apart are points B and C (because of larger transaction costs $\bar{g}^1 + \bar{g}^2$) the more likely there is to be no competitive equilibrium which is mutually beneficial. In fig. 4.3 the competitive equilibrium D is mutually beneficial but in fig. 4.4 it is not, and autarky would hold in this economy.

There is nothing really inefficient about this allocation; the seller is perfectly content to sell nothing at a price P^* and there is no demand at that price. The market is simply inactive. However, if an intermediary is to make his living by arranging transactions, there is no income to be derived from this equilibrium position. If the intermediary faces any fixed costs (he may have to publish the price P_h^* each day) then in the long run not only will the market be inactive but it will fail to exist! There will be no price P_h^* known by the economic agents. If the failure of a market to exist is due to the fact that turnover will occur at some future time at some uncertain event, then there will be strong reasons for reopening the market at that time. One must then deal with economies with

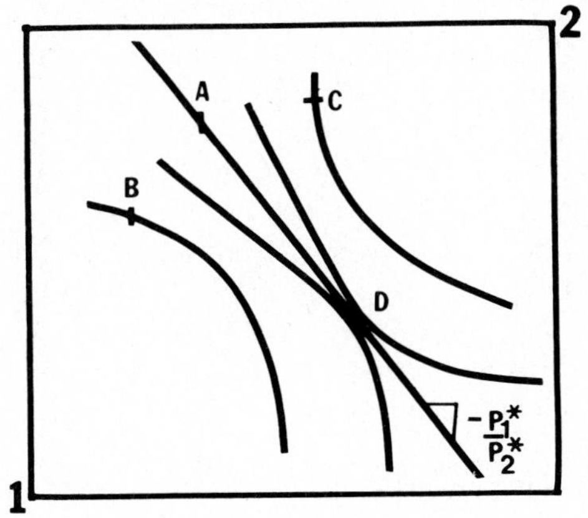

Figure 4.4

multiple (sequential) markets. It has been shown (Hart, 1975) that when markets are incomplete in this way, the resulting allocations may be inefficient.

If transaction costs are large, but not large enough to make markets inactive, the market may be thin (very few agents are actually buying or selling). Price-taking behavior is difficult to justify in a market with only a small number of active participants, and this leads all the usual problems of market inefficiency. Thin markets may lead to a situation with only one or two intermediaries, and the margin or premium prices, π, will not be determined competitively.

As above, transaction costs can be independent of the size of the commodity bundles actually exchanged. These are the set-up costs of transaction. Arranging the sale of apples for money may involve the services of a cash register operator, but the cost of those services really does not depend on the quantity or price of the apples sold. Of course, not all the costs of transaction are of this fixed, set-up variety. In order to sell cans of apple sauce, each can must be labelled with a price and the cost of labels and labelling labor depend directly on the number of cans sold.

Negotiation costs depend on the number of stipulations which must be included in a contract. The larger is the list of contingencies which must be incorporated in the exchange the more complicated the contracts become. The participants in the negotiation may even have to expend resources in pre-contractual definition and evaluation of the contingencies to be included in the contract. On the other hand, some resources may be used up just in gathering the participants in a market place. The set-up costs of negotiation make it advisable to make as many stipulations as possible. When people meet to negotiate the exchange of rights of a particular physical commodity, why do they not use the opportunity to arrange deliveries and receipts of the commodity in many successive time periods? While set-up costs may be spread across the collection of futures markets there is some advantage to limiting the number of periods. When markets meet to allocate property at some distant time, resources are being used for activities whose benefits are remote, and if individuals have a strong preference for present over future consumption, they might find it advantageous to put off the negotiation process in order to improve their current consumption opportunities. The set-up costs are not as significant if they can be discounted over a longer time horizon.

Example. Suppose there are two physical goods and two time periods, two individuals, and no production. Good k in period t is indexed $h = k + 2t$, for $k = 1, 2$, $t = 0, 1$. Both individuals have identical utility functions:

$$U^i(x^i) = x_1^i x_2^i (x_3^i x_4^i)^{1/\delta} .$$

The exponent is a discount factor; it is assumed that all commodities are goods, so $\delta \geqslant 0$. The individuals have endowments

$$\omega^1 = (1, 0, 1, 0), \qquad \omega^2 = (0, 1, 0, 1).$$

If the two individuals organize a futures market and transact all business at the beginning of the time period, they must use, respectively, the resource vectors

$$(\tfrac{1}{2}, 0, 0, 0) \quad \text{and} \quad (0, \tfrac{1}{2}, 0, 0)$$

in negotiating the contracts. Were they to organize only spot markets, one at time 1 and another later at time 2, then the transaction resources are, respectively,

$$(\tfrac{1}{3}, 0, 0, 0) \quad \text{and} \quad (0, \tfrac{1}{3}, 0, 0)$$

in period 1, and

$$(0, 0, \tfrac{1}{3}, 0) \quad \text{and} \quad (0, 0, 0, \tfrac{1}{3})$$

in period 2. By not organizing a futures market they use up $\tfrac{2}{3}$ units of each physical good instead of just $\tfrac{1}{2}$, but the spot markets push half of that cost into the future. The symmetry of this particular problem allows us to conclude that the spot market equilibrium consumption plan is the same for both individuals and is equal to

$$(\tfrac{1}{3}, \tfrac{1}{3}, \tfrac{1}{3}, \tfrac{1}{3}).$$

Similarly, the equilibrium allocation with a futures market gives each individual a consumption plan

$$(\tfrac{1}{4}, \tfrac{1}{4}, \tfrac{1}{2}, \tfrac{1}{2}).$$

If the subjective discount factor of the individuals is small,

$$\delta < \frac{\log\ 9/4}{\log 16/9} \cong 1.4.$$

then both parties prefer creating a futures market. However, when the discount factor is large,

$$\delta > 1.4,$$

it is mutually advantageous to delay negotiation of second period trades even though the set-up costs of negotiation have to be incurred again.

The set-up costs of a market produce non-convexities in the transaction technology and may result in discontinuities in the excess demand functions. It may be impossible to find a set of prices which reduces the excess demand to zero and hence the price system may fail to find an equilibrium allocation of scarce commodities. When the set-up costs are associated with the formation of the market, no marketeer interested in profits may be willing to set up the market, especially if variable transaction costs are large or supply and demand small so that the market is thin, even when established.

Heller (1972) has extended the Foley model to include the non-convexity of transaction technologies and found, using an argument similar to Starr's (1969) (see Chapter 3), that as long as set-up costs are small relative to the size of the economy, the price system will have only small distortions. However, the conclusion is dependent on the presence of governmental subsidies to marketeering firms to guarantee profitability. If the price system is not supplemented, it is possible that few will provide intermediation services, and thus some markets may fail to exist or may be non-competitive. Heller's model of transaction costs assumes that the set-up costs are independent of the number of agents trading, but when they depend on the number of agents, although not on the volume of trade, it is impossible to argue that set-up costs are small relative to the size of the economy.

Traders forfeit opportunities while they are trying to arrange mutual beneficial exchanges. Time is perishable and the theory of job search (Phelps et al., 1970) provides an explicit formulation of the costs of establishing contractual terms in the labor market. Even when there is a centralized clearinghouse for a particular market there may be costly delays in finalizing the terms of trade.

Example. Suppose that the excess demand for a perishable good declines with price but increases with time in a linear relation:

$$ED = a - bp + ct.$$

The equilibrium price rises over time as the good dissipates, so prompt discovery of equilibrium is in the buyer's interest. If an auctioneer adjusts price in proportion to the current excess demand,

$$\frac{\mathrm{d}p}{\mathrm{d}t} = ED,$$

beginning at a high price p_0, the time path of price is

$$p(t) = \frac{a}{b} - \frac{c}{b^2} + \frac{c}{b}t + \left(p_0 - \frac{a}{b} + \frac{c}{b^2}\right) \exp(-bt)$$

up until the time when excess demand hits zero:

$$t^* = ln(1/b - (a - bp_0)/c)/b.$$

A negative value for b implies that the market is unstable, and the closer the market comes to instability the more goods perish on the shelf as the equilibrium is negotiated. Even if the goods are not perishable, $c = 0$, the opportunity cost of the time spent searching for the equilibrium price will impose a transaction cost on the traders. ■

The negotiation of some contracts is confounded by the problem of the free rider. Suppose that it is very difficult to exclude individuals from enjoying the benefits of a "public" good such as an inoculation program for a contagious disease. The program is costly and must be financed by sacrifices by the individuals whose health is protected. However, each individual has an incentive to understate the benefit which he receives from the project and force the other individuals to pay a larger share of the program costs than is efficient. The misrepresentations may lead to underutilization of resources for the public good or involve large costs to prevent individuals from riding on their neighbors' coattails.

Example. Suppose that there are two goods: consumption, x, and public inoculations, y. Let there be two individuals with preferences

$$U^i(x, y) = x + 2\alpha_i\sqrt{y},$$

where α_i is a taste parameter indicating the relative desirability of public inoculations. While x varies with individual, the public inoculations are the same for both and neither person can exclude the other from benefiting from the inoculations. The technology of production requires that a unit of the consumption good is used up for every public inoculation. One way of determining the public choice is to charge each individual a separate per unit tax for public inoculations, t^i, sometimes called Lindahl prices (Milleron, 1972). If the ith individual has an endowment of consumption $\bar{x}^i$ and without loss of generality we take the price of consumption as 1, the budget of the consumer is

$$x^i = \bar{x}^i - t^i y^i.$$

The taxes must be adjusted so that the individuals agree on the public choice

$$y^1 = y = y^2,$$

and that there be equilibrium in the consumption market (including resource used up for inoculations)

$$x^1 + x^2 + y = \bar{x}^1 + \bar{x}^2.$$

It is easy to check that the individual's optimal choice is

$$x^i = \bar{x}^i - \frac{(\alpha_i)^2}{t_i},$$

$$y^i = \left(\frac{\alpha_i}{t^i}\right)^2.$$

The equilibrium conditions then require that tax rates satisfy

$$\frac{t^1}{t^2} = \frac{\alpha_1}{\alpha_2}$$

and

$$\frac{(\alpha_1)^2}{t^1} + \frac{(\alpha_2)^2}{t^2} = \left(\frac{\alpha_1}{t^1}\right)^2.$$

Thus, the equilibrium tax rates are

$$t^1 = \frac{\alpha_1}{\alpha_1 + \alpha_2} \quad \text{and} \quad t^2 = \frac{\alpha_2}{\alpha_1 + \alpha_2}$$

and the optimal number of inoculations is the efficient number

$$y = (\alpha_1 + \alpha_2)^2.$$

However, the ith consumer would be very naive to anticipate that a tax rate, which is personalized as above, is independent of his behavior. It is clear, from the above, that as α_i increases, the tax rate goes up. A moderately sophisticated consumer will find it desirable to understate the demand for public inoculations. The indirect utility function of the ith consumer is

$$U^i = \bar{x}^i + \alpha_i^2 / t_i.$$

When the consumer acts as though his taste parameter is α_i^* when it is in fact α_i, the utility is:

$$\begin{aligned} U^i &= \bar{x}^i - \alpha_i^{*2} / t_i + 2\alpha_i \sqrt{(\alpha_i^* / t_i)^2} \\ &= \bar{x}^i - \alpha_i^*(\alpha_i^* + \alpha_j^*) + 2\alpha_i(\alpha_i^* + \alpha_j^*). \end{aligned}$$

If the ith individual takes the other individual's parameter as given, then he will want to adjust his own misstatement of tastes:

$$\alpha_i^* = \alpha_i - \tfrac{1}{2}\alpha_j^*.$$

Only when the two simultaneously announce

$$\alpha_i^* = \tfrac{4}{3}\alpha_i - \tfrac{2}{3}\alpha_j$$

would there be no attempt to negotiate the tax rates. In this case the suboptimal number of inoculations agreed upon will be

$$y = \tfrac{4}{9}(\alpha_1 + \alpha_2)^2.$$

If $\alpha_i > \frac{4}{5}\alpha_j$, then the misstatements return to hurt the ith individual by lowering his utility. When the two individuals have approximately the same actual desire for public inoculations, then both are injured by their misrepresentations. See Chapter 17 for an extensive discussion of deception. ∎

All of the above illustrations of transaction costs are concerned with the negotiation of the contractual terms. Another important source of costs is the enforcement of the agreement. Not only will lawyers' fees be paid to assure that the exchange meets all legal requirements, but there may be legal costs to elicit the actual performance of the promises or to recover damage payments for breach of contract. The larger are the expected legal costs associated with breach the less likely will there be contractual agreement. The following example is based on work done by Shavell (1981, 1982).

Example. Suppose that a buyer is considering the purchase of a built-to-order machine which is expected to add R dollars to the net revenue of the buyer. The machine can be built by the seller but the cost, C, is uncertain and will not be known for some time. Were the buyer and seller to contract to build the machine and the costs turn out to be high the seller might refuse to perform as promised. The buyer can sue for breach of contract but must incur the legal expenses of suit and trial. Let f be the legal fee for drawing up and filing suit, let g be the buyer's projected payment for a trial lawyer, and let h be the seller's trial costs. For simplicity it will be presumed that the litigants agree on the expected damage payment, D, which a trial judgement will grant, and that expected damages exceed the buyer's legal fees, $f+g$. Hence, if the contract is breached the buyer will file suit. However, trial judgement will not be made because an out-of-court settlement is possible: the expected return to the buyer, $D-g$, falls short of the expected cost to the seller, $D+h$. The out-of-court settlement will be somewhere between these two amounts depending on the skill of each party in negotiation. Letting λ be a parameter denoting the settlement skill of the buyer, the financial payment for damages will be

$$S = \lambda(D+h) + (1-\lambda)(D-g).$$

Notice that the suit fee, f, is a sunk cost and does not influence this payment.

The seller decides to breach the contract if the cost of building the machine exceeds the cost of settlement, $C > S$. Let $\pi(C)$ denote the probability that costs of building are less than C. The expected cost of the contract to the seller is:

$$EC = \int_{C \leqslant S} C\,d\pi(C) + S(1-\pi(S)).$$

The expected value of the contract to the buyer is:

$$EV = R\pi(S) + (S-f)(1-\pi(S)).$$

A contract is mutual advantageous when the expected value exceeds the expected cost which occurs when

$$\int_{C \leqslant S} C\,d\pi(c) < R\pi(S) - f(1-\pi(S)).$$

If the legal fees for filing suit, f, increase, this decreases the advantage of contracting. An increase in trial fees for the buyer, g, decreases the settlement, S, and this will decrease expected value more than it decreases expected cost (assuming $R > S$) thus making the contract less advantageous. Increases in the trial fee for the seller, f, make settlement more expensive and this promotes performance and makes contracting more advantegeous. If the legal fees of the buyer are too much larger than the legal fees of the seller, no agreement will be reached and exchange will be thwarted.

CHAPTER 5

MARKETS AND UNCERTAINTY

The competitive price system can allocate uncertainties by enlarging the list of traded commodities to include goods distinguished by the state of nature. To be concrete, suppose that the physical characteristics of a service, an airplane trip from New York to Los Angeles, is coupled with four possible weather conditions,

s_1 = clear weather in New York and Los Angeles,
s_2 = clear weather in New York, cloudy weather in Los Angeles,
s_3 = cloudy weather in New York, clear weather in Los Angeles,
s_4 = cloudy weather in New York and Los Angeles,

to define four commodities, all of them airplane trips from New York to Los Angeles but available only in the corresponding state, s_1, s_2, s_3, or s_4. A consumption or production plan specifies a vector $x = (x_1, x_2, x_3, x_4)$, where x_i is the number of airplane trips in state s_i.

Since we enlarged the list of commodities from one to four, an equal extension of the list of prices must be made. Let p_i be the airfare from New York to Los Angeles in weather state s_i. One does not expect these prices to be equal; in fact, travelers would insist on paying less for a trip in state s_3 than in state s_2 since New York has more cloudy days than Los Angeles. When a buyer purchases a plane trip for state s_i, he must immediately deliver p_i units for account to the seller, and in return receives the right to travel in the specified weather condition. There are no "rain checks". If his ticket says "one flight in clear weather" and it is cloudy in Los Angeles or New York, he has no right to travel; the buyer has gambled and lost. The traveler may buy tickets for each of the four weather states and this hedge will assure travel to Los Angeles, but it a will cost $p_1 + p_2 + p_3 + p_4$ units of account.

This general approach to marketing uncertainty was developed by Arrow (1971a) and Debreu (1959). Let the physical characteristics, dates, and location of commodities be parameterized by a finite number of integers, $k = 1, 2, ..., K$, and let nature take on exactly one state, s, from a finite set of potential states,

$$S = \{s_1, ..., s_m\}.$$

A *contingent commodity plan* is an mK-tuple,

$$x = (x_{1s_1}, x_{2s_1}, ..., x_{Ks_1}, x_{1s_2}, ..., x_{Ks_2}, ..., x_{Ks_m})^{\mathrm{T}}.$$

If the state $s \in S$ occurs, the owner of x has legal rights of ownership to the bundle of goods

$$x_s = (x_{1s}, ..., x_{Ks})^{\mathrm{T}}.$$

The full contingent commodity plan is divided into m different subvectors identifying the quantities of physical goods or services legally owned in each of the m possible states:

$$x = (x_{s_1}, x_{s_2}, ..., x_{sm})^{\mathrm{T}}.$$

The ideal world of competitive market analysis assumes that an mK-dimensional price vector P exists specifying the value of contingent commodities in today's unit of account. A buyer of x in the competitive markets must immediately pay an amount Px, a certain expenditure, but uncertainty still remains about the delivered quantities of physical goods. The trade of contingent commodities allows individuals to shift the inherent natural risks to those who are most able or willing to bear them.

The standard general equilibrium model changes only its interpretation of the component parts. Survival of a consumer may depend critically on the state of nature, but no specific additional assumptions are made about the consumption set X^i. The consumers' preferences for contingent commodities include subjective beliefs about the likelihood of the uncertain states of nature, and while Savage (1954) has shown that with additional assumptions preferences may be represented by an expected utility indicator, the general approach of binary orderings does not have to be modified to incorporate uncertainty (see Chapter 6). The state of nature may dramatically influence the type and quantities of commodities which a producer can manufacture from his inputs; weather may influence a farmer or mechanical breakdowns may affect a manufacturer, but these impacts are included in the technology Y^j, now a subset of $\mathbb{R}^{mk}$. The set Y^j is known by the jth producer, but this does not mean that producers have perfect knowledge of the technology of production. Some states of nature capture the producer's uncertainty about his ability to transform inputs into outputs. For instance, a farmer may be uncertain about how much land can be tilled by a fixed number of men and tractors, but including a random productivity variable in the specification of nature transforms the farmer's uncertainty into an enlarged list of commodities.

The markets for contingent commodities meet once and determine the exchange prices for all contigent commodities, $P^* = (p^*_{1s_1}, ..., p^*_{Ks_m}) = (P^*_{s_1}, ..., P^*_{s_m})$, the demand of individuals, x^{i*}, $i = 1, 2, ..., I$, and the supply of producers, y^{j*}, $j = 1, ..., J$. For markets to be in equilibrium the following conditions must hold:

(1) x^{i*} is optimal with respect to $\succsim_i$ in the set of consumptions which satisfy $x^i \in X^i$ and $P^* x^i \leqslant P^* \omega^i + \Sigma_j \theta_{ij} P^* y^{i*}$,
(2) y^{i*} maximizes profit, $P * y^j$, on Y^j, and
(3) supply equals demand for all contingent commodities,

$$\sum_i x^{i*} = \sum_i \omega^i + \sum_j y^{j*}$$

Because all possible contingencies are accounted for in the definition of commodities, producers do not bear risk. When a producer's machine may or may not be operable due to random malfunctions, the producer simply sells outputs contingent upon the performance of his machine. Risk is born by the holder of the contingent commodity. The producer, paid prior to actual production, has a certain profit derived from payments for goods in either circumstance.

So far the model assumes that all individuals are capable of recognizing the true state of nature after uncertainties have been resolved. For example, the owner of a weather-contingent airplane ticket from New York to Los Angeles is assumed to know on the day of flight the weather in both cities. The owner of a bundle of goods contingent on the functioning of a producer's machine presumably knows when it is functioning or malfunctioning. Without this perfect knowledge individuals would not know if they legally owned a physical commodity.

Radner (1968) incorporated imperfect knowledge of the state of nature in this model of contingent commodity markets. An individual agent who does not learn s learns that the true state of nature belongs to some subset of the set of all states, S. The agent's imperfect knowledge characterizes an *information structure*, $\mathscr{S}$, a partition of the set S:

$$\mathscr{S} = \left\{ M_1, ..., M_q \mid M_j \subseteq S, M_j \cap M_k = \varnothing, j \neq k, \text{ and } \bigcup_{j=1}^{q} M_j = S \right\}.$$

The agent will learn which of the q subsets, $M_1, \ldots, M_q$, contains the true state of nature. If an individual obtains complete knowledge about nature, then his information structure is:

$$\mathcal{S}_c = \{ \{s_1\}, \{s_2\}, \ldots, \{s_m\} \}.$$

In such a case, he learns precisely which state of nature has occurred. An individual who obtains no information about nature has the information structure $\mathcal{S}_n = \{S\}$. He could never distinguish any state from any other. The typical information structure is found between these two extremes.

The limited capability of distinguishing states of nature restrict the contingent commodity plans which an individual would trade. For example, a traveler who learns the weather in New York but not the weather in Los Angeles,

$$\mathcal{S} = \{ \{s_1, s_2\}, \{s_3, s_4\} \},$$

would never want to buy just one ticket contingent on s_1. On the day of travel he would observe clear weather in New York but be unable to determine if he rightfully owns a trip to Los Angeles since it could be cloudy in Los Angeles. His contingent commodity contract is not compatible with his information structure. A plan is *compatible with an information structure* if for all $M \in \mathcal{S}$

$$s \in M \text{ and } s' \in M \text{ imply } x_s = x_{s'}.$$

When an individual has imperfect information, he should buy contingent commodities only if the plan is compatible with his information structure.

A consumption bundle x^i for consumer i is simultaneously restricted to belong to the survival set and to be compatible with his information structure. We define the set of such contingent commodity plans by

$$X^i(\mathcal{S}^i) = \{x^i \in X^i \mid \text{for all } M \in \mathcal{S}^i, x^i_s = x^i_{s'} \text{ if } s, s' \in M\}.$$

Similarly, the jth producer must limit his activities to the set of technically feasible productions which are compatible with his information structure, $\mathcal{T}^j$:

$$Y^j(\mathcal{T}^j) = \{y^j \in Y^j \mid \text{for all } M \in \mathcal{T}^j, y^j_s = y^j_{s'} \text{ if } s, s' \in M\}.$$

The compatibility restriction implies that an individual's contingent commodity plan must lie in a linear subspace of $\mathbb{R}^{mk}$ determined by the agent's partition, $\mathcal{S}$ or $\mathcal{T}$.

The requirement of informational compatibility creates certain difficulties in equilibrium analysis; some classical conditions are not applicable (free disposability cannot hold in general). However, for minor variations in these conditions Radner (1968) has shown that an informationally constrained competitive price equilibrium exists and that the resulting allocation is Pareto efficient relative to the given information structures.

The additional constraints imposed on the economy by the information structures lead to important new results. Two major conclusions are that some contingent markets are less active, and that the market power of some individuals is enhanced. To see the first point, let $\mathscr{A}(\mathscr{S})$ be the subspace of $\mathbb{R}^{mk}$ which is compatible with the information structure $\mathscr{S}$. Define the market trades of consumers and producers by

$$t^i = \omega^i - x^i, \qquad i = 1, ..., I,$$
$$t^j = y^j, \qquad j = 1, ..., J.$$

In discussing market trades it is not important to distinguish the type of agent, so let i be an index of traders going from 1 up to $I + J$. If H is a subset of $\{1, ..., I + J\}$, the net trade of the traders in the group H is

$$\sum_{i \in H} t^i.$$

Market clearing means

$$\sum_{i \in H} t^i + \sum_{j \notin H} t^j = 0.$$

Since the trade of agent i is compatible with his information, in aggregate it must be true that

$$\sum_{i \in H} t^i \in \sum_{i \in H} \mathscr{A}(\mathscr{S}^i).$$

$\mathscr{A}(\mathscr{S})$ is a linear subspace and is identical to $-\mathscr{A}(\mathscr{S})$. The market clearing condition implies that

$$\sum_{i \in H} t^i = -\sum_{j \notin H} t^j \in -\sum_{j \notin H} \mathscr{A}(\mathscr{S}^j) = \sum_{j \notin H} \mathscr{A}(\mathscr{S}^j),$$

and therefore the net trade of group H must belong to

$$\sum_{i \in H} \mathscr{A}(\mathscr{S}^i) \cap \sum_{j \neq H} \mathscr{A}(\mathscr{S}^j).$$

That is to say, the net trade of any group cannot depend upon information which is not known by the other members of the economy. If one particular agent can distinguish between s and state s', but no other trader can make this distinction, the agent is forced to trade equal bundles in states s and s' even though his information would permit otherwise. For example, if a manufacturer is the only agent who can distinguish whether a machine is malfunctioning, then he can only contract to supply a quantity which is producible in the worst situation. Similarly, when no traveler knows both the weather in New York and the weather in Los Angeles, airlines must sell consolidated airplane trips which do not distinguish between the four contingencies. This will happen even though airlines have complete weather information. Obviously when no one can distinguish between state s and s' these two potential contingent commodities collapse into just one commodity.

Radner bases information compatibility on the assumption that fraud is very costly, but the expected cost depends on the probability of proving that another person is breaching the contract. In some cases the expected damage due to fraudulent behavior does not justify dropping the assumption of good faith.

Example. With four states of nature, let the information structures of two consumers be

$$\mathscr{S}^1 = \{\{s_1, s_2\}, \{s_3, s_4\}\}$$

and

$$\mathscr{S}^2 = \{\{s_1\}, \{s_3\}, \{s_2, s_4\}\}.$$

Suppose that the consumers have identical unit endowments of a single good:

$$\omega^1 = \omega^2 = (1, 1, 1, 1),$$

and have identical logarithmic utility functions, $U(x) = \log x$. The information compatibility restriction prevents conditional trading. The consumers differ only in the probabilities they assign to the states of nature; they agree that states 2 and 4 will occur with probability 1/40, but consumer 1 thinks state 1 occurs with probability 9/40 while consumer 2 believes it occurs with probability 29/40. Consumer 2 cannot distinguish state s_2 from s_4, but we will not require that his consumption be informationally compatible. He chooses $(x_1^2, x_2^2, x_3^2, x_4^2)$ to maximize

$$29/40 \log x_1^2 + 1/40 \log x_2^2 + 9/40 \log x_3^2 + 1/40 \log x_4^2$$

$$\text{s.t.} \quad \sum_{h=1}^{4} p_h \cdot x_h^2 = \sum_{h=1}^{4} p_h \cdot 1.$$

Consumer 1 realizes that he can claim without fear of contradiction that the state is in s_4 when he thinks it is in s_2. He buys a bundle (y, y, z, z) but plans on consuming (y, z, z, z), when $y < z$. His object is to maximize

$$9/40 \log y + 1/40 \log z$$

$$\text{s.t.} \quad (p_1 + p_2)y + (p_2 + p_3)z = \sum_{h=1}^{4} p_h \cdot 1.$$

Equilibrium occurs at prices $p = (1131, 39, 1107, 123)$ and the equilibrium contracts are

$$x^1 = (18/39, 18/39, 62/41, 62/41),$$

and

$$x^2 = (60/39, 60/39, 20/41, 20/41).$$

Even though consumer 2 knows that his consumption in state s_2 will not be the contracted amount 60/39, but rather the smaller amount, 20/41, because of the fraudulent behavior of the first consumer, the second consumer improves his welfare by presuming good faith. This achieves an expected utility:

$$29/40 \log 60/39 + 11/40 \log 20/41 = 0.05$$

Restricting contracts so that $x_2^2 = x_4^2$ leads to a smaller expected utility of 0.0. ∎

It can also be argued that if information is garbled for some individuals, those agents with more precise knowledge will have a significant impact on some markets, in the sense of buying or selling a large proportion of the total exchanged commodities.

Example. Suppose there is one physical commodity and two states so that there are two contingent commodities. The economy consists of 100 consumers with identical preferences represented by the utility function $U = x_1^{2/3} x_2^{1/3}$. Each consumer has one dollar income. The sellers supply two units of commodity 1 and one unit of commodity 2, independent of price. If all consumers have complete information (they can distinguish state 1 from state 2) then the market clearing prices would be $p_1 = p_2 = 100/3$ and each consumer would buy a contingent consumption basket with $x_1 = 0.02, x_2 = 0.01$; but instead, suppose that all but one of the consumers lose their ability to distinguish states. These poorly informed consumers are forced to buy equal amounts of contingent goods, $x_1 = x_2$.

The one consumer with complete information may buy different quantities of the contingent goods. Markets clear if prices satisfy the equilibrium conditions,

$$\tfrac{2}{3}\frac{1}{p_1} + \frac{99}{p_1 + p_2} = 2,$$

$$\tfrac{1}{3}\frac{1}{p_2} + \frac{99}{p_1 + p_2} = 1.$$

An approximate solution of these equilibrium conditions is $p_1 = \frac{2}{3}, p_2 = 99$. At these prices the poorly informed majority will consume $x_1 = 0.01 = x_2$ and the single, well-informed consumer will consume $x_1 = 1.0, x_2 = 0.003$ (approximately). It is clear that the market power of the well-informed consumer has increased in the first market – instead of purchasing a hundredth of the total supply in state 1, he now purchases half the supply. It may be unreasonable to assume that he ignores his powerful position in the market. Non-competitive behavior may occur. ■

Markets can allocate risks even when commodities are not distinguished by states exactly as above, but such contingent commodities must be replaced by alternative instruments such as *securities* and *spot commodities*. Define m securities, one for each state of nature, so that the s th security sells for a price ϕ_s and promises the delivery of one monetary unit if and only if nature is in state s. Spot markets open for the K commodities after nature reveals its state. In these spot markets one unit of good k may be purchased at a price of π_{ks} monetary units. The spot and contingent markets differ because π_{ks} monetary units are exchanged for the commodity k only if state s occurs, whereas with contingent commodities p_{ks} monetary units are given up now, irrespective of the eventual state of nature. The securities allow individuals to transfer purchasing power between contingencies and the spot prices permit transfer of purchasing power between physical commodities (after uncertainty is resolved).

These two instruments are equivalent to a system of complete contingent markets. To illustrate the equivalence, consider an exchange model where $P^* = [p^*_{ks}]$ is the equilibrium contingent commodities prices and x^{i*} is the equilibrium demands of consumer i. That is, x^{i*} is the greatest element satisfying $P^*x = P^*\omega^i$ for preferences $\succsim_i$, and $\Sigma_i x^{i*} = \Sigma_i \omega^i$. Security and spot price take on the derived values

$$\phi^*_s = \sum_i \sum_k p^*_{ks} x^{i*}_{ks} \Big/ \sum_i P^*\omega^i$$

and

$$\pi^*_{ks} = \sum_i P^*\omega^i p_{ks} \Big/ \sum_i \sum_k p^*_{ks} x^{i*}_{ks}.$$

The consumer facing these prices (ϕ^*, π^*) would choose the quantities of securities, $z_1^i, ..., z_m^i$ and the quantities of spot consumptions, $x_{ls}^i, ..., x_{ks}^i$ to optimize $\succsim_i$ subject to

$$\sum_s \phi_s^* z_s^i = 0 \tag{1}$$

and

$$\sum_k \pi_{ks}^* x_{ks}^i = z_s^i + \sum_k \pi_{ks}^* \omega_{ks}^i, \quad \text{for each } s \in S. \tag{2}$$

However, the securities can be eliminated as a choice variable by substituting eq. (2) into (1). The remaining constraint on x becomes

$$\sum_s \phi_s^* \sum_k \pi_{ks}^* (x_{ks}^i - \omega_{ks}^i) = 0,$$

but by the definition of (ϕ^*, π^*) this is just

$$p^* x^i = p^* \omega^i.$$

At the security–spot prices (ϕ^*, π^*), preference optimization will lead to the same equilibrium demands, x^{i*}, that would have occurred with complete contingent markets.

The security and spot markets require just as many prices for the determination of equilibrium as do the contingent commodity markets. This is slightly surprising since $m \cdot K$ prices occur in the contingent commodity markets, while the security market require m prices and a spot market requires K prices, for a total of $m + K \leqslant mK$. To establish an equilibrium the full vector π^* of spot prices must be known ex ante, not just the vector $(\pi_{ls}^*, \pi_{2s}^*, ..., \pi_{ks}^*)$ corresponding to the eventual state of nature. The demand for securities depends on the planned consumption in each state; securities are used to finance spot purchases. Without prior knowledge of spot prices the consumer cannot decide on the most desirable consumption plan, so simultaneous determination of q^* and the full vector π^* must occur. Spot markets will be opened later but prices must be established now. Notice that since relative prices are the only relevant variables, each spot market determines only $K - 1$ relevant prices for a total of $m(K - 1) + m - 1 = mK - 1$. This is exactly the same number of relative prices established with contingent commodities.

Akerlof (1970) has argued that asymmetrical information about product quality will cause contingent markets to collapse. This has also been studied in the insurance literature under the heading *adverse selection*. Akerlof illustrated the problem using used automobiles. Random variations in the production process make some cars dependable and others are prone to breakdown ('lemons'). The commodity space should be enlarged to include good cars and bad cars. The owner of a car quickly discovers which quality product he owns, but it is very difficult for anyone else to discover the exact state of nature. Since no one but the owner has information to distinguish good cars from bad, distinct contingent markets will not exist (as Radner showed) and good cars and bad cars must sell at the same price. An owner of a 'lemon' can sell his car at the same price as a good car then turn around and buy a replacement at equal price in the hope that it is not a lemon. It would be in his self-interest to rid himself of his known lemon in the hope of getting a high quality replacement. Such behavior leads to an overall lowering of the average quality of the cars traded and it is possible that no price can produce an equilibrium with active trading. Akerlof presents the following numerical illustration.

Example. Suppose there are two types of traders. Traders of type 1 gain utility from the consumption of an other good and from the quality cars they own according to the utility function

$$U^1 = x^1 + \sum_{j=1}^{n} Q_j^1,$$

where x^1 is the quantity of the other good, Q_j^1 is the quality of the jth automobile, and n is the total number of cars owned. These traders are endowed in aggregate with N cars, whose qualities are uniformly distributed over the interval $[0,2]$; that is, the number of cars with quality in the interval $[Q, Q + \mathrm{d}Q]$ is $(N/2)\mathrm{d}Q$. (Some indivisibilities are ignored.) Traders of type 2 have utility functions

$$U^2 = x^2 + \tfrac{3}{2} \cdot \sum_{j=1}^{n} Q_j^2$$

and have no endowment of cars. Let the price of the other good be unity, the price of cars be p, and the average quality of cars marketed be μ. Any type 1 trader who owns a car of quality Q less than p will want to sell it since the gain in income allows him to buy some units of the other good which has higher marginal utility. The number of type 1 owned cars with quality in this range is $pN/2$, so the supply of cars is $S_2 = pN/2$. The average quality of these marketed cars is:

$$\mu = p/2,$$

since quality is uniformly distributed. If a type 1 trader observes that the price of cars is less than average quality marketed, he will buy cars because the expected marginal utility gain in the purchase of cars exceeds the loss in utility in terms of the forgone other good. If type 1 traders have income I^1 their demand for cars will be

$$D_1 = \begin{cases} \dfrac{I^1}{p}, & \mu > p, \\ 0, & \mu \leqslant p, \end{cases}$$

due to the linearity of utility. Similarly, the demand for cars by type 2 traders is:

$$D_2 = \begin{cases} \dfrac{I^2}{p}, & \tfrac{3}{2}\mu > p, \\ 0, & \tfrac{3}{2}\mu \leqslant p. \end{cases}$$

The adverse selection in this market, i.e. only the relatively bad cars are marketed, implies that average quality is half of price. The buyers, having zero demand at that price-average quality combination, drive P down to zero, where the market is nominally cleared, with price, supply, and demand all zero. The market fails to have positive equilibrium activity due to the extreme informational differences between buyer and seller. ■

Laffont (1975) has shown that the complete breakdown of the market could be prevented if one individual always believed optimistically that the average quality was positive. Whether or not the market actually vanishes, the trading volume will be greatly attenuated by the informational asymmetry, and in such thin markets individual traders may be so large relative to market size as to invalidate the fundamental price-taking assumption.

Another difficulty which occurs in markets which deal with uncertainty is *moral hazard*. Sometimes the relevant outcome of a situation depends not only on the unobserved state of nature but also on the activities of individuals. The likelihood of a fire in a warehouse depends on the precautionary measures taken; the breakdown of a machine is influenced by the operator's care. If a commodity has been sold contingent on a outcome, it would be in the self-interest of the seller to prevent that outcome from occurring. The agent faces a moral dilemma: Should he attempt to influence the natural processes that produce the contingency under which he must give up ownership rights to a commodity? Perhaps this can be phrased less pejoratively: How much effort should he make to assure that the contingency occurs? Trades of contingent commodities may be severely restricted if it is costly to detect those activities which influence the outcome. Since states of nature themselves may be difficult to observe (leading to restricted choice as discussed above), it would be nice if observable proxies could be used to define contingent commodities. Moral hazard makes such a proxy procedure impracticable.

The introduction of contingent commodities based on production uncertainty makes inaccurate the assumption of convexity of the technology of production. In a situation where machines may malfunction and the breakdown of one particular machine is not perfectly correlated with the breakdown of others, machines are not perfect substitutes for each other in a contingent world. With two machines there are four states of nature associated with their malfunctioning:

s_1: both machines operable,
s_2: machine 1 operable, machine 2 inoperable,
s_3: machine 1 inoperable, machine 2 operable,
s_4: both machines inoperable.

Machine 1 is not a substitute for machine 2 if nature takes on state s_2 or s_3. The non-convexity created by the indivisibility of machines may be smoothed out by large numbers of identical machines, but breakdown uncertainty requires that each machine be thought of as a distinct commodity.

Information is a valuable possession. It facilitates a much wider spectrum of contracts for the exchange of goods. The set of informationally compatible contingent activities will expand as new information structures provide a more accurate picture of nature. In the example above with 100 consumers with identical tastes but differing information, 99 of the consumers could not distinguish one state of nature from the other. The remaining consumer could. In that illustration the unique consumer bought one unit of the good to be delivered in state 1 and 0.03 units of the good to be delivered in state 2. The poorly-informed consumers were forced by information limitations to order 0.01 units to be delivered in either state. Had the 99 consumers acquired information about the state of nature, the equilibrium purchases of all 100 would equal 0.02 units for state 1 and 0.01 units for state 2. This would elevate individual utility by about 0.006 utils for each of the 99 and diminish by about 0.1 the utils of the unique consumer. Given this situation, there is incentive for the unique, well-informed consumer to set up a market for information and sell his knowledge to the 99 other consumers. What difficulties would one expect in treating information about nature as a marketed commodity just like any other service?

The most obvious complication is that memory is not destroyed when information is transmitted. If an inventor discovers that a particular production process is technically feasible, he may sell this knowledge to another person, but unless the knowledge is incorporated in a 'black box', the buyer can resell the exact same information to another buyer. Any of the buyers of information can become suppliers of information without relinquishing the rights to the knowledge they possess. It is very costly for the owner of 'information' to enforce property rights to his knowledge. Information is a difficult commodity to protect, unless the information system involves physical objects which can be controlled by the supplier of the information service. Any number of anecdotes about patent infringement could be produced to illustrate the point.

Another problem that must be faced when information is treated as a commodity is quantification. A consulting firm which has information about the fraction of products which will be defective in a particular production process must answer some obvious questions from a potential buyer: How accurate is the consulting firm's information? How much information is actually being provided? In some circumstances the answer may be a specified sample size or measure of dispersion, but these measures may only be partially adequate. Sample size says nothing about the precision of the sampling procedure itself, and variance is only one measure of dispersion. Uniform standards for measuring information are established only at a cost and therefore each piece of information may have to be treated as qualitatively, rather than quantitatively, different from the others. This topic is discussed at length in Chapter 9.

Related to the measurement problem is the potential for deception. When an information system is sold, the *right* to future knowledge is provided, not the knowledge itself. The seller claims he has a product which will narrow the range of values in which the state of nature is known to lie. The actual information will only be learned at some future data when a particular element $M \in \mathscr{S}$ is discovered to contain the true state of nature. Until the state is authenticated the accuracy of the structure $\mathscr{S}$ cannot be verified. A seller may claim that his information system is more informative than it really is and this deception about the quality of information can only be discovered by costly evaluation by the buyer. There can be fraud in the exchange of all kinds of commodities and services; the consumer protection movement in the United States is symptomatic of the scale of occurrence of deception and evaluation. Since information is an intrinsically difficult commodity to measure and hard to authenticate, the amount of deception and the cost of evaluation are much larger for information than for typical commodities.

A major component of an information system is the coding of messages; in essence, a language must be learned in order to understand the implications of the system's signals. Such set-up costs introduce non-convexities in the technology associated with the information. For instance, suppose that without information the technology is:

$$Y' = \{(y_{1s_1}, y_{2s_1}, y_{1s_2}, y_{2s_2}) \mid y_{1s_1} = -y_{2s_1}, y_{1s_2} =$$
$$= -y_{2s_2}, y_{2s_1} \geqslant 0\, y_{2s_2} \geqslant 0\},$$

where y_{1s_i} is labor in state s_i and y_{2s_i} is output in state s_i. Now assume that complete information could be purchased at the cost of one unit of labor, irrespective of the state of nature. The new technology would be

$$Y'' = \{(y_{1s_1}, y_{2s_1}, y_{1s_2}, y_{2s_2}) \mid y_{1s_1} = 1 - y_{2s_1}, y_{1s_2} =$$
$$= 1 - y_{2s_2}, y_{2s_1} \geqslant 0, y_{2s_2} \geqslant 0\}.$$

The technology of the firm with and without information about nature is

$$Y = Y' \cup Y''.$$

Even though Y' and Y'' are convex sets, their union, Y, is not convex; $y' = (-1, 1, -1, 1) \in Y'$ and $y'' = (-2, 1, -2, 1) \in Y''$, but $\frac{1}{2}y' + \frac{1}{2}y''$ is in neither Y' nor Y''. On this basis Radner (1968) argued that the set-up costs of an information system would destroy the classical convexity conditions.

Wilson (1975) has extended this argument to show that even without the fixed set-up cost, the interplay between the optimal selection of information systems and the production technology will lead to economies of scale even when the technology of physical production is free from such non-convexities. Wilson uses the following example to illustrate his argument.

Example. Let y_1 be output produced from inputs $y_2, ..., y_K$. The production plan y is technologically feasible in the state of nature s if it belongs to

$$Y(s) = \{y \mid y = \lambda \cdot (\bar{y}_1(\alpha, s), \bar{y}_2, ..., \bar{y}_K), \lambda \geqslant 0, 0 \leqslant \alpha \leqslant 1\}.$$

The variable λ is a scale factor and the variable α is an index of production technique. $(\bar{y}_1(\alpha, s), \bar{y}_2, ..., y_K)$ is the unit activity vector when the state of nature and technique are s and α, respectively. To be specific, assume the activity vector is determined by the function

$$\bar{y}_1(\alpha, s) = 1 - (\alpha - s)^2.$$

The producer improves output by choosing the technique as close to the state of nature as possible. The production plans, which could be obtained in some state of nature, are

$$\bigcup_{s\in S} Y(s),$$

a convex cone due to the concavity of $\bar{y}_1(\alpha, s)$ in s and the constant returns to scale of $Y(s)$.

Assume that the state of nature is uniformly distributed on the unit interval $S = [0,1]$, and that the firm has access to information structures indexed by a scalar Δ, where $1/\Delta$ is an integer. The information structure associated with Δ partitions the interval into $1/\Delta$ intervals of equal length:

$$\mathscr{S}(\Delta) = \{[0, \Delta), [\Delta, 2\Delta), ..., [1 - \Delta, 1)\}.$$

The information system $\mathscr{S}(\Delta)$ sends a message that the state lies in an interval $[k\Delta, k\Delta + \Delta)$ for some integer k. Given such a message the output maximizing choice of technique would be as follows:

$$\alpha = k\Delta + \Delta/2,$$

and the prior expected output from using this decision procedure would be

$$\eta(\Delta) = 1 - \frac{\Delta^2}{12}.$$

The information structure $\mathscr{S}(\Delta)$ costs the firm forgone output of an amount $c(\Delta)$, a convex function of interval length. For instance, when cost is proportional to the number of sets in the partition, it is proportional to $1/\Delta$, a convex function. Information about the state of nature may be used for any production scale factor. For any given scale factor λ, the optimal information structure maximizes expected output net of the cost of information:

$$y_1(\lambda) = \max_{0 \leqslant \Delta \leqslant 1} \lambda\eta(\Delta) - c(\Delta).$$

Even though the original technology $\cup_{s\in S} Y(s)$ exhibits constant returns to scale, the technology after optimal choice of information system,

$$Y = \{y \mid y = \lambda(y_1(\lambda)_1\, \bar{y}_2, ..., \bar{y}_K), \lambda \geqslant 0\},$$

exhibits increasing returns to scale. For given λ_1 and λ_2, let $\lambda = \omega\lambda_1 + (1-\omega)\lambda_2$, $0 \leqslant \omega \leqslant 1$. It follows that

$$\begin{aligned} y_1(\lambda) &\equiv \max_{\Delta} [\lambda\eta(\Delta) - c(\Delta)] \\ &= \max_{\Delta} [\omega(\lambda_1\eta(\Delta) - c(\Delta)) + (1-\omega)(\lambda_2\eta(\Delta) - c(\Delta))] \\ &\leqslant \omega \max_{\Delta_1}[\lambda_1\eta_1(\Delta_1) - c(\Delta_1)] + (1-\omega)\max_{\Delta_2}[\lambda_2\eta(\Delta_2) - c(\Delta_2)] \\ &= \omega y(\lambda_1) + (1-\omega)y(\lambda_2). \end{aligned}$$

Moreover, since $\eta(\Delta) = 1 - \Delta^2/12$ is strictly concave, the above weak inequality may be strengthened to a strict inequality. ■

Wilson concludes that the cost of information per unit of scale declines as the scale of operation increases. The benefits of information are proportional to the scale of production, so the net result of increasing the scale of production is to justify more information. It is not the fact that information is available, but that it is available in adjustable amounts, which leads to increasing returns to scale in production.

The treatment of information as a commodity traded on a market like any other commodity must address the possibility of market power due to small numbers of traders. Williamson (1975) has re-emphasized the fact that technological information is often acquired only by the operation of a particular production process. The idiosyncratic experience associated with this learning-by-doing puts only a small number of individuals in the position of being able to supply information about a part of the technology. Even if large numbers of people were originally competing for a particular job, first mover advantages may quickly produce monopolistic power for the individuals who first operate the production process. Hirshleifer (1971) has looked at the other side of the market and pointed out that knowledge of particular aspects of nature may be useful only to a limited number of individuals. Information about the durability of a car may only be of importance to the owner of that car. In such circumstances the limited number of potential buyers of an information system may introduce monopsonistic elements to the market determination of terms of exchange.

A final point to be made here is that possession of a unique information system may lead to speculation about the response of future spot markets. Hirshleifer (1971) has pointed out that an inventor can derive benefits from his technological knowledge in several ways. He may try to rent his knowledge for the royalties or he might speculate and distribute his information freely to all other agents. For instance, if an inventor discovers an extremely efficient technique for producing gas from coal, he might buy as much coal-bearing land as he can afford and only then announce to the world that he has made a major discovery. The inventor's gain will correspond to someone else's loss, and it could be argued that such behavior does not lead to any social benefit. Perhaps a more apt illustration would be an inventor who discovers that California is about to be hit by a major earthquake and speculates on the economic response of the population.

In conclusion, the provision of information can be extremely valuable to agents by expanding their degrees of freedom in allocating risk. However, to treat information as just another commodity which markets will allocate is to ignore many difficulties. Measurement, inappropriability, deception, non-convexities, monopoly–monopsony power, and speculative behavior may lead to inefficient use of informational resources.

CHAPTER 6

BEHAVIOR IN THE FACE OF UNCERTAINTY

In the previous chapter we saw how redistribution of risks might occur by extending the list of traded commodities and saw why it is unlikely that this extension would in fact occur. A common thread runs through the remainder of this book: organizations are institutions which are efficient at dealing with uncertainties and information when markets are not. In order to continue this line of reasoning, a coherent model of individual behavior in uncertain circumstances must be elucidated. This chapter defines the approach taken in economics and which is used in the following chapters.

A decision-maker's rewards are determined as a consequence of his actions and the state of nature which prevails. The state of nature which is relevant to the decision-making environment is denoted s, while the action variables which the decision-maker controls are summarized in an action vector α. The joint specification of action and state leads to a reward, r, valued by the decision-maker according to the function

$$r = \rho(\alpha, s).$$

As an example, the action may be the hiring of some number of workers, the state of nature might be the absentee rate, and the reward may then be the effective labor available, $r = (1-s)\alpha$. The variables r, α, and s are elements of R, the set rewards, A, the set of actions, and S, the state space, respectively.

The decision-maker may be unable to learn the state before he is forced to take an action. For a given action $\bar{\alpha}$, the relationship between state and reward, $r = \rho(\bar{\alpha}, s)$, is called an act. Because s is unknown, the consequence that will actually occur is unknown as well. In order to describe or prescribe the choice of action (or act) by a decision-maker, there must be a model of how the decision-maker evaluates situations where consequences of actions are not known with certainty.

Several approaches have been developed to handle decision-making in the face of uncertainty. (See Arrow, 1951c, for an extensive survey.) One very cautious proposal associated with Wald (1945) assumes that nature will always be in the worst possible state. The decision-maker must then protect himself by selecting the action which leads to the best consequence given that nature will take the state which generates the worst consequence for that act. This model is called the maximin criterion. Maximin is open to the criticism that it is too cautious a strategy and assumes nature is antagonistic, even if evidence proves otherwise. Savage (1951) proposed an alternative to the maximin criterion called the minimax regret criterion. Savage assumed that for each state the decision-maker calculates the best consequence and for each act notes the largest difference between consequence and this best consequence (regret). He selects the act which has the smallest maximum "regret." While this criterion is not as cautious as maximin, it is still a cautious criterion which assumes nature is antagonistic. To counter these objections followers of Jacob Bernoulli would suggest that in the face of insufficient reason, the decision-maker should treat each state as being equally likely and select the act which on average has the most desirable consequence. However, well-known gambling paradoxes (see Arrow, 1951c, p. 5) suggest that preferences do not depend just on average consequences. Other schools of thought have suggested that higher moments such as variance should be included in the decision-making criterion. Bernoulli (1730) suggested that if consequences are monetary, then one should treat preferences as though they were logarithms of consequences and select acts which maximize the expected value of these logarithms. Why should the desirability of consequences be determined by logarithms? Von Neumann and Morgenstern (1944) were the first to state a clear set of axioms implying that expected general utility is a reasonable criterion for choice in the face of uncertainty. Von Neumann and Morgenstern did not make any specific assumptions pertaining to the source of the probabilities used in their model. This is an area of continued debate. The works of Koopman (1940), Good (1950), Ramsey (1950), De Finetti (1964), and especially Savage (1954) have championed the development of personal or subjective probability. It is this approach that will be outlined below and followed subsequently.

A 'lottery' is a collection of alternative prizes along with a statement of the probabilities with which the prizes will be awarded. In the present formulation a simple lottery is the set of rewards $R = \{r_1, r_2, ..., r_n\}$ along with a probability vector $P = (p_1, p_2, ..., p_n)$, where $p_i \geqslant 0$, $i = 1, 2, ..., n$, $\Sigma_{i=1}^{n} p_i = 1$. *In this chapter, P denotes probability, not price.* The simple lottery will be denoted $\langle R, P \rangle$. A compound lottery is one in which prizes are lotteries themselves.

A decision-maker should be able to rank lotteries in terms of his desire to participate. The preferences, for lotteries, denoted by $\succsim$, is assumed to be a consistent binary relationship; that is, it satisfies the following.

Axiom 1. $\succsim$ is a complete, reflexive, and transitive binary relationship.

In addition, it is assumed that the decision-maker can reduce compound lotteries to simple lotteries by computing the joint likelihood of receiving consequences.

Axiom 2. The compound lottery which gives $\langle R, P\rangle$ with probability q, $0 \leqslant q \leqslant 1$, and $\langle R, P'\rangle$ with probability $1-q$, is viewed indifferently to the simple lottery $\langle R, qP+(1-q)P'\rangle$.

With this axiom a compound lottery may be denoted $\langle R, qP + (1-q)P'\rangle$. For mathematical simplicity it will be assumed that there exists a best simple lottery and a worst simple lottery.

Axiom 3. There exists lotteries $\langle R, P^{\mathrm{b}}\rangle$ and $\langle R, P^{\mathrm{w}}\rangle$ such that for all lotteries $\langle R, P\rangle$, it is true that $\langle R, P^{\mathrm{b}}\rangle \succsim \langle R, P\rangle \succsim \langle R, P^{\mathrm{w}}\rangle$.

Preferences are continuous if a sequence of lotteries moving from best to worst always passes through indifferences to any given lottery.

Axiom 4. For all lotteries $\langle R, P\rangle$ there exists a q, $0 \leqslant q \leqslant 1$, such that $\langle R, P\rangle \sim \langle R, qP^{\mathrm{b}} + (1-q)P^{\mathrm{w}}\rangle$.

When two lotteries ranked in a given order are combined each identically with a third lottery, then the resulting compound lotteries should be ranked in the same order.

Axiom 5. If $\langle R, P'\rangle \succsim \langle R, P''\rangle$ then,

$$\langle R, qP' + (1-q)P\rangle \succsim \langle R, qP'' + (1-q)P\rangle,$$

for all $0 \leqslant q \leqslant 1$ and $\langle R, P\rangle$.

Finally, if two compound lotteries give as prizes the worst and best simple lotteries, then their desirability depends only on the relative likelihood of getting the best simple lottery.

Axiom 6. $\langle R, qP^{\mathrm{b}} + (1-q)P^{\mathrm{w}}\rangle \succsim \langle R, q'P^{\mathrm{b}} + (1-q')P^{\mathrm{w}}\rangle$ if and only if $q \geqslant q'$.

A decision-maker who satisfies these axioms acts as though lotteries are ranked by a numerical measure which is the expected value of a utility function of the consequences. That is, there exists a continuous, real-valued function U defined on R such that

$$\langle R,P\rangle \gtrsim \langle R,P'\rangle, \quad \text{if and only if,} \sum_{i=1}^{n} U(r_i)P_i \geqslant \sum_{i=1}^{n} U(r_i)P'_i.$$

One such utility function can be defined as follows. The utility of reward r_i, $U(r_i)$, is that number between 0 and 1 such that

$$\langle R, e_i\rangle \sim \langle R, U(r_i)P^{\mathrm{b}} + (1-U(r_i))P^{\mathrm{w}}\rangle,$$

where $e_i = (0, ..., 1, ..., 0)$ is the ith unit vector. This number exists by the continuity axiom 4. Moreover, by axiom 6 it is unique. This does not, however, imply that this utility function is the only utility function which can represent the preferences $\gtrsim$. It can be shown that this utility function leads to an expected utility function which represents the preferences for lotteries.

Theorem 6.1. Define $U(r_i)$, $i = 1, ..., n$, by $\langle R,e_i\rangle \sim \langle R, U(r_i)P^{\mathrm{b}} + (1-U(r_i)P^{\mathrm{w}}\rangle$. Then $\Sigma_{i=1}^{n} U(r_i)P_i$ represents the preferences, $\gtrsim$, for $\langle R, P\rangle$, given axioms 1–6.

Proof. Let us show that the expected utility of $\langle R,P\rangle$ is $\Sigma_i U(r_i)P_i$:

$$\langle R,P\rangle \sim \left\langle R, \sum_{i=1}^{n} P_i e_i \right\rangle \sim \left\langle R, \sum_i P_i (U(r_i)P^{\mathrm{b}} + (1-U(r_i))P^{\mathrm{w}}) \right\rangle$$
$$\sim \left\langle R, \left(\sum_i U(r_i)P_i\right) P^{\mathrm{b}} + \left(1-\sum_i U(r_i)P_i\right) P^{\mathrm{w}} \right\rangle.$$

Let us assume that $\langle R,P\rangle \gtrsim \langle R,P'\rangle$. By the above it must be that

$$\left\langle R, \left(\sum_i U(r_i)P_i\right) P^{\mathrm{b}} + \left(1-\sum_i U(r_i)P_i\right) P^{\mathrm{w}} \right\rangle$$
$$\gtrsim \left\langle R, \left(\sum_i U(r_i)P'_i\right) P^{\mathrm{b}} + \left(1-\sum_i U(r_i)P'_i\right) P^{\mathrm{w}} \right\rangle.$$

By axiom 6 this is equivalent to

$$\sum_{i=1}^{n} U(r_i)P_i \geqslant \sum_{i=1}^{n} U(r_i)P'_i. \quad \blacksquare$$

As noted above, the utility function $U(r)$ is not the only representation of preferences. However, the class of representative functions consists only of affine transformations of U.

Theorem. The expected utility $\Sigma_{i=1}^n U(r_i)P_i$ defined above is unique up to a slope and intercept modification.

Proof. Suppose that $\tilde{U}(r) = aU(r) + b$. Then

$$\begin{aligned}\tilde{U}(\langle R,P\rangle) &= a\,U(\langle R,P\rangle) + b\\ &= a \sum_{i=1}^{n} U(r_i)P_i + b\\ &= \sum_{i=1}^{n} P_i(aU(r_i) + b)\\ &= \sum_{i=1}^{n} P_i(aU(\langle R,e_i\rangle) + b)\\ &= \sum_{i=1}^{n} P_i\tilde{U}(\langle R,e_i\rangle).\end{aligned}$$

Hence, $\tilde{U}$ is an expected utility indicator. Suppose that $\tilde{U}$ is an expected utility indicator representing $\succsim$. It must be shown that $\tilde{U}$ differs from U by an affine transformation. $\tilde{U}$ and U differ by a monotonic transformation ϕ since they both represent $\succsim$:

$$\begin{aligned}\tilde{U}(\langle R,P\rangle) &= \phi(U(\langle R,P\rangle))\\ &= \phi\left(\sum_{i=1}^{n} U(r_i)P_i\right).\end{aligned}$$

However,

$$\phi(U(\langle R,e_i\rangle) = \phi(U(r_i)) = \tilde{U}(r_i),$$

so

$$\tilde{U}(\langle R,P\rangle) = \sum_{i=1}^{n} \phi(U(r_i))P_i.$$

Differentiating $\tilde{U}$ twice with respect to P_i in both of these formulae gives $\phi''(U\langle R,P\rangle) = 0$ which means that ϕ is affine. ■

In summary, the expected utility criterion says that a decision-maker holding the beliefs that the state of nature $s \in S$ occurs with probability $P(s)$, will rank alternative actions, α, by calculating the expected utility,

$$\sum_{s \in S} U(\rho(\alpha, s))P(s),$$

and choose that action which maximizes this on the set A.

Nothing has yet been said about how the numerical evaluations of the relative likelihood of states of nature are determined. To begin this discussion, let us assume that in addition to S there has been specified a class of subsets of $S, \mathscr{S}$, with the following properties:

(1) $S \in \mathscr{S}$.

(2) If $E \in \mathscr{S}$, then $E^c \in \mathscr{S}$ (E^c is the complement of E in S).

(3) If $E_1, E_2, \ldots$ is a sequence of sets all of which belong to $\mathscr{S}$, then $\cup_{i=1}^{\infty} \in \mathscr{S}$.

That is, $\mathscr{S}$ is a σ-field of *events*. A probability measure, P, defined on $\mathscr{S}$ is a real-valued function which satisfies the properties:

(1) $P(E) \geqslant 0, E \in \mathscr{S}$.

(2) $P(S) = 1$.

(3) If $E_1, E_2, \ldots,$ is a sequence of pairwise disjoint events $(E_i \cap E_j = \varnothing, i \neq j)$, then $P(\cup_{i=1}^{\infty} E_n) = \Sigma_{i=1}^{\infty} P(E_i)$.

It will be assumed that the decision-maker has beliefs about the relative likelihood of the occurrence of events in $\mathscr{S}$. What we would like to show is that these 'qualitative' probabilities can be represented as 'quantitative' probability measures defined on $\mathscr{S}$. When relative likelihoods satisfy certain conditions this transformation can be uniquely effected.

If event E is deemed to be more likely than event F, this fact will be denoted

$$E \succsim^{\mathscr{L}} F.$$

As usual we will assume that relative likelihood is a consistent binary order on $\mathscr{S}$.

Axiom I. The relation $\succsim^{\mathscr{L}}$ is a complete, reflexive, transitive binary order.

We would also like to make the reasonable assumption that the null event is always viewed the least likely event and the state space, S, is the most likely event.

Axiom II. For all $E \in \mathcal{S}, S \succsim^{\mathcal{L}} E \succsim^{\mathcal{L}} \varnothing$.

For technical reasons it would be desirable to assume that a sequence of expanding events, each member of which is less likely than E, does not produce a more likely event than E when joined together.

Axiom III. If E is a given event and $F_1, F_2, \ldots$, is a sequence of events, $F_1 \subseteq F_2 \subseteq \ldots$ and such that $E \succsim^{\mathcal{L}} F_i$ for $i = 1, 2, \ldots$, then $E \succsim^{\mathcal{L}} \cup_{i=1}^{\infty} F_i$.

The above three axioms are not yet sufficient to guarantee the existence of a probability measure which represents the relative likelihood, $\succsim^{\mathcal{L}}$. In order to do that, the decision-maker must have a mental picture of an experiment with 'known' probability with which to calibrate $\succsim^{\mathcal{L}}$.

Axiom IV. There exists a random variable $X(s)$ mapping S into the reals such that this random variable has a uniform distribution on the unit interval $[0,1]$.

That is to say, there exists in the mind of the decision-maker an auxiliary experiment which produces a uniform distribution on $[0,1]$.

Given axioms I–IV the decision-maker's beliefs about relative likelihoods of events can be represented uniquely by a probability measure on $\mathcal{S}$. To this end, for any interval (a, b), $0 \leqslant a \leqslant b \leqslant 1$, let $F(a, b)$ be the event

$$F(a, b) = \{s \in S \mid X(s) \in (a, b)\}.$$

For each event $E \in \mathcal{S}$ define the probability measure of $E, P(E)$, by

$$F(0, P(E)) \sim^{\mathcal{L}} E.$$

Theorem 6.2. For all $E \in \mathcal{S}, P(E)$ exists, is unique, lies in $[0,1]$, and agrees with $\succsim^{\mathcal{L}}$ on $\mathcal{S}$, in the sense that $P(E) \geqslant P(E')$ if and only if $E \succsim^{\mathcal{L}} E'$ for all $E, E' \in \mathcal{S}$.

Proof. For any $E \in \mathcal{S}$, define $H(E)$ by

$$H(E) = \{b \in [0,1] \mid F(0, b) \succsim^{\mathcal{L}} E\}.$$

Since $F(0,1) = S$, axiom II implies that

$$F(0,1) \succsim^{\mathcal{L}} E,$$

and thus $H(E)$ is not empty. Let $b^* = \text{infimum } \{b \mid F(0, b) \succsim^{\mathscr{L}} E\}$ and let b_1, b_2 ..., be any decreasing sequence from $H(E)$ that converges to b^*. By the definition of F it must be that

$$F(0, b^*) = \bigcap_{i=1}^{\infty} F(0, b_i).$$

Taking the complements of this, applying deMorgan's rule, $(E_1 \cap E_2)^c = E_1^c \cup E_2^c$, and axiom III, it must be true that

$$F(0, b^*) \succsim^{\mathscr{L}} E.$$

By the definition of b^*, if $b < b^*$, then

$$F(0, b) \precsim^{\mathscr{L}} E.$$

Let b_1, b_2, ..., be a strictly increasing sequence of numbers converging to b^*; then

$$F(0, b^*) = \bigcup_{i=1}^{\infty} F(0, b_i).$$

By axiom III this implies

$$F(0, b^*) \precsim^{\mathscr{L}} E.$$

Therefore $F(0, b^*) \sim^{\mathscr{L}} E$ and we have existence. Uniqueness follows immediately. By definition of $P(E)$, $E \succsim^{\mathscr{L}} E'$ means

$$F(0, P(E)) \succsim^{\mathscr{L}} F(0, P(E')),$$

but by the uniform distribution on [0,1] this holds if and only if
$P(E) \geqslant P(E')$. ■

Several properties of probability distributions will be summarized here; more extensive developments may be found in any textbook on probability and statistics such as DeGroot (1970) or Parzen (1960). A real-valued function defined on S, $f(s)$, has an expected value

$$\mathrm{E}\{f\} = \sum_{s \in S} f(s) P(s).$$

In particular, if S is a subset of the real numbers, the mean of the variable s is the expected value of s:

$$\mathrm{E}\{s\} \equiv \bar{s} = \sum_{s \in S} s\,P(s).$$

The variance of S is the expected squared deviation of s from its mean:

$$\mathrm{var}\{s\} \equiv \sigma^2 = \mathrm{E}\{(s - \mathrm{E}\{s\})^2\} = \sum_{s \in S} (s - \mathrm{E}\{s\})^2 P(s)$$

The square root of the variance is called the standard deviation, σ.

The state of nature is sometimes comprised of a collection of several aspects. If the state is an ordered pair of numbers,

$$s = (s_1, s_2) \in S_1 \times S_2,$$

then the probability $P(s)$ is interpreted as the joint probability that each term takes on its respective value. The marginal probability of either term is found by summing across all possible values of the other term,

$$P_1(s_1) = \sum_{s_2 \in S_2} P(s_1, s_2)$$

$$P_2(s_2) = \sum_{s_1 \in S_1} P(s_1, s_2).$$

The variables s_1 and s_2 are independent when the joint probability is the product of the marginal probabilities:

$$P(s_1, s_2) = P_1(s_1) P_2(s_2).$$

The conditional probability of s_1 given a specific value of s_2 is defined to be

$$P_{1|2}(s_1 \mid s_2) = P(s_1, s_2) / P_2(s_2).$$

Similarly,

$$P_{2|1}(s_2 \mid s_1) = P(s_1, s_2) / P_1(s_1).$$

The covariance of s_1 and s_2 is the expected value of the product of $S_1 - \mathrm{E}\{s_1\}$ and $S_2 - \mathrm{E}\{s_2\}$:

$$\operatorname{cov}\{s_1, s_2\} = \mathrm{E}\{(s_1 - \mathrm{E}\{s_1\})(s_2 - \mathrm{E}\{s_2\})\}$$
$$= \sum_{s_1 \in S_1} \sum_{s_2 \in S_2} (s_1 - \bar{s}_1)(s_2 - \bar{s}_2) P(s_1, s_2).$$

The correlation coefficient is the ratio of the covariance to the product of standard deviations:

$$\operatorname{corr}\{s_1, s_2\} = \operatorname{cov}\{s_1, s_2\} / \sqrt{\operatorname{var}\{s_1\} \operatorname{var}\{s_2\}}.$$

The state space S has been taken to be a finite set but often it will be more appropriate to let S be the real numbers or an interval of real numbers. With a continuum of possible states any particular state is infinitesimal and therefore will occur with probability. This requires us to reinterpret probability distributions. A probability density function $P(s)$ is interpreted as follows: the probability that the state falls in the interval $[s, s + \mathrm{d}s]$ equals $P(s)\mathrm{d}s$ for suitably small $\mathrm{d}s$. The probability that the state is in an interval $[s', s'']$ is given by the integral

$$\int_{s'}^{s''} P(s)\mathrm{d}s.$$

All of the above properties carry over to continuous probability densities with integrals playing the role of summations.

We have now established that if a decision-maker's preferences and beliefs satisfy a collection of assumptions (axioms 1–6 and I–IV), then his probabilistic beliefs can be uniquely represented by a probability measure on the set of events and the preferences for consequences can be represented by a utility function, unique up to affine transformations, such that the decision-maker ranks actions according to his subjective expected utility

$$\sum_{s \in S} U(\rho(\alpha, s)) P(s).$$

The remainder of this chapter should be read under the assumption that this expected utility can be calculated by all decision-makers. It should be pointed out that the decision-makers do not choose actions because the expected utility is large. Rather, the actions that are selected happen to have large expected utility. The primary characteristics of the decision-maker are the orderings $\succsim$ and $\succsim^{\mathscr{L}}$, not $U(r)$ and $P(s)$. The expected utility is just a convenient analytic technique for characterizing the more fundamental behavioral assumptions.

Expected utility has grown to be a very popular theoretical criterion. However, in all fairness it must be pointed out that it has shortcomings just like other criteria. Not all individuals behave according to our axioms 1–6 and I–IV, and moreover they may have good reasons for not doing so. Some of the more obvious difficulties are spelled out in the remaining paragraphs of this section, but the reader might want to look at the surveys by Edwards (1961), Slovic and Lichtenstein (1971), and Kahneman and Tversky (1979) for more detailed analysis.

Allais (1953) developed a counterexample to axiom 5, which even the most sophisticated analysts find reasonable. Suppose that the rewards are monetary and there are four lotteries:

(1) $\langle(\$\,0, \$\,4000), (0.20, 0.80)\rangle$,

(2) $\langle(\$\,0, \$\,3000), (0.0\ \ , 1.0\ \ )\rangle$,

(3) $\langle(\$\,0, \$\,4000), (0.80, 0.20)\rangle$,

(4) $\langle(\$\,0, \$\,3000), (0.75, 0.25)\rangle$,

Many decision-makers, if given the choice between (1) and (2), choose (2) because they are afraid of giving up a sure \$ 3000 in the hope of winning only \$ 4000, even though the expected monetary value of (1) exceeds that of (2). The same decision-makers often choose (3) over (4). In neither (3) nor (4) is there any sure way of winning and the decision-maker opts for the lottery with the highest expected income. However, in making this pair of choices he has made a critical mistake. From the first choice, if he was maximizing expected utility, one could infer that

$$0.20\,U(0) + 0.80\,U(4000) < 1.0\,U(3000).$$

From the second choice, we know that

$$0.80\,U(0) + 0.20\,U(4000) > 0.75\,U(0) + 0.25\,U(3000),$$

or

$$0.05\,U(0) + 0.20\,U(4000) > 0.25\,U(3000),$$

or multiplying by 4

$$0.20\,U(0) + 0.80\,U(4000) > 1.0\,U(3000).$$

This contradiction arises from an apparent violation of axiom 5. Kahneman and Tversky (1979) found that in a sample of 100 individuals, 61 made the choices that Allais thought to be reasonable. Moreover, they found that when consequences are monetary losses rather than gains (+4000 is replaced by −4000, etc.) many individuals' preferences changed to (1) $\succsim$ (2) and (4) $\succsim$ (3). This too violates the expected utility assumption, but for apparently different reasons. With negative consequences the decision-makers seem to prefer a risky venture to a sure loss.

Kahneman and Tversky (1979) have identified two other common violations of the expected utility criterion: aversion to probabilistic insurance and the isolation effect. Probabilistic insurance can be analyzed with the following lotteries:

$$(5)\ \langle(\$\,4000, \$\,3000), (0.80, 0.20)\rangle,$$

$$(6)\ \langle(\$\,4000, \$\,3750), (0.0, 1.0)\rangle,$$

$$(7)\ \langle(\$\,4000, \$\,3800), (0.0, 1.0)\rangle,$$

$$(8)\ \langle(\$\,3800, \$\,3750, \$\,3000), (0.97, 0.01, 0.02)\rangle.$$

The lottery (5) involves a situation where an accident may occur with probability 0.20 which destroys a significant proportion of the decision-maker's wealth. Lotteries (6) and (7) are standard insurance policies against the above risks. The decision-maker pays a fixed premium ($ 250 and $ 200) to completely eliminate the risk. Many individuals desire such insurance. Let us assume that the individual is just indifferent between (5) and (6) and has strict preference for (7) over (5). The final lottery is probabilistic insurance; essentially, if the accident happens there is a 98 percent chance that the individual will be covered by the insurance policy. If he is insured, his premium is adjusted at random, with odds 97 to 1 that it will be $ 200 rather than $ 250. In most cases individuals choose the standard insurance policies (6) and (7) over probabilistic insurance, but this leads to a contradiction in the expected utility criterion. Let us set $U(3000) = 0$ and $U(4000) = 1$ without loss of generality. If (5) and (6) are viewed indifferently, then

$$U(3750) = 0.80\ U(4000) = 0.8.$$

Choice of (6) over (8), however, implies that

$$U(3750) > 0.97\ U(3800) + 0.01\ U(3750)$$

or

$$U(3800) < 0.817.$$

This implies that the slope of the utility function between 3750 and 3800 is less than 3.3×10^{-4}, while the slope between 3800 and 4000 exceeds 9.2×10^{-4}, contradicting the assumption that standard insurance (7) is desirable; gains in wealth from \$ 3800 are more desirable than equal losses and hence the individual is desirous of gambling on (5) rather than taking the sure income of (7).

The isolation effect is meant to capture the idea that, in Kahneman and Tversky's words, 'people often disregard components that the alternatives share and focus on the components that distinguish them'. Consider the following lotteries:

(9) you are given \$ 1000 and the lottery ⟨(\$ 0, \$ 1000), (0.5, 0.5)⟩,

(10) you are given \$ 2000 and the lottery ⟨(\$ 0, – \$ 1000), (0.5, 0.5)⟩,

(11) you are given \$ 1000 and the lottery ⟨(\$ 0, \$ 500), (0.0, 1.0)⟩,

(12) you are given \$ 2000 and the lottery ⟨(\$ 0, – \$ 500), (0.0, 1.0)⟩.

Many decision-makers would choose (11) over (9) and (10) over (12). In the first situation they decide to be cautious and in the second situation they gamble they will not loose the thousand dollars. These choices seen to assign two different utilities to the monetary values \$ 2000 and \$ 1500, contradicting the expected utility criterion. Apparently, the integration of a lottery into the utility function depends on the starting level of assets. A similar effect is observed with probabilities. Imagine the following sequential lotteries.

(13) There is a 75 percent chance that you will not get to play and will go home empty handed. If you play, you get the lottery ⟨(\$ 0, \$ 4000), (0.20, 0.80)⟩.

(14) There is a 75 percent chance that you will not get to play and will go home empty handed. If you play, you get the lottery ⟨(\$ 0, \$ 3000), (0.0, 1.0)⟩.

Most people choose the sequential lottery (14), apparently ignoring the common prospect of being sent home empty handed. However, the lottery (13) is equivalent to lottery (3) above and lottery (14) is equivalent to (4). As noted there, most individuals would choose (3) over (4), contradicting their choice of (14) over (13).

Objections have been raised about the way personal probabilities enter the expected utility criterion. Ellsberg (1961) developed the following. Suppose two urns contain 100 black or white balls each, the first urn containing an equal number of white and black balls while nothing is known about the second urn. The decision-maker is told that if he draws a black ball from an urn on the first try he will receive a \$ 1000 reward. Frequently, the decision-maker draws the ball from the first urn. This implies that he thinks the second urn has relatively fewer black than white balls. However, if the lottery is changed so that the reward is for drawing a white ball, most decision-makers still draw from urn 1. In a related example, a single urn contains 30 red balls and 60 other balls which may be white or black. There are five lotteries. Lottery 1 pays \$ 1000 if a red ball is drawn; lottery 2 pays \$ 1000 if a black ball is drawn; lottery 3 pays \$ 1000 if a red or white ball is drawn; lottery 4 pays \$ 1000 if a black or white ball is drawn; and lottery 5 pays \$ 1000 if a white ball is drawn. Many individuals would rather have lottery 1 than lottery 2 because they are unsure about the number of black balls and certain that 1/3 of all balls are red. Many individuals would select 4 rather than 3 since there is a 2/3 chance of getting a black or white ball but the odds on red or white is not known precisely. Many individuals would be indifferent between lotteries 2 and 5 based on a principle of insufficient reason. However, this gives the following contradiction of transitivity. Lottery 1 is preferred to 2 as above, and this is indifferent to 5 for reasons given. However, lottery 5 is equivalent to the compound lottery of getting lottery 2 with probability 1/2 and lottery 4 with probability 1/2. Suppose that the subjective probability of black is P and that of white is $2/3 - P$, then the compound gamble has a probability of $1/2 \cdot P + 1/2(2/3 - P) = 1/3$ of paying off irrespective of P. Hence, the compound lottery should be exactly equivalent to lottery 1, but this is a violation of transitivity.

Drèze (1974) records another example. The rewards are monetary and artistic, R = {\$ 1000, −\$ 1000, ticket to Beethoven concert, ticket to jazz concert}. The lotteries are:

(15) $\langle R, (0.5, 0, 0.5, 0)\rangle$,

(16) $\langle R, (0.5, 0, 0, 0.5)\rangle$,

(17) $\langle R, (0, 0.5, 0.5, 0)\rangle$,

(18) $\langle R, (0, 0.5, 0, 0.5)\rangle$.

Many individuals would choose (15) over (16), preferring to make up for their disappointment in missing out on the \$ 1000 by listening to Beethoven. The same individual may select (18) over (17), wanting to celebrate his escape from financial calamity by listening to jazz. However, compound lotteries of (15) and (18), and (16) and (17), with equal probabilities, give identical simple lotteries $\langle C, (0.25, 0.25, 0.25, 0.25)\rangle$, yet it would appear that (15) and (18) should dominate (16) and (17).

Although the above objections should be noted, we will continue to presume that decision-makers' tastes and beliefs are coherent enough so that they choose the action which

$$\text{maximizes } \sum_{s \in S} U(\rho(\alpha, s))\, P(s)$$

$$\text{subject to } \alpha \in A.$$

Further refinements will be made at some points. For example, it will sometimes be assumed that preferences are smooth enough so that appropriate continuous derivatives are defined. A choice of actions from an interval of the real numbers may then be characterized by the first-order condition:

$$\sum_{s \in S} U'(\rho(\alpha, s)) \frac{\partial \rho}{\partial \alpha} (\alpha, s)\, P(s) = 0.$$

It will often seem appropriate to take the decision-maker for a risk-averter. Following Arrow (1971b) and Pratt (1964), a decision-maker is risk averse if he would choose a lottery with no rewards over one with a fair gamble to win or lose. That is,

$$U(0) > P_1 U(r_1) + P_2 U(-r_2)$$

when

$$P_1 r_1 + P_2 (-r_2) = 0.$$

If we denote the maximum amount the decision-maker would pay and still be better than a fair gamble by π, it must be that

$$U(-\pi) \equiv P_1 U(r_1) + P_2 U(-r_2).$$

For small gambles we can approximate the utility functions by Taylor series around zero:

$$U(0) - U'(0)\pi = P_1 (U(0) + U'(0) r_1 + \tfrac{1}{2} U''(0) r_1^2) +$$
$$+ P(U(0) - U'(0) r_2 + \tfrac{1}{2} U''(0) r_2^2)$$

or

$$-U'(0)\pi = \tfrac{1}{2} U''(0)(P_1 r_1^2 + P_2 r_2^2),$$

where the fair gamble assumption has been used. Solving for the term π, we have

$$\pi = \tfrac{1}{2} \left(\frac{-U''(0)}{U'(0)} \right) (P_1 r_1^2 + P_2 r_2^2).$$

The amount the decision-maker would pay to be rid of a fair gamble is proportional to the variance of the gamble, $P_1 r_1^2 + P_2 r_2^2$, and a term which will be interpreted as the measure of risk aversion:

$$-U''(0) \,/\, U'(0).$$

Assuming that utility increases with rewards, this payment is positive when the utility is a concave function of reward, $U''(0) < 0$.

Example. Suppose that an investor can borrow any amount of money he wants at a fixed interest rate i and invest in a risky asset. The asset is expected to pay a dividend per dollar investment in either the amount s_1 or s_2. The investor thinks that the probability of s_k is P_k. The reward is the net income from borrowing an amount α,

$$r = \rho(\alpha, s) = \alpha(1 + s) - \alpha(1 + i),$$

and the optimal action is that borrowing which maximizes

$$\mathrm{E}\{U\} = P_1 U(\alpha(1 + s_1) - \alpha(1 + i)) + P_2 U(\alpha(1 + s_2) - \alpha(1 + i)).$$

The first-order condition which characterizes the optimal investment comes from setting the derivative of expected utility equal to zero:

$$0 = P_1 U'(\alpha(1 + s_1) - \alpha(1 + i))(s_1 - i) +$$
$$+ P_2 U'(\alpha(1 + s_2) - \alpha(1 + i))(s_2 - i).$$

If utility is a quadratic function of reward,

$$U = u_0 + u_1 r - \tfrac{1}{2} u_2 r^2, \qquad u_0, u_1, u_2 > 0,$$

and $s_1 < i < s_2$, then the optimal value of α must satisfy

$$0 = P_1(u_1 + u_2\alpha(s_1 - i))(s_1 - i) + P_2(u_1 + u_2\alpha(s_2 - i))(s_2 - i)$$

or

$$\alpha = \frac{P_1 u_1(s_1 - i) + P_2 u_1(s_2 - i)}{P_1 u_2(s_1 - i)^2 + P_2 u_2(s_2 - i)^2} \,.$$

Only when the expected return on the risky investment exceeds the cost of funds, $P_1 s_1 + P_2 s_2 > i$, will the investor borrow. The larger is u_2, the more risk averse is the decision-maker and the smaller is the optimal amount of borrowing. ■

In the above decision problem the choice of action was based on tastes and beliefs, but did not use any additional information about the unknown state of nature. What changes if the decision-maker has access to an information system which provides a message about the state of nature before actions must be chosen? The message may not tell exactly what value s takes but it may help by reducing the degree of uncertainty about s. Suppose that η is a random variable whose probability distribution varies with the state of nature; that is, η and s are not independent. The likelihood of receiving a message η when the true state is s is given by the conditional probability

$$P(\eta \mid s).$$

When the decision-maker observes a particular value of η, the probability of the unknown state should be modified according to Bayes' Theorem:

$$\begin{aligned} P(s \mid \eta) &= P(\eta \mid s) \cdot P(s) \,/\, P(\eta) \\ &= P(\eta \mid s)P(s) \Big/ \sum_{s \in S} P(\eta \mid s)P(s). \end{aligned}$$

The optimal decision should make use of any information which helps reduce the uncertainty of the state. The decision-maker must select a decision rule which specifies how each possible message will be used to determine the action. We will denote the decision rule by a function mapping the set of all possible messages, H, into the set of possible actions, A:

$$\alpha = \alpha(\eta).$$

For any decision rule the expected utility is given by

$$\begin{aligned} \mathrm{E}U[\alpha] &= \mathrm{E}\{U(\rho(\alpha(\eta), s))\} \\ &= \sum_{s \in S} \sum_{\eta \in H} U(\rho(\alpha(\eta), s))P(\eta \mid s)P(s). \end{aligned}$$

By reordering summations and grouping terms, the expected utility may be expressed as

$$\mathrm{E}U[\alpha] = \sum_{\eta \in H} \left[\sum_{s \in S} U(\rho(\alpha(\eta), s)) P(s \mid \eta) \right] P(\eta).$$

If $P(\eta) > 0$, maximizing expected utility requires for each η that the term in square brackets be maximized, but that term is nothing other than expected utility conditional upon η since $P(s)$ has been replaced by the posterior probability $P(s \mid \eta)$ using Bayes' Theorem.

Example. We will follow the previous example but assume that a message will be received forecasting the dividend payment. Let $H = \{\eta_1, \eta_2\}$ and

$$P(\eta_1 \mid s_1) = 0.9, \quad P(\eta_1 \mid s_2) = 0.1,$$

$$P(\eta_2 \mid s_1) = 0.1, \quad P(\eta_2 \mid s_2) = 0.9.$$

The message η_1 is a very strong indicator that the dividend will be s_1. The decision rule is a specification of how much to borrow depending on the dividend forecast; let $\alpha(\eta_1)$, $\alpha(\eta_2)$ be the respective borrowing. The posterior probabilities for the dividend given the forecast are calculated from Bayes' Theorem:

$$P(s_1 \mid \eta_1) = 0.9\, P_1 \,/\, (0.9\, P_1 + 0.1\, P_2),$$

$$P(s_2 \mid \eta_1) = 0.1\, P_2 \,/\, (0.9\, P_1 + 0.1\, P_2),$$

$$P(s_1 \mid \eta_2) = 0.1\, P_1 \,/\, (0.1\, P_1 + 0.9\, P_2),$$

$$P(s_2 \mid \eta_2) = 0.9\, P_2 \,/\, (0.1\, P_1 + 0.9\, P_2).$$

If each state was originally equally likely, $P_1 = P_2 = 1/2$, then the posterior probability of s_1 given η_1 is 0.9, etc. ■

CHAPTER 7

WHY ARE THERE BOSSES?

Almost every worker in the world has a boss at sometime in his or her life. The boss supervises, monitors, and inspects the performance of labor. He determines the wages paid, is instrumental in promoting or demoting, and often hires and fires the worker. The boss determines the daily work activities and modifies the plans made yesterday to suit the circumstances of today. The boss is frequently the most influential figure in the worker's life outside the immediate family.

Not every individual has a boss. A farmer plants, harvest, and sells those crops which he feels are best suited to the particular land he tills. No one dictates the choice of crop, method of cultivation, or the timing of his sale. The lawyer has a collection of clients whom he serves but his relationship to the man who wants a will drawn up is not one that involves supervision, direction, or subservience. The lawyer is the agent of his client but the client is not the boss. The small businessman who runs a dry-cleaner makes all the important decisions on location of his shop, hours of operation, equipment to use, advertisement policy, and price of cleaning shirts and skirts. The handyman who contracts to cut down a tree in someone's back yard and dispose of the timber is an independent contractor. He does not expect to be ordered to do the job in any particular way. He uses his own tools and uses his own methods.

Before the presence of a boss can be explained, the precise role of the boss must be delineated and differentiated from that of a mere employer. Five work situations will illustrate the functions of the boss. First, Joe, a corn farmer, supplements his own holdings of farm land by renting land from neighbors and by farming land owned by relatives. He pays a fixed rent to the neighbors regardless of the profit or loss he earns from the crops he grows, and the profit earned on his kins' land is shared among them. Joe has complete freedom to determine all aspects of the production process. In the second situation, George has a rubber tree in his yard which is so large that its roots are damaging his patio. He considered hiring a day-laborer and directing him how to cut down and remove the tree, but found instead a handyman who will dispose of the tree for a fixed fee. The handyman uses his own truck, chainsaw, and helpers and expects no guidance from George. Third, Jasmina is a lawyer in a large law firm. Cases are assigned to her by the senior partners of the firm and the clients ask her to develop briefs, appear in court, and other such tasks. The clients define the limits of Jasmina's activities but within those limits she is free to use her expertise to determine the best course of action. Fourth, Pat is an airline reservation agent who answers telephone requests for flight information and reservations. Once she plugs into the computer system and begins answering phone calls she is required to follow a strictly defined routine which tells how to greet the caller, how to respond to a request for flight times, and so forth. Airline supervisors may monitor conversations to be certain that she is working and following the stated procedures. Pat's work shift – day, night, or graveyard – is determined by a strict seniority system and the airline has only the right to determine the number of agents on each shift, not which agents work the shifts. The fifth work environment involves Jim, an employee of a laundry. The laundry business involves four work stations: sorting into hot, cold, and dry-clean; operating the commercial washer; drying and folding; and pickup and delivery. Each day some employees may be absent due to illness, or some machine may malfunction or the load may be heavy with dry-cleaning. The laundry manager assigns workers to stations as it seems most appropriate in the circumstance. Jim finds that some stations are more difficult than others and dislikes the uncertainty that he faces about the job conditions.

Each of the above situations involves the employment of humans in a production process. Which ones have a boss and what do these bosses do? The employer in all cases is responsible for the negotiation of the terms of the employment: what work must be done, who decides how to vary the tasks if an unusual circumstance occurs, and what is the compensation for the worker's effort. Once contract terms have been established the employer is responsible for monitoring the performance of the labor activities. Finally, if an event takes place that was not anticipated in the negotiation stage, the boss decides the most appropriate response and directs the worker to take the corresponding action.

While a boss has a role in contract negotiation, contract enforcement, and non-contractual decision-making, in this chapter particular emphasis will be placed on the boss as a decision-maker. The relatives of Joe must reach an agreement with him over what share of profits they receive in compensation for the land they lend him and they must make sure that the payment corresponds to the actual profit. However, they have no power to direct Joe's actions or overrule his choice of fertilizers. They are no more his boss then are the land owners who rent the land to him. For similar reasons George is not the handyman's boss. Jasmina is in a more complicated situation; the senior partners of the law firm are her bosses because they have contracted with her for the authority to assign cases to her as circumstances dictate. However, the clients are not bosses, even though they negotiate and control some aspects of the case. Within the sphere that Jasmina works she is in control of the decision-making process. The client does not dictate what precedent to cite in a brief nor do they tell her how to question a witness. These are judgments which she makes. Surprisingly, the airline reservation agent, Pat, does not have a boss as defined here, even though she is one of the most closely monitored workers in these scenerios. The airline has little to do with her labor once she has been taught the procedures for handling various types of customer requests. The monitoring is done to prevent shirking and to prevent agents from breaching the employment contract by using nonstandard procedures with customers. Pat may feel like a cog in a machine and have little discretion on the job, but she is not directed to take actions in an *ad hoc* fashion. The rules are clear and if she objects she is free to work for another airline or in some other profession. Unfortunately for Pat there are many other workers who are willing to follow the rules as stated by the airline and therefore she is in a weak position to influence the rules by either voicing complaints or exiting the airline. Finally, laundryman Jim does have a boss, even though he is not as closely monitored as Pat. The job description is not so complete that Jim knows exactly what he will have to do at the laundry each day. The manager has been granted the authority to readjust the station assignment as he sees fit, and therefore has an important role as a decision-maker.

It might be useful to contrast the terms "employer" and "boss" by listing synonyms along with terms that are not to be treated below as synonyms. Synonyms for boss are supervisor, manager, director, decision-maker, head, executive, commander, superintendent, master, overseer, chief, and leader. Crucial to these is that all have the authority to change the work assignment unilaterally. The boss is to be distinguished from the paymaster, hirer, monitor, inspector, enforcer, negotiator, payer, coordinator, recruiter, engager, enlister, instructor, proctor, and superior. All these terms refer to individuals who negotiate labor contracts or verify that they are carried out as agreed.

These illustrations allow us to distinguish between the terms "employer" and "boss". An employer is any representative of an enterprise who engages the services of workers for wages or salary. Not all employers are bosses, who superintend, manage, direct, and control the activities of workers. An employer may hire an individual to do a job without trying to control the methods used to accomplish the task. The question in the title does not ask why workers are hired, but why workers are hired to be directed.

The use of supervision and direction is often tied to the coordination and integration of many specific tasks performed by different workers. When a single worker produces a commodity that is directly consumed by the purchaser, the worker has direct incentives to produce the commodity in the most efficient manner. The farmer who rents land and equipment and grows crops for market does not need a supervisor to tell him the amount of seed to plant and how close the furrows should be. The hours he spends in the field harvesting need not be determined by anyone else. It is in his self-interest to put in the correct effort. If he does not make the decision correctly, then he must forgo the income that could otherwise be obtained. Hence, the value of a boss may be positively related to the degree of the division of labor. When the production of a commodity requires several separate labor tasks it may be advisable to let individual workers specialize in just one task, rather than trying to complete the entire product themselves. The division of the labor tasks among several individuals leads to the necessity of a coordinator; for the smooth fitting together of disparate mental or physical activities is difficult when each individual is concentrating solely on just one aspect of the entire production process.

Smith (1776) provides us with three reasons why division of labor and specialization lead to efficiency gains. By dividing the production into small distinct tasks the worker will, according to Smith, increase his physical dexterity and mental acuteness. Fewer mistakes will be made and a larger volume of high quality commodities or services may be handled. Smith also believed that by specialization and repetition less time would be lost moving from one activity to another. Finally, Smith suggested that the division of labor would facilitate the invention of methods and machines which help increase the productivity of the individual worker or decrease the effort that the worker must exert to complete his task.

Marglin (1974) has analyzed the arguments used by Smith and found that they are not completely convincing. In particular, Marglin does not see any reason why the three gains associated with the division of labor should be associated with the institution of hierarchy. It may be true that increased speed and accuracy in production can be achieved by repetition of the same few tasks, but this does not mean that there is a great need of detailed coordination with other workers. In fact, in the early stages of the Industrial Revolution the predominate system was "putting out". Work was done in the individual's cottage, but there was specialization in the production tasks. The worker received semi-finished product and sold back to the "putter-outer". All gains from increased dexterity were captured without bringing a monitor into the industry. Similarly, the loss of time setting up a particular production activity can be attenuated by performing one task sufficiently long so as to spread the fixed cost across a large number of commodities. This can be done by an individual worker and does not require the presence of a boss. Finally, extreme specialization does not necessarily imply that more time be spent thinking of labor-saving devices. In fact, Marglin argues that the lack of understanding of the total production process may actually hamper the invention of new methods and machines.

Alchian and Demsetz (1972) have argued that production takes place with supervision because of the measurement problems which occur when there are simultaneities in the total labor task. They argue that many production processes require the simultaneous effort of three or more workers to produce a single item. A worker often does not produce semi-finished products which are sequentially passed on to the next worker so that he can in turn contribute to the production of the final good. Unlike Adam Smith's pin factory where the semi-finished pins are put into buffer inventories to be passed on to the next production station, Alchian and Demsetz believe that many production processes require that the hands, eyes, and minds of all the workers be simultaneously active in the production. Production processes involve complicated rather than simple machines, and several laborers are needed to perform all the tasks that keep the complicated machine in continuous operation. Frequently, several laborers participate in an activity which involves physical objects or mental projects that are beyond the capabilities of one person. For example, the operation of a digital computer requires the synchronous performance of many tasks – card reading, monitoring the central processing unit, loading tapes and disks, taking output off the printer, and distributing to the output bins – and for a large computer system these tasks cannot be performed by just one worker. As another example, piano-movers must work in groups because of the size and weight of the pianos which they must handle.

Alchian and Demsetz feel that the inability to break the work process into distinct sequential stages leads to the introduction of monitoring and supervision. Simultaneity of the work causes problems because it is hard to measure the quality and quantity of effort and the contribution that the effort has made to the production of the final output. Since there are more than three workers, each worker must identify the effort of several others. If three laborers are lifting a piano up a flight of stairs, each one must distinguish not only how much the other two are together contributing, but must identify their separate efforts. This may be difficult for the workers since it must be done as they are themselves performing the production task. Moreover, there may be several combinations of the efforts of the other workers (along with worker's labor) to produce the resulting output. The knowledge of how fast the piano was carried up the stairs and how much vigor the worker put in himself may not be sufficient to identify the exertions of the other piano-movers. When several workers are concurrently operating distinct stations of a machine, it may be physically impossible to see the locations where other individuals work and it may also be impossible to infer their activities from the observable characteristics of the machine as it operates.

Workers may be able to observe the traits of fellow workers that indicate the quality and quantity of their contributions to the production. It might also be possible to arrange among the workers a system of monitoring that eliminates duplication of observations. Instead of each worker watching all other workers, each worker could be assigned a small number of colleagues to track during the production. However, if there are increasing returns to the scale of labor input at various stations, the simultaneous decrease in productive effort by all the workers will lead to a magnified drop in the output. It is also possible that when a worker monitors an additional worker the lost time for the additional observation is insignificant. That is, there may also be increasing returns to the task of inspection. Together these provide a rationale for assigning many workers to a single supervisor and letting the supervisor specialize completely in the inspection of the exertions of the producing workers.

Alchian and Demsetz's argument is not completely persuasive. Williamson (1975) has pointed out that the number of production processes that have the simultaneities suggested above is not large enough to explain the ubiquity of supervision. Many physical production processes consist of sequential modifications to a single object. The assembly line in an automobile plant is the most obvious example. A house is built by a sequence of workers adding various parts to the structure. Many mental production processes are also divisible into a sequence of tasks. The accounting department of a business breaks the problem into small subunits which are handled by separate accountants and then aggregated. In other words, there are many production processes which do have goods-in-progress which are used as a buffer inventory. Does Alchian and Demsetz's reasoning make sense in these circumstances?

Even when they are the synchronisms in the production activity, one might have a hard time explaining why observation costs are large. The piano-movers can combine the visual and tactile information which are side-products of the labor to make a judgement about the exertion of the other movers. The mover does not have to stop lifting in order to see whether the worker across the piano from him is grimacing, sweating, and straining. The physical proximity which makes the work indivisible may also attenuate observation costs.

In order to justify a single inspector one must assume that there are gains from specializing in observation; that is, one person can observe a given set of workers in less time than the total time it would take two persons to do the inspection. Moreover, the single monitor will be more desirable if there are increasing returns to scale from the increase in laborers. Neither of these assumptions are clearly true. The returns to observations could be constant, in which case letting every worker participate in the inspection system would be just as efficient as having a single monitor.

Alchian and Demsetz provide a rationale for specialization in inspection, observation, and enforcement of effort and quality of labor inputs, but do try to justify the special role the employer has in choosing the workers' tasks. Not only does a boss determine if a particular task has been successfully executed, but he determines which task is required of the worker. Alchian and Demsetz deny that this is a crucial element of the employment of labor when they say that the relation between boss and worker mirrors that between shopper and grocer.

It was Simon (1951) who first differentiated the employment contract from the sales contract and provided a theory for why authority for strategic planning and decision-making is placed in the hands of the monitor rather in the hands of one or more of the production workers. Simon's argument does not run counter to Alchian and Demsetz's theory of inspection; in fact the two complement each other. In a complex production process involving several workers there are bound to be important uncertainties not only about the environment but also the effort expended by the workers. The monitor of workers is usually in an excellent position to recognize the state of the environment at little cost. If circumstances require an adjustment of the tasks performed, the monitor's informational advantage may be used to improve the efficiency of the production process. The advantage of this delegation of authority to the employer will be modelled following Simon (1951). (See Williamson, 1980, for a less theoretical comparison of modes of organization.)

Work consists of performing one or more of a finite number of tasks, indexed $t = 1, ..., T$, which are distinguished by physical characteristics, location in space, or date of performance. The time devoted to a task t is denoted x_t and work is the vector $x = (x_1, ..., x_T)$. The quantity of work performed depends on effort, quality, and pace and it is assumed that such distinctions are already included in the list of tasks. Task t might be "packing boxes leisurely" and task $t + 1$ might be "packing boxes rapidly". Time provides the sole measure of the service provided.

Workers are capable of performing many tasks in a day. In one day the set of work assignments which the worker can perform is denoted X. If a worker knows how to do only tasks 1 and 2, then X might be

$$X = \{x \mid x_1 + x_2 = 1, 0 \leqslant x_1 \leqslant 1, 0 \leqslant x_2 \leqslant 1\}.$$

The work leads to the production of commodities which are valued by the employer, either because he consumes them or can exchange them for more desirable commodities. For analytic simplicity let us assume that the production process leads to only one type of commodity whose amount is denoted y. Production occurs with inherent uncertainties. The weather, health of workers, availability of operable equipment, creativity of workers, and properties of raw materials are only some of the unpredictable characteristics of the production environment. Using the variable s to denote the random state of nature, the maximum output is related to work and the state by a production function, $y = y(x, s)$.

The worker has preferences for work assignment and wage income, W (income is a proxy for those other goods which income buys) which will be represented by a utility function, $U(x, W)$. The combination of work assignment and wage income must be sufficient to keep the worker from taking another job. The next best job's utility is denoted $\bar{U}$. The employer must pay the worker in order to have any output but is not directly affected by the work assignment; the employer's utility is a function of output and wage paid to the worker, $V(y, W)$.

The informational aspects of the employment contract play a crucial role. We will presume that the worker can verify the work performed and the wages paid, but can observe neither the state of nature nor the output commodities. Two employment contracts will be contrasted: a contract with prespecified work assignments and a contract with authority to adjust work assignments. The informational asymmetries make a contingency contract impossible; as discussed in Chapter 5, the inability of the worker to check the state of nature opens up a potential for fraud by the employer.

Consider what terms the employer would offer the worker if the work assignment must be prespecified and independent of the state of nature. The employer must make a wage offer, W, and a work assignment, x, which is sufficiently attractive to keep the employee from switching to another job, yet he wants to make expected utility as large as possible. The terms x and W should be chosen to maximize

$$E\{V(y(x, s), W)\}$$

subject to the restrictions

$$x \in X, \quad \text{and} \quad U(x, W) \geqslant \bar{U}.$$

Designate the optimal preassigned contract x^*, W^*.

When an employer is given the authority to adjust the tasks to suit the state of nature, the employment contract must specify a range of work assignments from which the employer can choose. Symbolize the scope of authority by a set of work assignments, Γ. The employer will wait until the state of nature is known before committing himself to a particular work assignment in Γ. That is, the work x is chosen to maximize

$$V(y(x, s), W)$$

subject to

$$x \in X \quad \text{and} \quad x \in \Gamma.$$

The optimal work assignment rule is denoted $\hat{x}(s, W; \Gamma)$ to signify its dependence on the state and wage as well as the scope of authority. The wage, $\hat{W}$, paid by the employer is just sufficient to maintain employment. This implies that the worker's expected utility satisfies the following:

$$\mathrm{E}\{U(\hat{x}(s, \hat{W}; \Gamma), \hat{W})\} \geqslant \bar{U}.$$

In this chapter we only address the question of why authoritative terms of such contracts are desirable. Equilibrium terms of such contracts will be discussed in the following chapter.

The flexibility obtained by the authoritative contract has both positive and negative repercussions. The employer can obtain higher output on average by adjusting the tasks to suit the state of nature. On hot, smoggy days the output may be improved if more time is spent resting to recuperate from shorter periods of strenuous work, while continuous exertion may be more productive on mild, clear days. When machines are malfunctioning, more time needs to be spent on preventative maintenance than when the machines are operating smoothly. On the other hand, the authority introduces uncertainty from the worker's perspective. Some days the worker may have to exert more energy or perform odious tasks, and the worker lacks control of when this will occur. It will be presumed that the worker is fully aware of the likelihood of being asked to accept an assignment in Γ. This may come about because the worker can anticipate the optimal work rule, $\hat{x}$, or because the recurrence of certain tasks allow the worker to calculate relative frequencies.

Under what circumstances will the negative aspects of authority outweigh the positive? Only when the scope of authority is inappropriate will the worker and employer prefer predetermined work conditions. In very general circumstances, some degree of authority is mutually advantageous.

Theorem 7.1. If x^* does not maximize $U(x, W^*)$ subject to $x \in X$, then both employer and employee benefit from some authoritative employment contract.

Since x^* does not maximize $U(x, W^*)$ there must be a neighborhood of x^* in X that has work assignments which the worker prefers to x^*. Denote such a neighborhood Γ^*. By definition of $\hat{x}$, the employer must prefer that the work be $\hat{x}(s, W^*; \Gamma^*)$ just as much as x^*, for all possible states. Thus, authority to choose the work from the set Γ^* is desired by both employer and employee.

The only condition where authority is possible detrimental is when by coincidence the work chosen to maximize the employer's expected utility happens to also maximize the worker's utility. Even when this happens this does not necessarily make authority disadvantageous, because the employer may be able to reward the worker with a sufficiently high wage to compensate for the authority to assign less desirable tasks.

Example. Suppose that the preferences of the worker for x_1 and x_2 and wage income are

$$U(x_1, x_2, W) = x_1 + x_2 - 1 - \tfrac{1}{2}(x_1^2 + x_2^2) + W,$$

and suppose that the employer's preferences are

$$V(y, W) = 2y - W.$$

The remainder of the environment is specified as follows:

production function:

$$y(x_1, x_2, s) = sx_1 + x_2 - \tfrac{1}{2}(x_1^2 + x_2^2);$$

utility opportunity:

$$\bar{U} = 1;$$

possible work assignments:

$$X = \{(x_1, x_2) \mid x_1 \geqslant 0, x_2 \geqslant 0, x_1 + x_2 \leqslant 1\};$$

probability distribution:

$$P(s) = \{\tfrac{1}{2}, \ \text{if } s = 0 \ \text{ or } s = 2; 0, \text{otherwise}.$$

The state of nature represents the productivity of the first task and may be zero or two with equal probability. If the employment contract does not authorize adjustment of the work assignment, the optimal predetermined work assignment and corresponding wage are

$$x_1^* = 0.5 = x_2^*$$

and

$$W^* = 1.25.$$

By treating the uncertain state as a constant, equal to its mean of 1, the employer finds equal time in each task optimal and can expect a utility of

$$\mathrm{E}\{V^*\} = 0.25.$$

On the other hand, when the employer has the authority to choose (x_1, x_2) after observing the productivity of task one, utility maximization leads to the work assignment rule

$$\hat{x}_1 = s/2; \; \hat{x}_2 = 1 - s/2$$

Since the predetermined assignment (0.5, 0.5) is the most desirable possible work from the employee's perspective, this assignment rule is bound to lower the expected utility of the worker. However, the employer can raise his wage offer to $\hat{W} = 1.50$ to maintain the overall attractiveness of the job. By so doing the employer's expected utility increases to $E\{\hat{V}\} = 0.50$. Authority is desirable even though it means a less attractive work environment for the employee. ■

In summary the authority vested in the employer is mutually beneficial for the following reasons. Division of labor into a sequence of small tasks performed by specialized workers is productive because it allows the workers to accumulate task-specific skills, minimize set-up costs, and facilitate technological progress. When work involves synchronized labor of various types, the measurement of effort either by observing output or monitoring workers is difficult, so inspectors of labor inputs are desirable. The individual who holds the position of inspector has an advantage over the workers in efficiently acquiring information about the uncertain aspects of production. The workers' inability to verify the inspector's conclusions about the state of nature prevents the use of a contingency contract for employment of labor and thus narrows the choice of employment contracts to those which prespecify a work assignment independent of the state of nature or those which give the inspector authority to unilaterally adjust the assignments to best correspond to the state. Under very general conditions the *ex post* flexibility provided by an authoritative contract makes it desirable to incorporate the role of director with the role of monitor in the position of the boss.

CHAPTER 8

THE TERMS OF AUTHORITY

In the previous chapter the use of authority in the decision-making of an organization was rationalized. What remains to be explained is how much authority appears in the employment of labor. In order to accomplish this the employment contract will be described by a probability distribution over the set of possible work assignments. This distribution is determined by the optimal assignment rule used by the employer to adjust work to production uncertainties. The assignment rule is endogenously determined since it may be influenced by the number of workers employed and this is determined by the wages found in the labor market.

The tasks performed by workers are indexed $h = 1, ..., \ell$, and the work assigned is an ℓ-tuple $x = (x_1, ..., x_\ell)$. We will assume for simplicity that all workers are capable of performing the work if it belongs to a set $X \leqslant \mathbb{R}^\ell$, although workers may have different tastes for work assignments. The workers, indexed $i = 1, ..., m$, have preferences for work and wage income which are represented by utility functions

$$U^i(x, W).$$

The employers, designated $j = 1, ..., n$, use the work to produce output, y. For the time being, it will be assumed that the employer has need for at most one worker. This will be changed subsequently. The output is also influenced by the random state of nature according to the production function

$$y^j = y^j(x, s).$$

The profit from employment, the differences between output and wage assuming the price of output is unity, determines the employer's utility

$$V^j(y^j - W^j).$$

There may be differences of opinion about the relative likelihoods of states of nature so the jth employer's subjective beliefs about the random variable s are incorporated in a density function, $f^j(s)$, such that

$$f^j(s) \geqslant 0, \quad \text{for all } s \in S,$$

and

$$\int_S f^j(s)\,\mathrm{d}s = 1.$$

Employers hire workers at given wages and are granted the authority to choose the work assignment after nature has determined its state. The employer will find it optimal to choose from the set X the work which maximizes output conditional upon the observed state of nature. Denote the solution of the problem

$$\text{maximize } y^j(x, s)$$

$$\text{subject to } x \in X$$

as $x^j(s)$ and call it the work assignment rule. Given the work assignment rule and the subjective probability of the state of nature, the employer can determine the frequency his employee will have to perform each task. This resulting probability density is designated $g^j(x)$, where

$$g^j(x) \geqslant 0, \quad \text{for all } x \in X,$$

and

$$\int_X g^j(x)\,\mathrm{d}x = 1.$$

Given the optimal use of authority, the employer must decide if the worker should even have been hired. The expected output which the employer can have from employment is

$$\bar{y}^j = \int_S y^j(x^j(s), s)\, f^j(s)\,\mathrm{d}s.$$

A risk neutral employer will be able to afford to hire a worker if the wage he pays, W^j, does not exceed the expected output (which equals expected revenue). When wage exceeds $\bar{y}^j$ the employer will drop out of the labor market.

The employer makes a job offer to all workers consisting of a job description,

$g^j(x)$, and a wage, W^j. Workers who accept such a contract will be paid the given wage but will not know with certainty the tasks involved. For example, a secretary might be hired only knowing that there is an equal probability that the task assigned will be typing or taking shorthand dictation. Workers are free to choose any job offer which has been made or to remain self-employed and receive a utility $\bar{U}^i$. They observe the entire spectrum of job offers and can calculate for each employer the expected utility derived from the announced wage income and job description,

$$\bar{U}^{ij}(W^j) = \int_X U^i(x, W^j)\, g^j(x)\, \mathrm{d}x.$$

The worker is unconcerned with the manner in which the job description is derived from the work assignment rule and the state probability density. If the worker and employer have a recurring contractual relationship, the employee may detect misuses of authority when the empirical frequency of tasks differs from the contractual frequency given by $g^j(x)$.

The worker's choice of the most attractive job offer may be formulated as a linear integer assignment problem. Maximize by choice of $\alpha_{i0}, \alpha_{i1}, \ldots, \alpha_{in}$:

$$\alpha_{i0}\, \bar{U}^i + \sum_{j=1}^{n} \alpha_{ij}\, \bar{U}^{ij}(W^j)$$

subject to

$$\sum_{j=0}^{n} \alpha_{ij} = 1$$

and

$$\alpha_{ij} \in \{0, 1\}.$$

The choice variables are integer assignment variable with the interpretation that $\alpha_{i0} = 1$ means that self-employment is optimal and $\alpha_{ij} = 1$ means that employer j has the most attractive job available. The constraints specify that the worker must choose exactly one employer. The job consists of full-time submission to the authority of that employer.

A job offer spectrum $(g^1(x), W^1, \ldots, (g^n(x), W^n)$ is in equilibrium when the optimal assignments from the above problem, $\alpha = [\alpha_{ij}]$, also satisfy the condition

$$\sum_{i=1}^{m} \alpha_{ij} = \begin{cases} 1, & \text{if } W^j \leqslant \bar{y}^j, \\ 0, & \text{if } W^j > \bar{y}^j, \end{cases}$$

for $j = 1, ..., n$. If $W^j \leqslant \bar{y}^j$, then the jth employer wants to hire exactly one worker and the above condition then states that exactly one worker accepts his job offer. When $W^j > \bar{y}^j$, no worker is desired and the above condition states that no worker should accept the job offer.

In this simple model where employers hire at most one worker, the job description, $g^j(x)$, is fixed by the technology and the beliefs about the uncertainty. Only wage is adjustable. Market pressures will increase wage offers of jobs whose job descriptions do not attract workers and decrease wages on more desirable jobs until equilibrium is established. Equilibrium is illustrated in fig. 8.1.

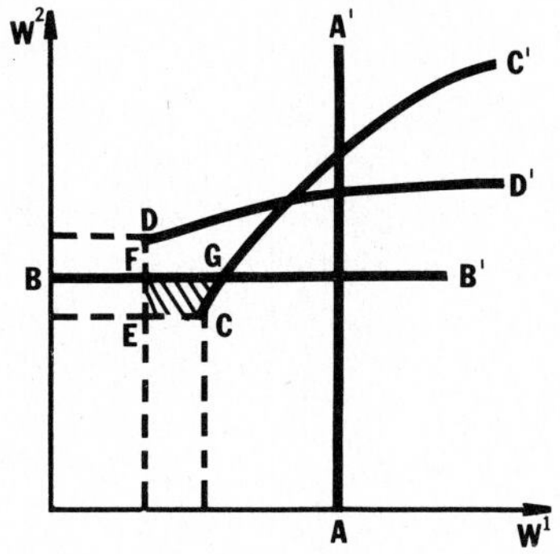

Figure 8.1

There are two employers and two workers. Line AA' in the wage space represents the dividing line between profit and loss for employer $j = 1$. To the left of AA', the wage W^1 is low enough that employer 1 can profit from an employee; to the right of AA' a worker would not cover his wage with the revenues he generates. Similarly, BB' divides the wage space according to the profitability of a worker for employer $j = 2$. Curve CC' divides the wage space according to the preferences of worker $i = 1$. Below and to the left of point C both wages are so low that worker 1 rejects employment. Salaries below the curve CC' lead worker 1 to choose employer $j = 1$ since his wage is significantly larger than that of employer 2. Curve DD' is the analogous curve for worker $i = 1$. When wages are in the shaded region, $CEFG$, the workers and employers have reached an equilibrium where worker $i = 1$ accepts the offer of employer $j = 2$ and worker $i = 2$ accepts the offer of employer $j = 1$.

It should be pointed out that equilibrium may result in one or more pairs of workers and employers deciding that there is no mutually beneficial employment. In fig. 8.2 the equilibrium salaries must lay in region $ECGF$. In this region

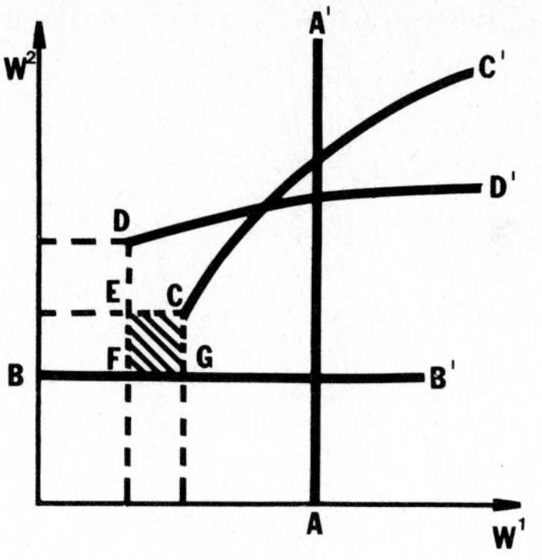

Figure 8.2

worker $i = 1$ decides to be self-employed and employer $j = 2$ decides not to employ a worker. Worker $i = 2$ and employer $j = 1$ strike an employment bargain. One should not view this as a situation of unemployment. The remainder of the chapter presumes that all workers find work with the employers and are not self-employed.

The job conditions are determined only on the supply side: the function relating optimal work and state of nature, $x^j(s)$, and the subjective beliefs about nature, $f^j(s)$, together determine the job description, $g^j(x)$. This is completely independent of labor market conditions. The next task is to show how the job description may be endogenously determined, in part by the preferences of the workers.

The only change to be made in the above model is to permit employers the option of hiring several workers. (There is no longer a need to assume that the number of employers equals the number of workers.) Let L be the number of workers employed by the employer and denote the total contribution of those workers toward output by

$$y^j(L, x, s).$$

The employer j with work force L observes the state of nature s and selects the task assignments for the typical worker,

$$x^j(s, L),$$

to maximize output. By the nature of the employment relation, the work selection is done after workers are hired and nature is observed.

Prior to hiring workers the employer calculates that the expected net revenue associated with L workers is

$$\int_S y^j(L, x^j(s, L), s)\, f^j(s)\, \mathrm{d}s - W^j L,$$

where $W^j L$ is the cost of hiring L full-time employees. The employer selects the work force to maximize the expected net revenue. Denote the optimal number of workers by

$$L^j(W^j).$$

When this has been done the employer can calculate the job conditions (a probability density on X from the composite function $x^j(s, L^j(W^j))$ and the subjective beliefs, $f^j(s)$. Denote the calculated job description by $g^j(x, W^j)$ where

$$g^j(x, W^j) \geqslant 0, \quad \text{for all } x \in X,$$

and

$$\int_X g^j(x, W^j)\, \mathrm{d}x = 1.$$

Unlike the previous model the job conditions are endogenously determined. As salary adjusts, so do the optimal work force sizes and hence so do the optimal work assignments.

Workers observe the spectrum of job offers,

$$((g^1(x, W^1), W^1), \ldots, (g^n(x, W^n), W^n)),$$

and select the employer whose offer maximizes their expected utility, exactly as before. More than one worker may find employer j's offer the most attractive. If $\alpha = [\alpha_{ij}]$ is the array of workers' assignment variables, equilibrium will occur when

$$\sum_{i=1}^{m} \alpha_{ij} = L^j(W^j), \quad \text{for } j = 1, \ldots, n.$$

If output is zero when the number of workers is zero, $y^j(0, x, s) \equiv 0$, then equilibrium may occur with some employers hiring no workers. The choice of optimal work force removes the requirement that $W^j \leqslant \bar{y}^j$.

We will now analyze a market for workers who operate or repair machines, focusing on the market impacts of employer's changing riskiness of technology. Workers are hired in this example because they can operate machinery or repair machinery when it malfunctions. For a particular employer, j, let s^j be the number of worker-days needed to repair machines. This is a random variable. Let $x_1 L$ denote the total worker-days of labor used in operating machines and let $x_2 L$ denote the total worker-days used for repair work. Labor can be transformed into output by the jth employer according to the relation

$$y^j = \beta^j x_1 L - \tfrac{1}{2}(x_1 L)^2 - \tfrac{1}{2}(x_2 L - s^j)^2 .$$

The first two terms are the total production of machine-operating labor and the last term is the loss in revenue which occurs if there is a deviation from the required number of repairmen. The coefficient β^j varies with employer, reflecting perhaps the size of the employer's capital stock.

Labor is hired as above, the employer has L workers and each worker's time is allocated between operating and repairing according to $x = (x_1, x_2)$, where it is assumed that each worker supplies one worker-day of labor

$$X = \{(x_1, x_2) \mid x_1 + x_2 = 1\}.$$

Non-negativity constraints will be ignored.

Suppose the employer believes that the number of worker-days needed to repair machines has a mean η^j and a standard deviation δ^j. To ensure that non-negativity constraints are not violated it might also be assumed that η^j is large compared to δ^j and that the probability density has a compact support. The employer maximizes the expectation of y^j subject to $x \in X$. The optimal time spent operating machines will be

$$x_1^j(L, s^j) = \tfrac{1}{2} + (\beta^j - s^j)/2L,$$

and the optimal size work force will be

$$L^j(W^j) = \eta^j + \beta^j - 2W^j.$$

The workers hired by employer j grant the employer the authority to select operation time x_1 with a frequency given by a probability distribution with mean

$$E\{x_1\} = \tfrac{1}{2} + (\beta^j - \eta^j)/(2\eta^j + 2\beta^j - 4W^j)$$

and standard deviation

$$\sigma^j = \sqrt{E\{(x_1 - E\{x_1\})^2\}} = \delta^j / (2\eta^j + 2\beta^j - 4W^j).$$

To simplify the analysis assume that all employers believe that the expected number of worker-days needed for repair work equals the coefficient of productivity of the machines, $\eta^j = \beta^j$. Because of this, when the salary increases the job description changes only by an increase in the authority required, σ^j, and there is no change in the expected time spent operating and repairing machines (see fig. 8.3). For employers with less predictable machines the authority curve in fig. 8.3 will be uniformly higher and steeper.

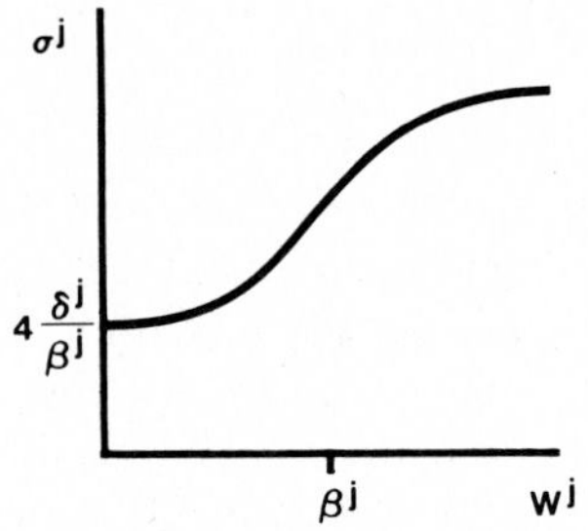

Figure 8.3

Assume that workers have utility functions of the separable form:

$$U^i(x, W) = \psi^i(W) - D^i(x),$$

where ψ^i is the value of income and D^i is the disutility of labor. Separability implies that the marginal utility of income is not influenced by the job conditions. Let us make a Taylor series approximation of expected utility around $x = (\frac{1}{2}, \frac{1}{2})$ keeping only terms of degree two or less:

$$E\{U^i(x, W^j)\} = \psi^i(W^j) - \tfrac{1}{2}(\sigma^j)^2 A^i - \bar{D}^i,$$

where

$$A^i = D^i_{x_1 x_1} - 2D^i_{x_1 x_2} + D^i_{x_2 x_2}$$

and

$$\bar{D}^i = D^i(\tfrac{1}{2}, \tfrac{1}{2}).$$

A^i is evaluated at $x = (\frac{1}{2}, \frac{1}{2})$. The worker i would pay an amount approximately equal to

$$\tfrac{1}{2}\,(\sigma^j)^2\, A^i/\psi^{i\prime}$$

to eliminate the authority which employer j asks for. A^i will be treated as a measure of the worker's aversion to authority. When the worker views the tasks as perfect substitutes,

$$D^i(x) = D^i(x_1 + x_2),$$

the worker does not care how much authority the employer wants so long as the total supply of labor time is the same. In this case the value of A^i will be zero and the worker would not pay to reduce the authority of the employer. This brings into relief the assumption made here that the amount of authority is measured by the spread of the distribution of the random variables x_1 and x_2. The tastes of a worker can be described by a family of indifference curves, as in fig. 8.4 (Arrow, 1971b, and Pratt, 1964, use a similar analysis). Workers with greater aversion to authority will have flatter indifference curves.

Suppose there are two employers where $\delta^1 > \delta^2$. The first employer has less predictable machines and must have greater authority to adjust the repair/operating task assignment. Also, suppose there are two types of workers where $A^1 < A^2$. Workers of type 1 are less averse to working under authority. If there are N^i workers of type i, the salaries that would induce the employer $j = i$ to

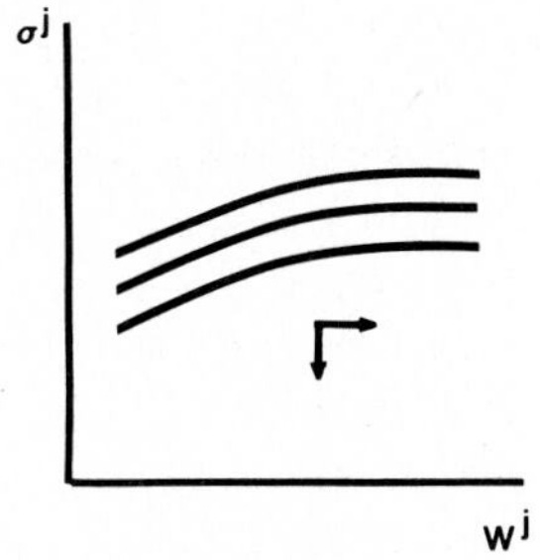

Figure 8.4

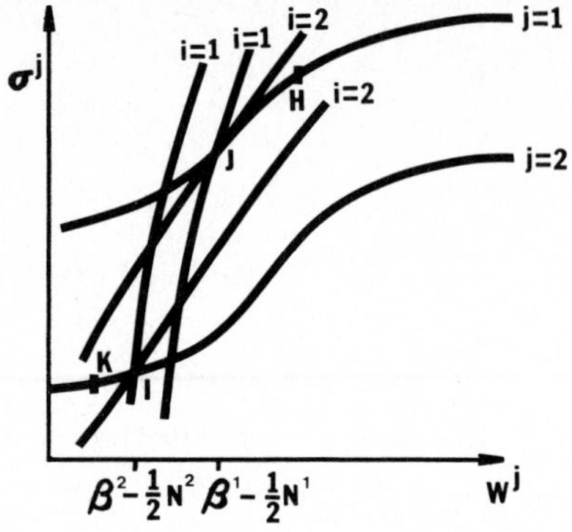

Figure 8.5

hire all the workers of that type is $W^j = \beta^j - \frac{1}{2}N^i$. Equilibrium will be achieved if these salaries lead to workers of type i accepting employer $j = i$'s offer, as in fig. 8.5. Since the indifference curves of $i = 1$ are so much steeper than $i = 2$, type 1 workers accept the offer J and type 2 workers accept the offer I. There is no tendancy for salaries or job authority to adjust from these values.

Only dramatic shifts in workers' attitudes towards authority will influence salaries and authority. If A^1 increases slightly, the indifference curves of $i = 1$ will rotate clockwise slightly. The workers of type 1 will be less satisfied with the offer J than before but will still choose the authoritarian employers offer. J will not change.

If one member of type 1 workers was to change aversion to authority and become a type 2 worker, equilibrium salaries and job descriptions must adjust. The salary offered by employer 2 will fall along the authority curve from I to K; K is 1/2 units less salary. Simultaneously employer 1 will find his salary rising by 1/2 to reduce his excess demand for workers. Employer 2 reduces the authority he requires from his workers while employer 1 increases his authority.

If the productivity of operating time required for machine repair increases at the same time that the expected time required for machine repair increases ($\beta^j = \eta^j$ goes up), employer j will increase the salary he offers. If the number of workers remains constant, the salary increase will be just sufficient so that job authority is unchanged. There is a shift in the authority curve as well as a movement along it. The workers of the employer will be better off than before.

If the predictability of machines decreases, the salary of workers is unaffected, but the required authority necessary to justify that salary and work force, will rise. The workers' expected utility will fall.

Equilibrium in job markets like these may not produce an efficient allocation of resources. Consider an economy with two employers and three types of

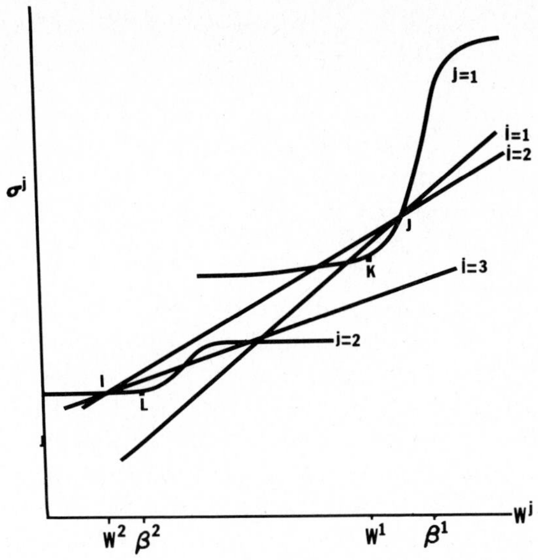

Figure 8.6

workers, as in fig. 8.6. Only one indifference curve is drawn for each worker type. Workers of type 1 are the least averse to authority and workers of type 3 are the most averse to authority. The preferences are chosen such that workers of type 1 would accept offer J rather than offer I; workers of type 3 would accept I rather than J. The single worker of type 2 is indifferent between the two offers, but we assume that he has selected offer I. If the salary of employer 1 were to fall by 1/2 units, he would want to hire one additional worker; if the salary of employer 2 where to rise by 1/2 units, he would want to fire one worker. By construction of the indifference curves all workers would be better off if this salary adjustment where made. Worker 1 is better off at K than at J and would still prefer the more authoritarian employer. Worker 3 would be better off at L than at I and would still prefer to work in the less authoritarian situation. Since the authority curve of $j = 1$ intersects worker 2's indifference curve with a steeper slope than employer 2's, the worker 2 will want to switch employers and accept offer K.

Are the employers better off by this salary adjustment? Substitution of the optimal work force and task assignment back into the revenue function allows us to calculate the expected profit of the employer as a function of his salary:

$$\mathrm{E}\{y^j\} - W^j L^j(W^j) = -\tfrac{1}{2}(\beta^j + \delta^{j^2}) + (W^j - \beta^j)^2 .$$

The closer W^j is to β^j, the flatter the expected profit relationship. By construction, W^2 is closer to β^2 than W^1 is to β^1. From this we conclude that a rise in W^2 by 1/2 units and a fall in W^1 by 1/2 units will increase the total expected profits of the employers 1 and 2.

In summary, fig. 8.6 illustrates an economy with multiple equilibria. Not all equilibria are efficient since equilibrium I–J is dominated by L–K. All parties would be better off if worker 2 worked for employer 1. However, there is no tendency for I–J to change since salaries are determined by the labor market, not by fiat.

This chapter is a tentative step toward a general model of the equilibrium terms of authority. The contractual mode studied here permits the employer to authoritatively select the tasks performed by workers. The motivation for such an investigation is simple. Authoritarian allocation of resources is a prevalent technique for distributing scarce resources, not only in centralized economies but also in economies with strong property rights. Most of us voluntarily work for a boss who tells us how to use a large proportion of our time. Not only should economists investigate conditions which result in such widespread use of authority, but they should also investigate the limits and terms of such authority.

A model of the equilibrium of a system of job markets was developed; authority was a primary ingredient. Employers desired authority because of the uncertainties they faced and workers were willing to submit to authority because their income was supplemented by such submissive behavior. The matching of workers to jobs was carried out by a market mechanism, which also determined the equilibrium terms of authority. By postulating specific changes in workers' attitudes toward authority or changes in employers' beliefs about uncertainties, the model was able to predict changes in salary levels as well as levels of authority.

CHAPTER 9

MEASURING INFORMATION

Information provides value to a decision-maker by decreasing the uncertainty prior to commitment to a line of activity. In this chapter we begin studying the use of information and communication in organizations by creating measures of the amount and quality of information implicit in a communication system. It is particularly useful when a unique scalar measure of the informativeness of any information system exists, but unfortunately the complex, multiple attributes of most communication networks makes simple measures misleading. Very simple messages are sometimes more informative than long and complex ones because they identify situations that are critical for the proper selection of actions. The newspaper headline "WAR!" immediately identifies a crucial feature of the environment, while a detailed official communique may obfuscate the situation. Moreover, some messages provide much greater information when combined with other messages than the simple sum of separate contributions. Learning that it will rain and that your umbrella is broken may be more valuable than the separate values of weather information and umbrella information.

This chapter's major results are Blackwell's Theorem and the axiomatic derivation of Shannon's measure of information. Shannon's measure, based upon the entropy of the random environment, provides a well-defined, scalar measure of information content and can be justified with a few restrictions on the decision-maker's surprise at learning the state of nature. Blackwell's Theorem, on the other hand, identifies several identical ways of defining the relative informativeness of communication systems. One definition brings into relief the limitations of the Shannon measure by pointing out that the Shannon measure will sometimes rate one communication network as more informative than another when there are decision-makers who would rationally choose the latter even if it was more costly.

Suppose the space of all possible states of nature is finite,

$$S = \{s_1, s_2, ..., s_m\}.$$

Let the probability of each state of nature be designated P_i, $i = 1, 2, ..., m$ where $P_i \geqslant 0$ and $\Sigma_{i=1}^{m} P_i = 1$. When P_i lies close to 1 and he discovers that the true state of nature equals s_i, the decision-maker should not be surprised. But when P_i is near 0, the discovery that s_i is the true state should be quite surprising. Define the decision-maker's "surprise" upon discovering s_i by a monotonically decreasing function of the initial probability,

$$\psi(P_i),$$

so the decision-maker's expected surprise equals

$$\mathrm{E}\{\psi(P)\} = \sum_{i=1}^{m} P_i\, \psi(P_i).$$

Viewed prior to learning the true state of nature, this measures the initial ignorance about the state of nature. We can stipulate reasonably that surprise must be zero when the state of nature is certain, $\psi(1) = 0$. This implies that the discovery of the true state of nature reduces the decision-maker's ignorance to zero. The decrease in ignorance upon learning the state will be considered a measure of the information acquired,

$$\begin{aligned} H(P) &= \mathrm{E}\{\psi(P)\} - \psi(1) \\ &= \mathrm{E}\{\psi(P)\}. \end{aligned}$$

What general assumptions about the information function $H(P)$, each of which should be plausible if not reasonable, will imply that only one kind of function is possible? The following axioms lead directly to the Shannon "entropy" measure developed in connection with thermodynamics and communication theory. See Watanabe (1969) for a detailed discussion.

It will be assumed that H is a real-valued, continuous, symmetric function defined on the m-dimensional simplex $\Delta^m = \{(P_1, P_2, ..., P_m) \mid P_i \geqslant 0, i = 1, 2, ..., m$ and $\Sigma_{i=1}^{m} P_i = 1\}$. Symmetry means

$$H(P_1, P_2) = H(P_2, P_1).$$

We might interpret this as saying the surprise function does not depend on the state of nature, $\psi_i(P) = \psi(P)$.

Axiom I. H is a real-valued, continuous, symmetric function on Δ^m.

If the state space is increased by an event s_{m+1}, $S = \{s_1, ..., s_m, s_{m+1}\}$, but the new event is impossible, $P_{m+1} = 0$, the information provided by learning the state of nature is unchanged. Equivalently, states of nature which cannot occur make no contribution to our ignorance.

Axiom II. $H(P_1, ..., P_m, 0) = H(P_1, ..., P_m)$.

The information function on Δ^m is denoted H_m and on Δ^{m+1} is denoted H_{m+1}. If all events are equally probable, then increasing the number of events increases the information. That is, assuming all events are equally likely, if there are more events the prior ignorance is larger.

Axiom III.

$$H_{m+1}\left(\frac{1}{m+1}, ..., \frac{1}{m+1}\right) > H_m\left(\frac{1}{m}, ..., \frac{1}{m}\right).$$

The final axiom pertains to the information associated with pairs of random variables. When there are two variables which are uncertain, s and η, the joint information function $H(P_{s\eta})$ is a function from the $m + n$-dimensional simplex Δ^{m+n} into the real numbers. If η is known to take on the value η_j, then the conditional information measure depends functionally on the posterior distribution $P_{s|\eta j} = (P(s_1 \mid \eta_j), ..., P(s_m \mid \eta_j))$ say, $H(P_{s|\eta j})$. The fourth axiom relates the joint to the conditional information function.

Axiom IV. If s and η are any random variables, then

$$H(P_{s\eta}) = H(P_\eta) + H(P_{s|\eta}),$$

where $H(P_{s|\eta}) = \Sigma_{j=1}^{\eta} H(P_{s|\eta_j}) P(\eta_j)$ is the expected conditional information.

When s and η are independent random variables then $P(s|\eta_j) = P(s)$ and hence axiom IV implies that

$$H(P_{s\eta}) = H(P_\eta) + H(P_s).$$

Axioms I–IV narrow considerably the class of functions which are admissible information measures. In fact, only one class of surprise functions will do – the logarithmic functions – and the resulting information measure will be called the Shannon measure.

Theorem. If the information function H satisfies axioms I, II, III, IV, then

$$H(P) = -b \sum_{i=1}^{m} P_i \log P_i,$$

where b is a constant.

Proof. Let $f(m) = H_m(1/m, ..., 1/m)$. By axiom III, $f(m)$ is an increasing function of m. Let s be a random variable that takes on m^k values with equal probability, $1/m^k$. Let η be independent of s and take on m values of equal probability $1/m$. Therefore (s, η) takes on m^{k+1} values with equal probability $1/m^{k+1}$. Axiom IV implies

$$H(P_{s\eta}) = H(P_s) + H(P_\eta)$$

or

$$f(m^{k+1}) = f(m^k) + f(m).$$

This clearly implies

$$f(m^k) = kf(m).$$

Let m and n be two integers such that $n \leqslant m$. Choose an integer ℓ such that

$$m^k \leqslant n^\ell \leqslant m^{k+1}.$$

As k gets very large, ℓ must get very large. By axiom III:

$$f(m^k) \leqslant f(n^\ell) \leqslant f(m^{k+1}).$$

But then

$$kf(m) \leqslant \ell f(n) \leqslant (k+1)\, f(m).$$

Divide these inequalities by $\ell f(m) > 0$ to get

$$\frac{k}{\ell} \leqslant \frac{f(n)}{f(m)} \leqslant \frac{k}{\ell} + \frac{1}{\ell}. \tag{9.1}$$

Notice that log is an increasing function so that

$$\log m^k \leqslant \log n^\ell \leqslant \log m^{k+1},$$

and hence

$$\frac{k}{\ell} \leqslant \frac{\log n}{\log m} \leqslant \frac{k}{\ell} + \frac{1}{\ell}. \tag{9.2}$$

Inequalities (9.1) and (9.2) imply

$$\left| \frac{f(n)}{f(m)} - \frac{\log n}{\log m} \right| \leqslant \frac{1}{\ell}, \quad \text{for all } \ell.$$

As k gets very large $1/\ell$ must approach zero; hence

$$\frac{f(n)}{f(m)} = \frac{\log n}{\log m}, \quad \text{for all } n \leqslant m.$$

Reordering we have

$$\frac{f(m)}{\log m} = \frac{f(n)}{\log n} = b = \text{constant} > 0.$$

We thus have for $b = 1$ (this sets base of logarithm):

$$H\left(\frac{1}{m}, ..., \frac{1}{m}\right) = \log m, \quad \text{for } m \text{ integer.}$$

What if the probabilities are not all equal? We shall assume that probabilities are rational but not equal. (The extension to real numbers will not be argued here, other than to say we can approximate any real by a rational arbitrarily close.) That is, $P_i = m_i/m$, where $\Sigma_i m_i = m$. Now suppose s takes on m values with equal probability $1/m$. Group the events of S into n sets, $S_i, i = 1, ..., n$, where the number of events in set S_i is m_i. Now we say that event η has value η_i if $s \in S_i$. (s, η) takes on m values each of equal probability. For a given $\eta = \eta_i$, s can take on m_i values with equal probability, so by the above result:

$$H(s|\eta_i) = \log m_i.$$

Since the probability of η_i equals $P(s \in S_i) = m_i/m$, the expected value of surprise is

$$H(P_{s|\eta}) = \sum_{i=1}^{n} \frac{m_i}{m} \log m_i = \sum_i P_i \log m_i.$$

By the above result:

$$H(P_{s\eta}) = \log m.$$

Applying axiom IV we have

$$\log m = H(P_\eta) + \Sigma P_i \log m_i,$$

or

$$\begin{aligned} H(P_\eta) &= \log m - \sum_i \log m_i P_i \\ &= \left(\sum_i P_i\right) \log m - \sum_i P_i \log m_i \\ &= \sum_i P_i (\log m - \log m_i) \\ &= -\sum_i P_i \log \frac{m_i}{m} \\ &= -\sum_{i=1}^{n} P_i \log P_i. \quad \blacksquare \end{aligned}$$

Theorem 9.1. $H(P) = -b\ \Sigma_i P_i \log P_i$ satisfies axioms I, II, III, and IV.

Proof. Since $\lim_{P\to 0} P \log P = 0$, we can see that axiom II is satisfied. Since $-\Sigma(1/m)\log(1/m) = \log m$ is an increasing function of m, axiom III is satisfied.

$$\begin{aligned} H(P_\eta) + H(P_{s|\eta}) &= -\sum_j P(\eta_j)\,[\log P(\eta_j) + \sum_i P(s_i|\eta_j) \log P(s_i|\eta_j)] \\ &= -\sum_j P(\eta_j) \sum_i (\log P(\eta_j)\, P(s_i|\eta_j) + P(s_i|\eta_j) \log P(s_i|\eta_j)) \\ &= -\sum_j P(\eta_j) \sum_i P(s_i|\eta_j) \log\,[P(\eta_j)\, P(s_i|\eta_j)]) \\ &= -\sum_j \sum_i P(\eta_j)\, P(s_i|\eta_j) \log\,[P(\eta_j)\, P(s_i|\eta_j)] \\ &= H(P_{s\eta}). \quad \blacksquare \end{aligned}$$

These conclusions may be interpreted as saying that the restrictions on possible functions H summarized in the four axioms eliminate all but one "surprise" measure $\psi(P_i)$; the only measure of surprise compatible with the axioms is $\psi(P_i) = -\log P_i$, where the base of the logarithm is arbitrary. Notice that $\log(1) = 0$ so the measure of information, the difference between prior and posterior ignorance, exactly equals initial ignorance.

What properties does the Shannon measure of information have? The following theorems hold for $H(P) = -\Sigma_i P_i \log P_i$.

Theorem 9.2. $H(P_{s\eta}) \leqslant H(P_s) + H(P_\eta)$ with equality if and only if s and η are independent.

The proof of this theorem is based on Gibb's lemma, a result of independent interest.

Gibb's lemma. The values of $x_1, \ldots, x_m$ which maximize $\Sigma_{i=1}^m P_i \ell n\, x_i$ subject to $x_i \geqslant 0$, $\Sigma_{i=1}^m x_i = 1$ are $x_i = P_i$, assuming $P_i \geqslant 0$, $\Sigma_{i=1}^m P_i = 1$.

The proof follows from the Kuhn–Tucker conditions:

$$P_i/x_i - \lambda \leqslant 0, \qquad x_i \geqslant 0,$$

$$x_i\,(P_i/x_i - \lambda) = 0,$$

and

$$\sum_{i=1}^{m} x_i = 1.$$

Since $P_i = \lambda x_i$, we can sum to find

$$\sum_i P_i = 1 = \lambda \sum_i x_i = \lambda,$$

which gives the lemma. ■

Proof of Theorem 9.2. Define $x(s, \eta) \equiv P(s) \cdot P(\eta)$. By Gibb's lemma:

$$-H(P_{s\eta}) = \sum_s \sum_\eta P(s, \eta) \log P(s, \eta) \geqslant \sum_s \sum_\eta P(s, \eta) \log x(s, \eta),$$

with equality only when s and η are independent. But

$$\begin{aligned}\sum_s \sum_\eta P(s, \eta) \log x(s, \eta) &= \sum_s \sum_\eta P(s, \eta)\,(\log P(s) + \log P(\eta))\\ &= \sum_s P(s) \log P(s) + \sum_\eta P(\eta) \log P(\eta)\\ &= -H(P_s) - H(P_\eta).\end{aligned}$$

This gives the desired result. ■

A corollary of this theorem says that conditional information is less information except when there is independence.

Corollary. $H(P_{s|\eta}) \leqslant H(P_s)$ with equality if and only if s and η are independent.

Proof. By axiom IV, $H(P_{s\eta}) = H(P_\eta) + H(P_{s|\eta})$. It follows from the above theorem that

$$H(P_\eta) + H(P_{s|\eta}) \leqslant H(P_s) + H(P_\eta)$$

or

$$H(P_{s|\eta}) \leqslant H(P_s),$$

with equality only when s and η are independent. ■

Suppose that s is completely determined by η; that is, there exists a function $s = f(\eta)$. In this case $P(s|\eta)$ will be either zero or one depending on $s \neq f(\eta)$ or $s = f(\eta)$.

Theorem 9.3. If s is completely determined by η, then $H(P_{s|\eta}) = 0$.

Proof. $P(s|\eta) \log P(s|\eta) \equiv 0$ since $P(s|\eta)$ equals zero or one and $\log(1) = 0$ and $0 \log(0) = 0$. ■

If the set of all states of nature has m elements, then an upper bound can be placed on the Shannon measure.

Theorem. $H_m(P) \leqslant \log m$ with equality if and only if $P_i = 1/m$ for all $i = 1, \ldots, m$.

Proof. For fixed m, let us maximize $H_m(P)$ on the simplex Δ^m:

$$\max - \sum_{i=1}^{m} P_i \log P_i$$

subject to

$$P_i \geqslant 0, \quad \sum_i P_i = 1.$$

The first-order conditions are

$$-1 - \log P_i - \lambda \leqslant 0$$

and

$$P_i(-1 - \log P_i - \lambda) = 0.$$

But there cannot be a corner solution since if P_i approaches 0, $-\log P_i$ approaches $+\infty$, violating $-1 - \log P_i - \lambda \leqslant 0$. Hence,

$$-1 - \log P_i = \lambda, \quad \text{for all } i.$$

Hence, $P_i = P_j$ and thus $P_i = 1/m$ for all i. ■

One definition drawn from communication theory, which will be useful later, is the rate of transmission, $T(s \mid \eta)$.

Definition. $T(s \mid \eta) = H(P_s) - H(P_{s \mid \eta})$.

Intuitively, the rate of transmission measures the decrease in ignorance we would have if we could observe a related part of the state of nature. Some properties of the rate of transmission are:

Theorem 9.4. $T(s \mid \eta) \geqslant 0$.

Proof. This is a restatement of the previous corollary.

Theorem 9.5. $T(s \mid \eta) = T(\eta \mid s)$.

Proof.

$$\begin{aligned} T(\eta \mid s) &= H(P_\eta) - H(P_{s\eta}) + H(P_s) && \text{by axiom IV} \\ &= H(P_s) - H(P_{s\eta}) + H(P_\eta) \\ &= H(P_s) - H(P_{s \mid \eta}) && \text{by axiom IV} \\ &= T(s \mid \eta). \quad ■ \end{aligned}$$

Example. Suppose that there are three states of nature and two possible messages and probabilities:

$$[P(s_i, \eta_j)] = \begin{bmatrix} 9/30 & 1/30 \\ 1/30 & 9/30 \\ 5/30 & 5/30 \end{bmatrix} .$$

The prior probability distribution of s gives equal probabilities of 1/3 to the three states and the conditional probabilities are

$$[P(s_i | \eta_j)] = \begin{bmatrix} 9/15 & 1/15 \\ 1/15 & 9/15 \\ 5/15 & 5/15 \end{bmatrix} .$$

The Shannon measure of initial ignorance equals

$$H(P_s) = -\sum_{i=1}^{3} 1/3 \log 1/3 = 0.477.$$

The Shannon measure when message η_1 is received equals

$$H(P_{s|\eta_1}) = -(9/15 \log 9/15 + 1/15 \log 1/15 + 5/15 \log 5/15) = 0.371.$$

It can be easily verified that $H(P_{s|\eta_2}) = 0.371$. Since each message has equal probability, the expected Shannon measure after observing η is

$$H(P_{s|\eta}) = (1/2)\, 0.371 + (1/2)\, 0.371 = 0.371.$$

The decrease in surprise due to information η equals the rate of transmission:

$$T(s | \eta) = 0.477 - 0.371 = 0.106. \quad \blacksquare$$

Shannon's measure evaluates information systems without placing them in any particular decision-making context. We shall now compare information structures by calculating the maximum expected utility which is obtained using the information. If all decision-makers, irrespective of their utility function, would choose one information system over another, then it might be inferred that this behavior reveals that the former has more information than the latter. It should be noted that in the following we compare only expected benefits and ignore the cost of information; when an actual choice between information systems is made, both attributes must be taken into account. The argument follows that of Marschak and Miyasawa (1968).

Again, for simplicity assume that all random variables take on one of a finite number of possible values. The state and messages associated with two distinct information systems are drawn from sets:

$$S = \{s_1, \ldots, s_m\},$$

$$H = \{\eta_1, \ldots, \eta_n\},$$

$$H^* = \{\eta_1^*, \ldots, \eta_{n^*}^*\}.$$

Probability distributions will be given in matrix notation as follows

$P = [P(s_i, \eta_j)]$, $m \times n$ matrix of joint probabilities,

$\Pi = [P(s_i | \eta_j)]$, $m \times n$ matrix of posterior probabilities,

$\Lambda = [P(\eta_j | s_i)]$, $m \times n$ matrix of likelihoods of messages,

$$Q = \begin{bmatrix} P(s_1) & . & . & . \\ . & P(s_2) & . & . \\ . & . & . & . \\ . & . & . & P(s_m) \end{bmatrix},$$ $m \times m$ diagonal matrix of marginal probabilities of state, the same for both P and P^*.

For ease of reading, a typical element of a matrix, say P, will be denoted $P_{s\eta}$ rather than P_{ij}. The analogous definitions of matrices for the information system η^* are denoted P^*, Π^*, and Λ^*.

It will also be convenient to assume that only a finite set of actions are possible,

$$A = \{\alpha_1, ..., \alpha_\ell\}.$$

Utility depends on the action and state of nature and can then be summarized by a matrix,

$U = [U(\alpha_i, s_j)]$, $\ell \times m$ matrix of utilities.

A decision function, specifying the action taken for each possible message, is represented by a decision matrix

$D = [D(\eta_i, \alpha_j)]$, $n \times \ell$ matrix,

where $D_{\eta\alpha} = 1$ if action α is taken when message η is received, and $D_{\eta\alpha} = 0$ if some other action is taken. The set of all possible decision matrices is a collection of non-negative matrices with a single 1 in each row and otherwise 0.

The utility which a decision-maker expects when a decision matrix D is used equals

$$\mathrm{E}U[D, U, P] = \sum_{s=1}^{m} \sum_{\alpha=1}^{\ell} \sum_{\eta=1}^{n} P_{s\eta} D_{\eta\alpha} U_{\alpha s} = \mathrm{tr}(PDU),$$

where $\mathrm{tr}(PDU)$, the trace of the matrix PDU, is the sum of all the diagonal elements. The optimal decision matrix $\hat{D}$, is defined by

$$\mathrm{tr}(P\hat{D}U) \geqslant \mathrm{tr}(PDU), \quad \text{for all decision matrices } D.$$

When all decision-makers, that is, all utility functions U, place the maximum expected utility of information system η above that of η^*, we will say that η is revealed more informative than η^*.

Condition *U*. $\mathrm{E}U[\hat{D}, U, P] \geqslant \mathrm{E}U[\hat{D}^*, U, P^*]$, for all matrices U.

This rating of information systems cannot be complete. Some information systems will be ranked higher by one U but ranked lower for another, preventing us from inferring a revealed informativeness. Please notice that the inequality must be true for all $\ell \times m$ matrices, not just positive matrices or monotonic matrices or risk averse matrices. All decision-makers must declare η more desirable than η^* before condition U will rank η as more informative than η^*.

An alternative ordering of information systems is based on the randomization of the likelihood matrix. Suppose that the probability of receiving η^* in state s is determined as a random event conditional upon the message η which itself is randomly conditional on s.

Condition *B*. There exists a Markov matrix B (i.e. $B \geqslant 0$ and $\Sigma_{\eta^*=1}^{n^*} B_{\eta\eta^*} = 1$ for all $\eta = 1, ..., n$ such that

$$\Lambda^* = \Lambda B,$$

or equivalently,

$$P(\eta^* | s) = \sum_{\eta \in H} P(\eta | s)\, B_{\eta\eta^*}.$$

A message η^* provides no additional information beyond what is contained in η if the following condition holds.

Condition *G*. $P(s | \eta, \eta^*) = P(s | \eta)$ for all (s, η, η^*).

The condition G is one way of formalizing the concept that η^* is just a "garbled" version of η.

Finally, a condition which is slightly more difficult to interpret but very important is,

Condition ϕ. For all convex, real-valued functions on the unit simplex, ϕ, it is true that

$$\sum_{\eta} \phi(\Pi_\eta)\, P(\eta) \geqslant \sum_{\eta^*} \phi(\Pi^*_{\eta^*})\, P^*(\eta^*),$$

where Π_η is the ηth column of Π, $\Pi_\eta = (P(s_i \mid \eta), ..., P(s_m \mid \eta))^T$.

For a given utility function U consider defining a function ϕ by

$$\phi(\Pi_\eta) \equiv \max_{\alpha(\eta)} \sum_{s \in S} U(\alpha(\eta), s) P(s \mid \eta).$$

This is always a convex function of Π_η. To see this let Π_η and $\overline{\Pi}_\eta$ be two vectors and let α and $\overline{\alpha}$ be the corresponding solutions of the maximization. Let $\Pi_\eta(\lambda) \equiv \lambda \Pi_\eta + (1 - \lambda)\overline{\Pi}_\eta$ be a convex combination of the two vectors, $0 \leqslant \lambda \leqslant 1$. Simple algebra gives the following:

$$\sum_s U(\lambda\alpha + (1 - \lambda)\overline{\alpha}, s)(\lambda P(s \mid \eta) + (1 - \lambda)\overline{P}(s \mid \eta))$$

$$= \lambda \sum_s U(\alpha, s) P(s \mid \eta) + (1 - \lambda) \sum_s U(\overline{\alpha}, s) \overline{P}(s \mid \eta)$$

$$- \lambda \left[\sum_s U(\alpha, s) P(s \mid \eta) - \sum_s U(\lambda\alpha + (1 - \lambda)\overline{\alpha}, s) P(s \mid \eta) \right]$$

$$- (1 - \lambda) \left[\sum_s U(\overline{\alpha}, s) \overline{P}(s \mid \eta) - \sum_s U(\lambda\alpha + (1 - \lambda)\overline{\alpha}, s) \overline{P}(s \mid \eta) \right].$$

By the optimality of α and $\overline{\alpha}$ the terms in square brackets are positive, which gives the inequalities:

$$\phi(\Pi_\eta(\lambda)) \geqslant \sum_s U(\lambda\alpha + (1 - \lambda)\overline{\alpha}, s)(\lambda P(s \mid \eta) + (1 - \lambda)\overline{P}(s \mid \eta))$$

$$\geqslant \lambda \phi(\Pi_\eta) + (1 - \lambda)\phi(\overline{\Pi}_\eta),$$

demonstrating the convexity. Using this definition of ϕ, condition ϕ is nothing other than a restatement of condition P with the arbitrary U generating the arbitrary, convex function ϕ.

The conditions P, B, G, and ϕ all seem to rank information systems in quite different ways, but a very important result in the analysis of the information content of messages is the following result due to Blackwell (1950), showing a close interdependence.

Blackwell's Theorem. Conditions U, B, and ϕ are equivalent and condition G implies but is not implied by the other three.

The theorem will be proved in the following stages:

$$U \Rightarrow B \Rightarrow \phi \Rightarrow U, \quad G \Rightarrow B, \quad B \nRightarrow G.$$

U implies B. By condition U, for all U and Q,

$$\mathrm{tr}(P\hat{D}U) = \mathrm{tr}(Q\Lambda\hat{D}U) \geqslant \mathrm{tr}(P^*\hat{D}^*U) = \mathrm{tr}(Q\Lambda^*\hat{D}^*U).$$

By the optimality of $\hat{D}^*$, it must be that for all decision matrices, D^*,

$$\mathrm{tr}(Q\Lambda^*\hat{D}^*U) \geqslant \mathrm{tr}(Q\Lambda^*D^*U).$$

Let us assume that $Q = (1/m)I$; that is, all states are equally likely. Putting the two inequalities together gives for all D^*:

$$\mathrm{tr}(\Lambda\hat{D}U) \geqslant \mathrm{tr}(\Lambda^*D^*U).$$

Consider the situation where there are exactly as many actions as there are messages in H^*: $\ell = n^*$. Letting the square matrix D^* equal the identity matrix the above inequality is

$$\sum_{s,\eta,\alpha} \Lambda_{s\eta}\hat{D}_{\eta\alpha}U_{\alpha s} \geqslant \sum_{s,\eta^*} \overset{*}{\Lambda}_{s\eta^*}U_{\eta^* s}$$

or

$$\Gamma = \sum_{s,\eta^*} U_{\eta^* s}\left(\sum_{\eta} \Lambda_{s\eta}\hat{D}_{\eta\eta^*} - \Lambda^*_{s\eta^*}\right) \geqslant 0.$$

The function Γ is a bilinear form in U and D. If we restrict utilities to the unit interval and D to the set of Markov matrices, there must exist a saddle-point of Γ, minimized with respect to U and maximized with respect to D:

$$\Gamma(U^0, D) \leqslant \Gamma(U^0, D^0) \leqslant \Gamma(U, D^0),$$

for all U, D limited as above. The inequality derived above shows that when $U = U^0$,

$$\Gamma(U^0, \hat{D}) \geqslant 0,$$

and by the saddle-point conditions we conclude that there exists a D^0 such that for all U,

$$\Gamma(U, D^0) = \sum_{s,\eta^*} U_{\eta^* s}\left(\sum_{\eta} \Lambda_{s\eta}D^0_{\eta\eta^*} - \Lambda^*_{s\eta^*}\right) \geqslant 0.$$

Since utility is arbitrary on the unit interval, place +1 in exactly one element of U and put to 0 elsewhere. The above inequality implies

$$\sum_{\eta} \Lambda_{s\eta} D^{0}_{\eta\eta^*} - \Lambda^*_{s\eta^*} \geqslant 0.$$

If strict inequality occurs, by summing across s and η^* and using the fact that Λ, D^0, and Λ^* are Markov matrices, the contradiction "$1 > 1$" occurs. Hence, equality must hold for all s and η^*; in matrix notation this says

$$\Lambda D^0 = \Lambda^*.$$

Since D^0 is Markov it is the matrix B desired.

B implies ϕ. Define a matrix M by

$$M_{\eta\eta^*} = B_{\eta\eta^*} P(\eta)/P(\eta^*).$$

Because B is a Markov matrix, we have

$$\sum_{\eta^*} M_{\eta\eta^*} P(\eta^*) = P(\eta),$$

which leads to the following,

$$\begin{aligned}\sum_{\eta} P(\eta)\,\phi(\Pi_\eta) &= \sum_{\eta}\sum_{\eta^*} M_{\eta\eta^*} P(\eta^*)\,\phi(\Pi_\eta)\\ &= \sum_{\eta^*} P(\eta^*)\left(\sum_{\eta} M_{\eta\eta^*}\,\phi(\Pi_\eta)\right).\end{aligned}$$

The matrix M has columns which sum to 1 since

$$\begin{aligned}\sum_{\eta} M_{\eta\eta^*} &= \sum_{\eta} B_{\eta\eta^*} P(\eta)/P(\eta^*)\\ &= \sum_{\eta} B_{\eta\eta^*}\left(\sum_{s} P(\eta, s)\right)\Big/P(\eta^*)\\ &= \sum_{s}\left[\sum_{\eta} P(\eta|s)\,B_{\eta\eta^*}\right] P(s)/P(\eta^*)\\ &= \sum_{s} P(\eta^*|s)\,P(s)/P(\eta^*)\\ &= P(\eta^*)/P(\eta^*)\\ &= 1,\end{aligned}$$

where the definition of B was used to simplify the term in square brackets. By the property of convex functions we have

$$\sum_{\eta} M_{\eta\eta^*}\,\phi(\Pi_\eta) \geqslant \phi\left(\sum_{\eta} M_{\eta\eta^*}\,\Pi_\eta\right).$$

The term on the right-hand side of this inequality may be simplified using the definition of M and B:

$$\phi\left(\sum_{\eta} \frac{B_{\eta\eta^*}P(\eta)}{P(\eta^*)}\,P(s|\eta)\right) = \phi\left(\sum_{\eta} \frac{B_{\eta\eta^*}P(\eta\mid s)P(s)}{P(\eta^*)}\right)$$

$$= \phi\left(\frac{P(\eta^*|s)\,P(s)}{P(\eta^*)}\right)$$

$$= \phi(P(s|\eta^*)) = \phi(\Pi^*_{\eta^*}).$$

Hence,

$$\sum_{\eta} P(\eta)\,\phi(\Pi_\eta) \geqslant \sum_{\eta^*} P(\eta^*)\,\phi(\Pi^*_{\eta^*}),$$

which was to be shown.

ϕ implies U. As verified in the comments on condition ϕ, the function

$$\phi(\Pi_\eta) \equiv \max_{\alpha} \sum_{s} U(\alpha, s)\,P(s|\eta)$$

is convex. Multiplying by $P(\eta)$ and summing gives

$$\sum_{\eta} \phi(\Pi_\eta)\,P(\eta) = \mathrm{E}U[\hat{D}, U, P].$$

Condition ϕ therefore implies condition U.

G implies B. By assumption:

$$P(s|\eta, \eta^*) = \frac{P(s, \eta, \eta^*)}{P(\eta, \eta^*)} = P(s|\eta) = \frac{P(s, \eta)}{P(\eta)},$$

which implies that

$$P(\eta^*|\eta) = \frac{P(\eta, \eta^*)}{P(\eta)} = \frac{P(\eta, \eta^*|s)}{P(\eta|s)} = \frac{P(s, \eta, \eta^*)/P(s)}{P(s, \eta)/P(s)}.$$

Cross multiplying and summing with respect to η gives

$$\sum_{\eta} P(\eta^* | \eta) P(\eta | s) = P(\eta^* | s).$$

Since $P(\eta^* | \eta)$ is a probability distribution the matrix

$$B_{\eta\eta^*} = P(\eta^* | \eta)$$

is the desired Markov matrix.

B does not imply G. From the definition of B:

$$\sum_{\eta} P(\eta | s) B_{\eta\eta^*} = P(\eta^* | s)$$
$$= \sum_{\eta} P(\eta, \eta^* | s)$$

or

$$\sum_{\eta} [P(\eta, \eta^* | s) - P(\eta | s) B_{\eta\eta^*}] = 0.$$

If the term in square brackets is identically zero, then $B_{\eta\eta^*} = P(\eta^* | \eta)$ and reading the proof of "G implies B" backwards gives condition G. However, the term in square brackets may be positive or negative as long as the sum equals zero, so B does not necessarily imply G.

This concludes the proof of Blackwell's Theorem. ■

The relationship between the equivalent measures of informativeness, U, B, and ϕ, and the Shannon transmission can now be specified. If we have two signals, η and η^*, which provide information about the unknown state of nature, we might say that the signal with the large rate of transmission provides more information.

Condition *T.* $T(s | \eta) \geqslant T(s | \eta^*)$.

The condition ϕ is equivalent to U and B as stated in Blackwell's Theorem and condition ϕ requires *all* convex function's ϕ to rank η and η^* the same way.

Theorem 9.6. Condition ϕ implies condition T but not conversely.

Proof. Condition T can be reexpressed as

$$H(P_s) - H(P_{s|\eta}) \geqslant H(P_s) - H(P_{s|\eta^*})$$

or

$$-H(P_{s|\eta}) \geqslant -H(P_{s|\eta^*}).$$

That is,

$$\sum_\eta P(\eta) \sum_s P(s|\eta) \log P(s|\eta) \geqslant \sum_\eta P(\eta^*) \sum_s P(s|\eta^*) \log P(s|\eta^*).$$

Define the particular ϕ function as follows:

$$\phi(\Pi_\eta) = \sum_s P(s|\eta) \log P(s|\eta).$$

Differentiating twice gives:

$$\frac{\partial^2 \phi}{\partial P(s|\eta)^2} = 1,$$

$$\frac{\partial^2 \phi}{\partial P(s|\eta)\, \partial P(s|\eta')} = 0, \qquad \eta \neq \eta'.$$

The Hessian of this function is positive definite and therefore $-H(P_{s|\eta})$ is convex. By condition ϕ it is clear that the above equality must hold.

Conversely, the condition T only implies the inequality of ϕ for the particular ϕ function given above. Thus, it does not imply condition ϕ. ∎

The analysis of this chapter provides several definitions of "more informative". The strongest requirement, condition G, has the advantage of easy verification; if the posterior distribution of the state given the two messages η and η^* is independent of η^*, then η is more informative than η^*. Condition G is violated if, for some s, η, and η^*, the posterior distribution is even slightly sensitive to η^* and therefore will often be unable to rank information systems. For example, suppose that η^1 and η^2 are two observations of a random variable whose unknown mean is s. Suppose that $\eta \equiv \eta^1$ and for some η_i^1:

$$\eta^* \equiv \begin{cases} \eta^1 + \epsilon, & \text{if } \eta^1 \neq \eta_i^1 \text{, where } \epsilon \text{ is random noise,} \\ (\eta^1, \eta^2), & \text{if } \eta^1 = \eta_i^1 . \end{cases}$$

That is, η^* is a noisy version of η except in the unlikely case that η equals η_i^1, when another observation is made. If the prior probability of η_i^1 is suitably small, almost certainly η^* contains less information than η but condition G will never be satisfied, not even if $P(\eta_i^1) = 0$.

The equivalent conditions U, B, and ϕ seem to be the most suitable for ranking information systems because they prevent two decision-makers from disagreeing on the relative informativeness. Unfortunately, these conditions cannot be verified by simple constructions. Either the maximum expected utilities must be compared for all utility functions, or we must solve a system of linear inequalities $\Lambda^* = \Lambda B, B \geqslant 0, \Sigma_j B_{ij} = 1$.

The condition T, using Shannon's measure, is the weakest condition. There may well be decision-makers who would chose to use an information system which is less informative according to its rate of transmission. However, the Shannon measure is calculated easily and therefore is a useful analytic tool.

Example. Consider a decision problem. There are three states, $S = \{s_1, s_2, s_3\}$, and two messages, $H = \{\eta_1, \eta_2\}$, $H^* = \{\eta_1^*, \eta_2^*\}$. Probability matrices are:

$$P = \begin{bmatrix} 9/30 & 1/30 \\ 1/30 & 9/30 \\ 5/30 & 5/30 \end{bmatrix}, \quad P^* = \begin{bmatrix} 6/30 & 4/30 \\ 3/30 & 7/30 \\ 6/30 & 4/30 \end{bmatrix},$$

$$\Pi = \begin{bmatrix} 18/30 & 2/30 \\ 2/30 & 18/30 \\ 10/30 & 10/30 \end{bmatrix}, \quad \Pi^* = \begin{bmatrix} 12/30 & 8/30 \\ 6/30 & 14/30 \\ 12/30 & 8/30 \end{bmatrix}.$$

Information system η is very successful in predicting whether s_1 or s_2 has ocurred, but does not distinguish these from s_3 well. On the other hand, η^* is slightly better at distinguishing s_3 from s_1 or s_2, but very poor at distinguishing between s_1 and s_2. The rates of transmission are easily calculated,

$$T(s|\eta) = 0.106, \qquad T(s|\eta^*) = 0.018,$$

and indicate that η is much more informative than η^*. Suppose there are two actions, $A = \{\alpha_1, \alpha_2\}$, and the utility function is

$$U = \begin{bmatrix} 6 & 6 & 0 \\ 0 & 0 & 10 \end{bmatrix}.$$

This utility puts little premium on distinguishing s_1 from s_2 but a large premium on isolating s_3. The optimal decision matrix for each information system is

$$\hat{D} = \hat{D}(\eta, \alpha) = \begin{bmatrix} 1 & 0 \\ 1 & 0 \end{bmatrix},$$

and

$$\hat{D}^* = \hat{D}^*(\eta^*, \alpha) = \begin{bmatrix} 0 & 1 \\ 1 & 0 \end{bmatrix} .$$

Maximum expected utilities are

$$\operatorname{tr} P\hat{D}U = \operatorname{tr} \begin{bmatrix} 2 & 2 & 0 \\ 2 & 2 & 0 \\ 2 & 2 & 0 \end{bmatrix} = 4$$

and

$$\operatorname{tr} P^*\hat{D}^*U = \operatorname{tr} \begin{bmatrix} 4/5 & 4/5 & 2 \\ 7/5 & 7/5 & 1 \\ 4/5 & 4/5 & 2 \end{bmatrix} = 4.2.$$

The decision-maker with the above utility matrix will find it optimal to take the information system with a lower transmission rate because it is slightly more effective at isolating a very important state. ■

CHAPTER 10

THE VALUE OF COMMUNICATION IN TEAMS

Hierarchical organization and authority have a comparative advantage over markets when uncertainty is prevalent and informational asymmetries exist naturally. Multi-member organizations confront two forms of uncertainty: external and internal. Shaping the environment are external random variables beyond the control of the organization. The health of workers, operating characteristics of machinery, and demand for its products are all influenced by shocks which are external to the decision-making of the organization's members. Internal uncertainties are created by the behavior patterns chosen by members. When decision-makers adjust their choice of activity to suit the observed circumstances, their actions have a calculated uncertainty, and even when a member knows the pattern which guides other decision-makers' responses to observations, unless he also possesses knowledge of their observations his predictions of their actions will be imprecise. External uncertainty is reduced by observation. Internal uncertainty is reduced by communication.

This chapter analyzes the benefits of communication in organizations, leaving for the next chapter the task of evaluating the costs of reducing internal uncertainty. Four communication problems will be examined. In the first, a decentralized firm, producing two goods with interdependent costs, would like to base output choices on both prices; since prices are available only to the respective salesmen, this requires communication. What if the communication network is noisy? How valuable is the reduction of noise and how does the value change as costs becomes more interdependent? Second, a single decision-maker, making sequential but interdependent decisions, has a communication problem of sorts. Should he delay the first decision while more evidence accumulates? This not only reduces external uncertainty but also uncertainty about the second stage decision. Third, a firm may centralize its information acquisition but still face a problem of communicating instructions. If there are errors in instructions to any one of the interdependent agents, no member should blindly execute orders, even if his orders are very precise. In the fourth, an organization can facilitate communication by grouping projects into departments. For informational purposes, projects which face common uncertainties should segregate in different departments.

A well-defined decision problem is needed to evaluate the communication system of an organization. Marschak and Radner (1972) found it useful to eliminate the game theoretic difficulties created by conflicting preferences of the members by assuming that the organization acts as a team. A *team* is a group of interdependent decision-makers who share a common objective. The team members acquire information which helps improve the match of their actions and the state of nature, but they do not necessarily share the information. Actions, being dependent upon the information, are coordinated by selecting decision policies which help forecast the final action. Failure to anticipate the actions of other decision-makers may lead a member to distinctly awkward choices.

The model of a team will follow the notation of Chapter 6 for decision-making under uncertainty, modified to incorporate a multitude of decision-makers. Decision-makers are indexed by the letter i, the index taking on values in the set of names $N = \{1, 2, ..., n\}$. Member i controls an activity by choosing the value of his action, α_i. The joint effect of the actions,

$$\alpha = (\alpha_1, \alpha_2, ..., \alpha_n)^{\mathrm{T}},$$

and the state of nature, s, determines a reward according to the function,

$$r = \rho(\alpha, s).$$

Rewards accrue to the team, not to the individual members, and are evaluated by a common utility function,

$$V(r).$$

It will be convenient to deal directly with the composition of the utility and reward functions

$$U(\alpha, s) = V(\rho(\alpha, s)).$$

The member named i acquires information which helps identify the state of nature; the value of the information is given by a random variable, η_i. The collection of information variables of the team,

$$\eta = (\eta_1, \eta_2, ..., \eta_n),$$

has a relative likelihood of occurring which depends on the true but unknown state of nature through the conditional distribution

$$P(\eta \mid s).$$

The state of nature has a probability distribution

$$P(s).$$

We will use the arguments of the probability function P to denote a different functional form as well as value of the random variable to eliminate the cumbersome notation $P_{\eta|s}(\eta|s)$ and $P_s(s)$. Team harmony is encapsulated in the assumption that U is a utility function common to all members and that the joint probability of the random variables, $P(\eta|s)\,P(s)$, is also commonly held by all decision-makers.

The team uses the information to determine the action by specifying for each member a decision rule,

$$\alpha_i(\eta_i),$$

mapping the set of possible values of the information variables, H_i, into the set of implementable actions, A_i. For given decision rules the expected utility of the team is expressed as

$$\mathrm{E}U[\alpha(\eta)] = \int_H \int_S U(\alpha(\eta), s)\, P(\eta|s)\, P(s)\, \mathrm{d}s\, \mathrm{d}\eta,$$

where $H = \mathrm{X}_{i=1}^{n} H_i$ and $\alpha(\eta) = (\alpha_1(\eta_1), ..., \alpha_n(\eta_n))^T$. It should be pointed out that the information of the ith member may or may not be the same as the jth member. In general, the actual decision $\alpha_j(\eta_j)$ is a random variable from the perspective of another decision-maker.

Example. Let α_1 be an output commitment made by a salesman and let α_2 be the number of machines installed by the production department. The state consists of the price of output, s_1, and the price of machinery, s_2. If the cost of labor needed to assume production of α_1 given α_2 machines is denoted $C(\alpha_1, \alpha_2)$, then profit equals

$$U(\alpha, s) = \alpha_1 s_1 - \alpha_2 s_2 - C(\alpha_1, \alpha_2).$$

The production department orders machines according to a purchasing policy,

$$\alpha_2(s_2).$$

The salesman observes the price of output before contracting to deliver according to the sales policy

$$\alpha_2(s_1).$$

If the joint probability of the prices is $P(s_1, s_2)$, then the expected profit is

$$\int_{S_1}\int_{S_2} (\alpha_1(s_1)s_1 - \alpha_2(s_2)s_2 - C(\alpha_1(s_1), \alpha_2(s_2)))P(s_1, s_2)\mathrm{d}s_1\,\mathrm{d}s_2. \quad \blacksquare$$

A team makes optimal use of its information system when it chooses its decision rules to maximize expected utility. The conditions characterizing the optimal team decision rule are somewhat more complicated than those for a single decision-maker because both the state and the actions are random variables from the perspective of any one team member. Radner (1962) derived the following necessary conditions.

Theorem 10.1 (Person-by-person optimality). If $\alpha(\eta)$ is the optimal team decision rule, then for each $i \in N$ and for all $\eta_i \in H_i$, it must be true that

$$0 = \mathrm{E}\{U_{\alpha_i}(\alpha(\eta), s) \mid \eta_i\},$$

where $U_{\alpha_i} = \partial U / \partial \alpha_i$.

Proof. Write a decision rule as a small deviation from the optimum,

$$\alpha(\eta) + \epsilon\, \gamma(\eta),$$

where ϵ is a diagonal matrix and $\gamma(\eta)$ is an arbitrary team decision rule. Optimality requires that for all $\gamma(\eta)$

$$\frac{\partial \mathrm{E} U[\alpha(\eta) + \epsilon\, \gamma(\eta)]}{\partial \epsilon_{ii}} = 0,$$

when ϵ equals zero. Evaluating this partial derivative gives the equivalent first-order condition

$$E\{U_{\alpha_i}(\alpha(\eta), s) \cdot \gamma_i(\eta_i)\} = 0,$$

and since $\gamma_i(\eta_i)$ can take on arbitrary values this implies

$$E\{U_{\alpha_i}(\alpha(\eta), s) | \eta_i\} = 0, \quad \text{for all } \eta_i \in H_i. \quad \blacksquare$$

That is to say, given the other members' decision rules, the ith person must use a decision rule such that the action taken when η_i is observed equates the conditional expected marginal utility of the ith person's action to zero. The conditional expectation is taken after modifying the beliefs according to Bayes rule; that is, if $\eta_{-i} \equiv (\eta_1, ..., \eta_{i-1}, \eta_{i+1}, ..., \eta_n)$ are the information variables of all members but i, then

$$P(\eta_{-i}, s | \eta_i) = P(\eta | s) P(s) / P(\eta_i).$$

The person-by person optimality conditions have the general form of a system of non-linear integral equations (see Akbari et al., 1980, and Hess and Kalaba, 1978). Some simplifying assumptions are reasonable and permit the easy solution of the person-by-person optimality conditions.

Assumption Q. The teams' utility is linear quadratic in the actions with a quadratic form that is constant. That is,

$$U(\alpha, s) = w(s) + v(s)^{\mathrm{T}} \alpha + \tfrac{1}{2} \alpha^{\mathrm{T}} Q \alpha,$$

where $v(s)$ is a n-vector of functions and Q is a $n \times n$ matrix of constants.

Assumption L. The regression of $v_i(s)$ on η_i is linear. The regression of η_j on η_i is linear. That is,

$$E\{v_i(s) | \eta_i\} = b_{i0} + b_{i1} \eta_i$$

and

$$E\{\eta_j | \eta_i\} = c_{ij0} + c_{ij1} \eta_i.$$

The assumption of quadratic utility may be justified as a second-order approximation of a more general function (see, however, Malcomson, 1978). The linear regression assumption is useful because the normal probability distribution along with many other distributions satisfy it. See Mardia (1970) and Johnson and Kotz (1972). Together assumptions Q and L allow us to conclude that the team optimal decision rules will be affine (that is, linear except for a non-zero intercept).

Theorem 10.2. If the team utility function satisfies assumption Q and the probability distributions satisfy assumption L, then there is a decision rule of the form

$$\alpha_i(\eta_i) = a_{i0} + a_{i1}\,\eta_i,$$

which satisfies the person-by-person optimality condition.

Proof. Write out the optimality conditions using assumption Q:

$$0 = \mathrm{E}\{v_i(s) + \sum_{j=1}^{n} q_{ij}\,\alpha_j(\eta_j)\,|\,\eta_i\}.$$

If we choose affine decision rules such that

$$0 = b_{i0} + \sum_j q_{ij}(a_{j0} + a_{j1}\,c_{ij0}),$$

$$0 = b_{i1} + \sum_j q_{ij} a_{j1}\,c_{ij1})$$

then the optimality conditions must hold. To check, simply substitute assumption L into the person-by-person optimality conditions:

$$0 = \mathrm{E}\{v_i(s)\,|\,\eta_i\} + \sum_j q_{ij}(a_{j0} + a_{j1}\,\mathrm{E}\{\eta_j\,|\,\eta_i\})$$

$$= b_{i0} + \sum_j q_{ij}(a_{j0} + a_{j1}\,c_{ij0}) + \left(b_{i1} + \sum_j q_{ij} a_{j1}\,c_{ij1}\right)\,\eta_i.$$

Speyer et al. (1980) show that decision rules are also affine in the case of normal random variables and exponential utility. ■

The maximum expected utility may be expressed in terms of the moments of $v(s)$ and $\alpha(\eta)$ when utility is quadratic.

Theorem 10.3. If the team utility satisfies assumption Q, then the maximum expected utility equals

$$\mathrm{E}U[\alpha] = \mathrm{E}\{w(s)\} + \tfrac{1}{2}\,\mathrm{E}\{v(s)^{\mathrm{T}}\alpha(\eta)\},$$

where α satisfies the person-by-person optimality conditions.

Proof. Multiply the optimality conditions by $\alpha_i(\eta_i)$ and take expectations with respect to η_i to get

$$0 = \mathrm{E}\left\{v_i(s)\,\alpha_i(\eta_i) + \sum_j q_{ij}\,\alpha_i(\eta_i)\,\alpha_j(\eta_j)\right\}.$$

(Notice that $\mathrm{E}\{\mathrm{E}\{x\,|\,y\}\} = \mathrm{E}\{x\}$.) Summing across i gives:

$$0 = \mathrm{E}\{v(s)^{\mathrm{T}}\alpha(\eta) + \alpha(\eta)^{\mathrm{T}}Q\alpha(\eta)\}.$$

Add $\mathrm{E}\{2w(s) + v(s)^{\mathrm{T}}\alpha(\eta)\}$ to both sides to get:

$$\mathrm{E}\{2\,w(s) + v(s)^{\mathrm{T}}\alpha(\eta)\} = 2\,\mathrm{E}\{w(s) + v(s)^{\mathrm{T}}\alpha(\eta) + \tfrac{1}{2}\alpha(\eta)^{\mathrm{T}}Q\alpha(\eta)\},$$

from which the theorem is evident. This result does not depend on assumption L. ∎

Example. Consider a specific communication problem. Two salesman must make field decisions on how many orders for goods they should accept. The ith salesman attends the market for good i where he learns the price s_i and sells the quantity α_i. The production process involves the joint use of some facilities and personnel, so costs are interdependent. Specifically, the cost function is

$$C(\alpha_1, \alpha_2) = \tfrac{1}{2}\alpha_1^2 + q\,\alpha_1\,\alpha_2 + \tfrac{1}{2}\alpha_2^2,$$

where q is a numerical measure of the degree of interdependence. The salesmen do not directly discern the other good's price. Instead, a message is relayed through headquarters, where mistakes in comprehension or reporting can occur. If s_i is the price of good i, the message received by member j equals

$$s_i + e_i,$$

where e_i is an error term introduced by the transmission. The organization must design sales policies relating price information to sales,

$$\alpha_i(s_i, s_j + e_j),$$

in order to maximize expected profit,

$$\mathrm{E}\{s_1\,\alpha_1(s_1, s_2 + e_2) + s_2\,\alpha_2(s_2, s_1 + e_1) -$$
$$- C(\alpha_1(s_1, s_2 + e_2), \alpha_2(s_2, s_1 + e_1))\}.$$

With the above, quadratic cost function, the utility function satisfies assumption Q.

Suppose that (s_1, s_2) are independent normal random variables with means $(\bar{s}_1, \bar{s}_2)$ and unitary variances. The error terms will be assumed to have independent normal distributions with zero means and precisions τ_1 and τ_2 (the precision is the reciprocal of the variance and measures the accurancy of the message). The posterior distribution of s_i given s_j and $s_i + e_i$ is also normal with a linear regression,

$$\mathrm{E}\{s_i | s_j, s_i + e_i\} = \frac{\bar{s}_i}{1 + \tau_i} + \frac{\tau_i}{1 + \tau_i}(s_i + e_i).$$

(See Mood and Graybill, 1963, for a derivation of properties of multivariate normal distributions.)

We can use theorem 10.2 to characterize the optimal decision rules as affine functions:

$$\alpha_i(s_i, s_j + e_j) = a_{i0} + a_{i1}\,s_i + a_{i2}(s_j + e_j).$$

The above coefficients, a_{ik}, must satisfy the following system of linear equalities:

$$a_{11} + q\,a_{22} = 1,$$

$$a_{12} + q\,\frac{\tau_2}{1 + \tau_2}\,a_{21} = 0,$$

$$a_{21} + q\,a_{12} = 1,$$

$$a_{22} + q\,\frac{\tau_1}{1 + \tau_1}\,a_{11} = 0,$$

$$a_{10} + q\,a_{20} = -q\,\frac{\bar{s}_2}{1 + \tau_2}\,a_{21},$$

$$a_{20} + q\,a_{10} = -q\,\frac{\bar{s}_1}{1 + \tau_1}\,a_{11}.$$

Table 10.1

$$\alpha_1 = a_{10} + \frac{1+\tau_1}{1+(1-q^2)\tau_1}\, s_1 - \frac{q\tau_2}{1+(1-q^2)\tau_2}\,(s_2+e_2),$$

$$\alpha_2 = a_{20} + \frac{1+\tau_2}{1+(1-q^2)\tau_2}\, s_2 - \frac{q\tau_1}{1+(1-q^2)\tau_1}\,(s_1+e_1),$$

where

$$a_{10} = \frac{q}{1-q^2}\left(\frac{q\bar{s}_1}{1+(1-q^2)\tau_1} - \frac{\bar{s}_2}{1+(1-q^2)\tau_2}\right),$$

$$a_{20} = \frac{q}{1-q^2}\left(\frac{q\bar{s}_2}{1+(1-q^2)\tau_2} - \frac{\bar{s}_1}{1+(1-q^2)\tau_2}\right).$$

Straightforward but tedious linear algebra leads to the solution for the optimal output decision rules as exhibited in table 10.1. These sales policies depend on the underlying parameters in a complex way, but several important regularities should be noticed. When salesman i has great confidence that his message will be understood, his actions will be very sensitive to his own good's price. Technically, the coefficient a_{i1} increases with τ_i. With better lines of communication the salesman can be confident that the other salesmen will not drive up the marginal cost through the inderdependence term, $q\alpha_1\alpha_2$. The response of α_i to $s_j + e_j$ depends on the sign of q. When q exceeds zero, a report of a high price of the other good will lead salesman i to decrease the orders he accepts. As the precision of the received message, τ_j, increases, the sensitivity of α_i to $s_j + e_j$ increases.

From theorem 10.3 the maximum expected utility can be calculated using the affine decision rules:

$$\begin{aligned} EU &= \tfrac{1}{2}\,\mathrm{E}\{s_1(a_{10} + a_{11}s_1 + a_{12}(s_2+e_2)) + \\ &\quad + s_2(a_{20} + a_{21}s_2 + a_{22}(s_1+e_1))\} \\ &= \tfrac{1}{2}(a_{10}\bar{s}_1 + a_{20}\bar{s}_2 + a_{11}\,\mathrm{E}\{s_1^2\} + a_{21}\,\mathrm{E}\{s_2^2\} + (a_{12}+a_{22})\,\mathrm{E}\{s_1 s_2\}, \end{aligned}$$

where use has been made of the fact that the communication errors are independent random variables with zero mean. Since s_i is an independent random variable with mean $\bar{s}_i$ and variance 1, expected profit may be further simplified:

$$\mathrm{E}U = \tfrac{1}{2}(a_{10}\bar{s}_1 + a_{20}\bar{s}_2 + a_{11}(1+\bar{s}_1^2) + a_{21}(1+\bar{s}_2^2) + (a_{12}+a_{22})\bar{s}_1\bar{s}_2).$$

Since the coefficients of the optimal decision rules are exhibited in table 10.1, we can calculate how any parameter influences the maximum expected utility. Of particular importance is the sensitivity of expected utility to the decision of communication.

Theorem 10.4. In the above team problem the maximum expected utility is a monotonic increasing, concave function of communication precision, τ_i. Hence, the marginal value of more accurate communication,

$$MVC_i = \frac{\partial \mathrm{E}U}{\partial \tau_i},$$

is positive and decreasing with precision τ_i.

Straightforward differentiation of EU, using table 10.1, gives

$$\frac{\partial \mathrm{E}U}{\partial \tau_i} = \tfrac{1}{2}\,\frac{q^2}{1+(1-q^2)\tau_i},$$

which is clearly positive and decreasing in τ_i (see fig. 10.1).

If the organization experiences an increase in its cost interdependence, as measured by q, the marginal value of communication increases, as indicated by the counter-clockwise rotation in fig. 10.1. If one could buy communication accuracy at a constant cost per unit of precision, the organization would increase precision up to the point where the marginal value of communication equals the cost of communication. Increased interdependence will increase the chosen amount of accuracy in the communication system, regardless of whether the dependency is an economy ($q < 0$) or diseconomy ($q > 0$). This is not true in

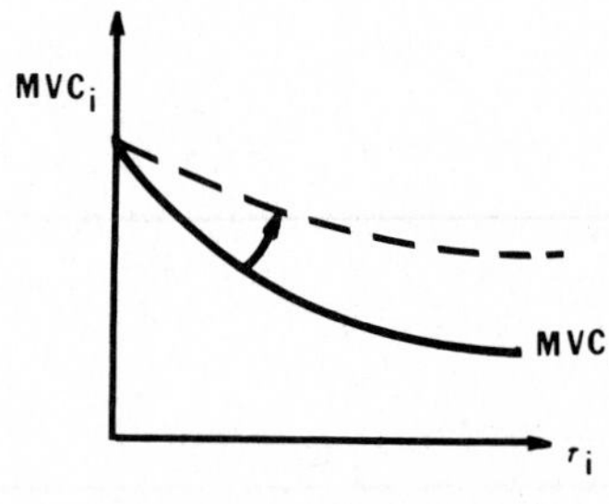

Figure 10.1

general. An increased diseconomy may force the team to choose decision rules so insensitive to information that communication is less valuable at the marginal, as will be seen in the next model.

Example. Communication is thought of as occurring between different decision-makers but it may also be across time. Consider a monopolist producing two closely related products, facing demand curves

$$x_1 = I_1(s) - \alpha_1 + q\,\alpha_2$$

and

$$x_2 = I_2(s) - \alpha_2 + q\,\alpha_1,$$

where x_i is the quantity of good i demanded if the price of the two goods are (α_1, α_2). The income of consumers has a random effect on demand, $I_i(s)$. The parameter q measures the degree to which the goods are gross substitutes ($q > 0$) or complements ($q < 0$). For simplicity let us assume that the income terms are

$$I_i(s) = 1 + s,$$

and that each commodity can be produced at a constant one dollar unit cost. Profits are therefore,

$$\begin{aligned} U &= \alpha_1 x_1 + \alpha_2 x_2 - (x_1 + x_2) \\ &= -2(1+s) + (s-q)(\alpha_1 + \alpha_2) - \alpha_1^2 + 2q\alpha_1\alpha_2 - \alpha_2^2. \end{aligned}$$

The monopolist can improve his expected profits by acquiring information about the random income term, say by doing market surveys or household interviews. Suppose that good 1 must have its price advertised to attract customers and the timely development of an advertising campaign mandates the specification of price α_1 before the market survey is complete. The sequential choice of prices introduces internal uncertainty. The profitability α_1 is influenced by the price later chosen for good 2 and that price, α_2, depends on the unfinished market survey. Suppose that sample of the kth household produces a forecast of s, denoted s_k which has a normal distribution with a mean equal to s and a variance equal to 1. Although a total of m households will be sampled, the price α_1 must be chosen after only ℓ surveys are made, $\ell < m$. If the random variable s is a unit normal random variable, sample means provide all relevant information:

$$\eta_1 = \frac{s_1 + \ldots + s_\ell}{\ell},$$

$$\eta_2 = (\eta_{21}, \eta_{22}) = \left(\frac{s_1 + \ldots + s_\ell}{\ell}, \frac{s_{\ell+1} + \ldots + s_m}{m - \ell}\right).$$

That is, the second price is chosen knowing not only $\eta_1 \equiv \eta_{21}$, but also the sample mean of the $m - \ell$ households surveyed after fixing the first price.

The demand interdependence forces the monopolist to consider the expected price of good 2 when choosing price α_1. When price α_2 is selected, the price of good 1 is already known. The optimal price rules must satisfy the person-by-person expected profit maximizing conditions:

$$0 = \mathrm{E}\{s|\eta_1\} - q - 2\alpha_1(\eta_1) + 2q\,\mathrm{E}\{\alpha_2(\eta_{21}, \eta_{22})|\eta_1\},$$

$$0 = \mathrm{E}\{s|\eta_{21}, \eta_{22}\} - q - 2\alpha_2(\eta_{21}, \eta_{22}) + 2q\,\alpha_1(\eta_{21}).$$

Standard rules on sampling from normal probability distributions give the following regressions:

$$\mathrm{E}\{s|\eta_1\} = \frac{\ell}{\ell + 1}\eta_1,$$

$$\mathrm{E}\{\eta_{21}|\eta_1\} = \eta_1,$$

$$\mathrm{E}\{s|\eta_{21}, \eta_{22}\} = \frac{\ell}{m+1}\eta_{21} + \frac{m - \ell}{m+1}\eta_{22},$$

and

$$\mathrm{E}\{\eta_{22}|\eta_1\} = \frac{\ell}{\ell + 1}\eta_1.$$

Using theorem 10.2 the optimal decision rules are affine, and the solution is found in table 10.2.

The maximum expected utility can be calculated easily using theorem 10.3:

$$\begin{aligned} \mathrm{E}U &= \mathrm{E}\{-2(1+s)\} + \tfrac{1}{2}\mathrm{E}\{(s-q)(\alpha_1 + \alpha_2)\} \\ &= -2 + \tfrac{1}{2}\mathrm{E}\{s(\alpha_1 + \alpha_2)\} - \tfrac{1}{2}q\,\mathrm{E}\{\alpha_1 + \alpha_2\}. \end{aligned}$$

Table 10.2

$$\alpha_1(\eta_1) = \frac{-q/2}{1-q} + \tfrac{1}{2}\,\frac{1}{1-q}\,\frac{\ell}{\ell+1}\,\eta_1,$$

$$\alpha_2(\eta_{21}, \eta_{22}) = \frac{-q/2}{1-q} + \tfrac{1}{2}\left(\frac{\ell}{m+1} + \frac{q}{1-q}\,\frac{\ell}{\ell+1}\right)\eta_{21} + \tfrac{1}{2}\,\frac{m-\ell}{m+1}\,\eta_{22}.$$

Substituting the optimal decision rules from table 10.2 and noting that the covariance of s_k and s equals 1 allows us to simplify this formula:

$$\mathrm{E}U = \tfrac{1}{2}\,\frac{q^2}{1-q} - 2 + \tfrac{1}{2}\left(\frac{m}{m+1} + \frac{1+q}{1-q}\,\frac{\ell}{\ell+1}\right).$$

Expected utility is a monotonic increasing and concave function of both m and ℓ. Treating the sample sizes as continuous variables implies that the marginal value of information, $\partial \mathrm{E}U/\partial m$ is positive and falling, and the marginal value of communication, $\partial \mathrm{E}U/\partial \ell$, is positive and decreasing. Suppose that each sample of a household costs t dollars, and that the advertising costs decrease as more time is made available to promote product 1. If the advertising expense can be cut in proportion to $m - \ell$, then total cost of sampling and promotion equals

$$mt - (m - \ell)h,$$

where h is the per time period savings on advertising. With this specification the optimal number of samples and the optimal time to fix the price of good 1 are

$$m^* = \frac{1}{\sqrt{2(t-h)}} - 1$$

and

$$\ell^* = \sqrt{\frac{1+q}{1-q}}\,\frac{1}{\sqrt{2h}} - 1,$$

under the presumption that q is not so large that $\ell^* > m^*$. ℓ^* is a monotonic increasing function of q; that is, as the two goods become closer substitutes it becomes crucial to communicate accurate estimates of the demand. If, however, q is negative but increases in magnitude, the demand for communication declines. If the last $m - \ell$ observations indicate a large demand because of high income, the increase in the price of the second good has the added benefit of pushing some customers over into the other good's market. ■

The communication problems just discussed occur in a decentralized decision-making organization. Highly centralized organizations have informational difficulties, too. Imagine an organization producing two goods. The central decision-maker chooses the quantities to maximize profits, correctly accounting for any cost interdependence, and sends instructions to the production units. Instructions may be garbled so it is not clear that the production units should follow instructions regardless of the noise in the command system. Radner (1961) developed a model of these errors in instruction which implies that orders should always be hedged against when noise is in the communication system.

Example. Consider a firm wich observes the prices (s_1, s_2) of its two outputs and chooses production quantities (α_1, α_2) to maximize profit:

$$U = s_1 \alpha_1 + s_2 \alpha_2 - \tfrac{1}{2}\alpha_1^2 - q\alpha_1\alpha_2 - \tfrac{1}{2}\alpha_2^2.$$

The optimal quantities,

$$\alpha_1^* = \frac{1}{1-q^2}(s_1 - qs_2),$$

and

$$\alpha_2^* = \frac{1}{1-q^2}(s_2 - qs_1),$$

are sent to the production units, but the instructions received have random noise attached:

$$\eta_1 = \alpha_1^* + e_1,$$

$$\eta_2 = \alpha_2^* + e_2.$$

What are the optimal production rules for the firm? Should $\alpha_i(\eta_i) = \eta_i$; that is, should production units follow orders?

Suppose that (s_1, s_2) was drawn from a bivariate normal distribution with zero means, unit variances, and zero covariances, and that error terms, e_i, are independent normal random variables with zero mean and precision τ_i. Theorems 10.1 and 10.2 imply that production rules should be affine and satisfy the person-by-person optimality conditions:

$$0 = \mathrm{E}\{s_1 \mid \eta_1\} - a_{11}\,\eta_1 - q\,a_{21}\,\mathrm{E}\{\eta_2 \mid \eta_1\},$$

$$0 = \mathrm{E}\{s_2 \mid \eta_2\} - a_{21}\,\eta_2 - q\,a_{11}\,\mathrm{E}\{\eta_1 \mid \eta_2\}$$

(intercepts are zero since s_i has a zero mean). The optimal production policies are found in table 10.3.

Only when both instructions are infinitely precise will the production units follow instructions. Even when instruction to unit 1 is perfectly precise, $\tau_1 = \infty$, its coefficient a_{11} is smaller than 1; less output will be produced than was required by the instruction. If the unit 1 did not hedge this way, the error in instruction to unit 2 might drive the marginal cost of good 1 above the price of good 1. As accuracy of instruction improves for good i, production unit i pays closer attention to its instructions as does the other production unit:

$$\frac{\partial a_{11}}{\partial \tau_1} > 0, \quad \frac{\partial a_{21}}{\partial \tau_1} > 0,$$

$$\frac{\partial a_{11}}{\partial \tau_2} > 0, \quad \frac{\partial a_{21}}{\partial \tau_2} > 0.$$

Table 10.3

$$\alpha_1 = a_{11}\,\eta_1 = \left(1 - \frac{1 + \gamma\tau_2 + q\delta\,\tau_1}{(\gamma\tau_1 + 1)(\gamma\tau_2 + 1) - q^2\delta^2\,\tau_1\,\tau_2}\right)\eta_1,$$

$$\alpha_2 = a_{21}\,\eta_2 = \left(1 - \frac{1 + \gamma\tau_1 + q\delta\,\tau_2}{(\gamma\tau_1 + 1)(\gamma\tau_2 + 1) - q^2\delta^2\,\tau_1\,\tau_2}\right)\eta_2,$$

where $\gamma = (1 + q^2)/(1 - q^2)^2$ and $\delta = 2q/(1 - q^2)^2$.

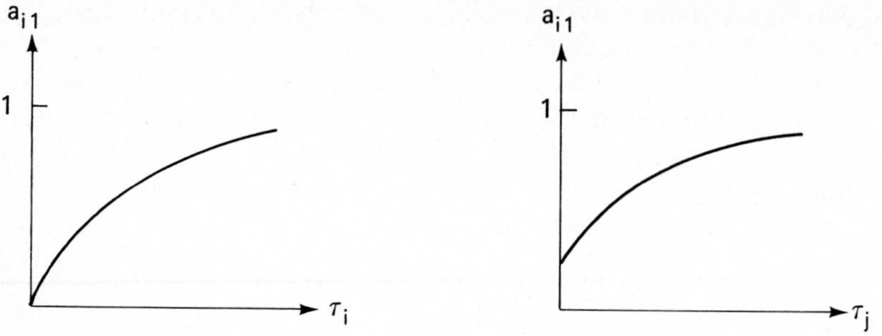

Figure 10.2

See fig. 10.2. The coefficients are concave functions of precision. From theorem 10.3 we can write the maximum expected utility as

$$\mathrm{E}U = \tfrac{1}{2}\mathrm{E}\{s_1\alpha_1 + s_2\alpha_2\} = \tfrac{1}{2}\,\frac{1}{1-q^2}\,(a_{11} + a_{21}).$$

The marginal value of more precise instructions is positive and decreasing in τ_i from the monotonicity and concavity of a_{i1}. When the instructions are equally precise, $\tau_1 = \tau_2 = \tau$, the marginal value of precise communication equals

$$\frac{\partial \mathrm{E}U}{\partial \tau} = \frac{1}{\tau + 1 - q^2}\ .$$

As the degree of interdependence, q, increases in magnitude, the marginal value of precise instructions increases. ■

As a final application of team decision theory consider how an organization should be departmentalized. At any given time the organization has several projects it can invest its resources in. The profitability of project i depends on the resources allocated to it, α_i, and the state of nature, s, according to a function

$$\rho_i(\alpha_i, s).$$

The organization only has a given amount of resources to allocate

$$\sum_{i \in N} \alpha_i = \hat{\alpha}.$$

If there were no costs to communication, the organization would wait until the state had been discovered and choose the allocation $\alpha_i(s)$, $i \in N$, to

$$\text{maximize } U(\alpha, s) = \sum_{i \in N} \rho_i(\alpha_i, s)$$

$$\text{subject to } \sum_{i \in N} \alpha_i = \hat{\alpha}.$$

This fully integrated organization may be very costly in terms of information and communication. Cremer (1980) suggests the following analysis of alternative organization forms. An organization form is a partition of the projects into departments:

$$O = \{J_1, ..., J_k\},$$

$$\bigcup_{i=1}^{k} J_i = N \quad \text{and} \quad J_i \cap J_j = \phi, \quad \text{if } i \neq j.$$

A department $J \in O$ is allocated a fixed quantity of the resource, $\overline{\alpha}_J$, and upon observing the state maximizes

$$\sum_{j \in J} \rho_j(\alpha_j, s)$$

subject to

$$\sum_{j \in J} \alpha_j = \hat{\alpha}_J.$$

The allocation $\hat{\alpha}_J$, $J \in O$, is chosen to maximize the total expected payoff of each department.

Suppose that $\overline{\alpha}_i = \mathrm{E}\{\alpha_i(s)\}$ is the expected value of the fully integrated organization, $O = N$. Approximate the profit function near $\overline{\alpha}_i$ by a quadratic function

$$\rho_i = \gamma_i(s) q_i (\alpha_i - \overline{\alpha}_i) - \tfrac{1}{2} q_i (\alpha_i - \overline{\alpha}_i)^2.$$

For any given department and departmental resources the solution of the department's maximization problem must satisfy the optimality conditions:

$$\gamma_j(s) q_j - q_j(\alpha_j(s) - \overline{\alpha}_j) = \lambda_J(s)$$

and

$$\sum_{j \in J} \alpha_j(s) = \hat{\alpha}_J,$$

where $\lambda_J(s)$ is the shadow price of the resource constraint. The solution of these equations is:

$$\lambda_J(s) = q_J(\gamma_J(s) + \overline{\alpha}_J - \hat{\alpha}_J),$$

$$\alpha_j(s) = \gamma_j(s) - \frac{q_J}{q_j}(\gamma_J(s) + \overline{\alpha}_J - \hat{\alpha}_J),$$

where

$$q_J = 1 \Big/ \Big(\sum_{j \in J} q_j^{-1}\Big),$$

$$\gamma_J(s) = \sum_{j \in J} \gamma_j(s),$$

and

$$\overline{\alpha}_J = \sum_{j \in J} \overline{\alpha}_j.$$

Theorem 10.3 allows us to express the maximum expected profit for the department as a function of departmental resources:

$$\rho_J(\hat{\alpha}_J) = q_J\, \mathrm{E}\{\gamma_J(s)\}(\hat{\alpha}_J - \overline{\alpha}_J) - \tfrac{1}{2} q_J(\hat{\alpha}_J - \overline{\alpha}_J)^2$$
$$+ \tfrac{1}{2} \sum_{j \in J} q_j\, \mathrm{E}\{\gamma_j(s)^2\} - \tfrac{1}{2} q_J\, \mathrm{E}\left\{\Big(\sum_{j \in J} \gamma_j(s)\Big)^2\right\}.$$

If we take the organization form O as given, the optimal allocation to the departments maximizes

$$\sum_{J \in O} \rho_J(\hat{\alpha}_J)$$

subject to

$$\sum_{J \in O} \hat{\alpha}_J = \hat{\alpha}.$$

Since $\rho_J(\hat{\alpha}_J)$ is quadratic the optimal solution is easily found to be

$$\hat{\alpha}_J = \overline{\alpha}_J,$$

and the maximum expected utility for the organizational form is

$$\rho(O) = \tfrac{1}{2} \sum_{i \in N} q_i \, \mathrm{E}\{\gamma_i(s)^2\} - \tfrac{1}{2} \sum_{J \in O} q_J \, \mathrm{E} \left\{ \left(\sum_{j \in J} \gamma_j(s) \right)^2 \right\}.$$

The first term is independent of the assignment of projects to departments. Only the last term varies as the organizational form changes.

Consider an organization with three projects which wants to unite project 1 with either project 2 or 3 to form a department. The two organizational forms to be compared are

$$O \;= (\{1, 2\}, \{3\}),$$

$$O^* = (\{1, 3\}, \{2\}).$$

For analytic simplicity suppose $q_i = 1$ and $\mathrm{E}\{\gamma_i(s)\} = 0$ for all i. The difference between the profitability of the organizational forms is

$$\rho(O) - \rho(O^*) = -\tfrac{1}{2}[\tfrac{1}{2}\,\mathrm{E}\{(\gamma_1(s) + \gamma_2(s))^2\} + \mathrm{E}\{\gamma_3(s)^2\}]$$

$$+\tfrac{1}{2}[\tfrac{1}{2}\,\mathrm{E}\{(\gamma_1(s) + \gamma_3(s))^2\} + \mathrm{E}\{\gamma_2(s)^2\}].$$

Organization O is more profitable if

$$\mathrm{var}[\gamma_2(s)] - 2\,\mathrm{cov}[\gamma_1(s), \gamma_2(s)] > \mathrm{var}[\gamma_3(s)] - 2\,\mathrm{cov}[\gamma_1(s), \gamma_2(s)].$$

If project 2 is more uncertain than project 3, then this will tend to make it optimal to group project 2 into a department with 1. On the other hand, if project 1 and 2 are much more positively correlated than are 1 and 3, project 2 should *not* be joined with project 1. The reasoning is that since both projects move up and down together, the advantage of a flexible allocation within the department is wasted. Projects should be in groups which have strong negative correlations between their profitabilities in order to take advantage of interdepartmental communication.

CHAPTER 11

COST OF COMMUNICATION

A communication system consists of more than a communication device. Translators, recorders, interpretors, languages, and lexicons play fundamental roles in transmitting information. It would be beyond the scope of this book to explore the economic problems associated with designing minimum cost communication systems where all these aspects are variable. Instead this chapter will be concerned only with the choice of an organization's language, the symbols and vocabulary used to communicate from one member to another their knowledge of the environment. Studies of these issues are stylized; we will abstract from many important issues of cognitive psychology and communication science in order to make some progress toward an understanding of the cost of communication. Much of the following is based on Watanabe's (1969) exposition of information theory.

The cost of a communication system may not depend simply on the number of different signals which might be transmitted. For example, let the state of nature be the quality of a worker's contribution to production, where quality may be classified in five ways, S = {excellent, good, average, below average, poor}. Prior to communication it was thought that the probabilities of these qualities were $P = (5/15, 4/15, 3/15, 2/15, 1/15)$. Consider two communication systems, one which does not distinguish between {excellent} and {good} quality work, and another which does not distinguish qualities below {good}. That is, the two communication networks induce the following partitions of S:

$$\mathscr{S} = \{ \{\text{excellent, good}\}, \{\text{average}\}, \{\text{below average}\}, \{\text{poor}\} \},$$

and

$$\mathscr{S}^* = \{ \{\text{excellent}\}, \{\text{good}\}, \{\text{average, below average, poor}\} \}.$$

Just because $\mathscr{S}$ has more messages to contend with does not mean that it is more costly. Suppose the channel of communication is limited to symbols "A" and "B". The communication system $\mathscr{S}$ might be coded with the following lexicon:

excellent, good	$\Leftrightarrow$ "A",
average	$\Leftrightarrow$ "B",
below average	$\Leftrightarrow$ "AA",
poor	$\Leftrightarrow$ "AB";

while the system $\mathscr{S}^*$ has the lexicon:

excellent	$\Leftrightarrow$ "A",
good	$\Leftrightarrow$ "AA",
average, below average, poor	$\Leftrightarrow$ "B".

Even though $\mathscr{S}$ has a larger lexicon, the number of symbols which must be transmitted is expected to be

$$\frac{9}{15}\cdot 1+\frac{3}{15}\cdot 1+\frac{2}{15}\cdot 2+\frac{1}{15}\cdot 2=\frac{18}{15},$$

which exceeds that of $\mathscr{S}^*$:

$$\frac{5}{15}\cdot 1+\frac{4}{15}\cdot 2+\frac{6}{15}\cdot 1=\frac{19}{15}.$$

It can easily be checked that no other lexicon for $\mathscr{S}^*$ will make the expected number of symbols transmitted smaller than 19/15 and thus the cost of implementing $\mathscr{S}^*$ will be greater than the cost of $\mathscr{S}$.

In the previous chapter the information was treated as a random variable, η, a special form of encoding information. η takes on values of real numbers, often just integers, as when

$$H=\{1, ..., m\}.$$

The symbols used to transmit decimal representation of this information are "0", "1", ..., "9". Generalizing this, a communication system transmits the fact that the state lies in one of the sets in the partition $\mathscr{S}$ by using symbols from a set of characters

$$\chi = \{\chi_1, \chi_2, ..., \chi_q\},$$

and a lexicon of the form

$$L = \{(M, w(M) | M \in \mathscr{S} \text{ and } w(M) = \chi^1 \parallel \chi^2 \parallel .. \parallel \chi^{\ell_M}, \text{ where}$$
$$\text{where } \chi^i \in X, i = 1, ..., \ell_M\}.$$

The notation "$\|\cdot\|$" refers to concatenation or juxtaposition of symbols and $w(M)$ is the word associated with message M. The longer the word, the more resources used to encode, transmit, and decode the information.

The organization must take care to select a lexicon which economizes on the communication of symbols, for an arbitrary choice of language may force decision-makers and workers to spend inordinate effort encoding and interpreting communication. For example, suppose that of eight workers exactly one has special talents at a special task, but to discover the worker requires exhaustive inspection. To minimize the cost of identifying their talents, the group is divided in half and assigned identical four-person tasks. The subgroup with higher productivity is again subdivided and given two-person tasks. Finding the most productive pair, they are assigned individual tasks and the more productive worker is judged to have special talent. This communication procedure requires three repetitions of the monitoring, compared with worker-by-worker monitoring which would be expected to be repeated 3.5 times. The difference expands dramatically as the number of workers increases. In what follows this procedure will be generalized to allow for more than two symbols and for non-uniform probabilities.

Partition the set of messages $\mathscr{S}$ into no more than q sets, where q equals the number of symbols in χ, and denote this partition,

$$G^1 = \{G_1^1, G_2^1, ..., G_{h_1}^1\}, \qquad h_1 \leqslant q.$$

Each of the elements of G^1, say, G_i^1, can be partitioned in a similar fashion:

$$G_i = \{G_{i1}^2, G_{i2}^2, ..., G_{ih_2}^2\}, \qquad h_2 \leqslant q.$$

Continuing this procedure until each message in $\mathscr{S}$ is identified, we have created a lexicon for G using the symbols χ. If $M \in G_i^1$, then the first symbol in the word for M is χ_i. Similarly, $M \in G_{ij}^2$ implies that the second symbol in the word for M is χ_j.

This procedure can be illustrated by a tree with $\mathscr{S}$ at the trunk and the elements of $\mathscr{S}$ as peripheral branches. Fig. 11.1 provides one example for $q = 3$. The

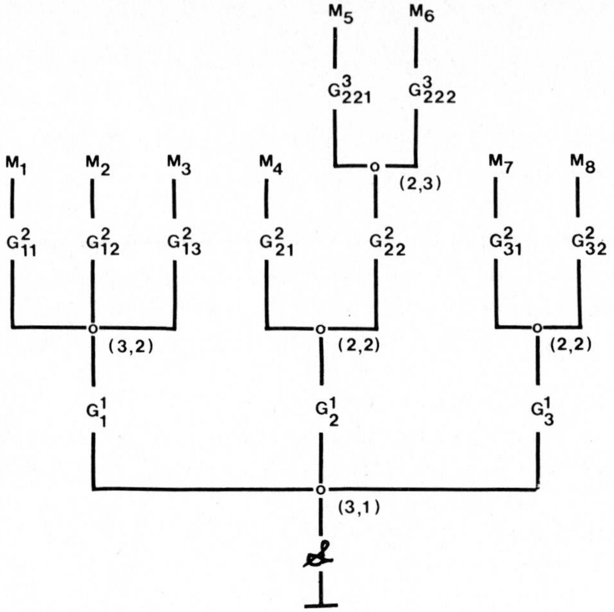

Figure 11.1

tree consists of branching points and branches to which we will assign special numbers. Each branching point has a degree and rank; the degree equals the number of branches attached to the point and the rank is the number of branches between the branching point and the base. Each branch has a probability and a rank, where the probability equals the sum of the probabilities of those messages connected to that branch, and the rank is the number of branching points between this branch and the base. For example, $P(G^2_{22}) = P(M_5) + P(M_6)$, and $r(G^2_{22}) = 2$. The rank of the peripheral branch terminating in M_i tells us how many symbols are used to identify that message. Denoting that rank ℓ_i and the corresponding probability P_i, the number of symbols which is expected to occur in communicating a message using this lexicon tree is

$$E\{\ell\} = \sum_{i=1}^{m} P_i \ell_i .$$

We can place a lower bound on this expected word length using Shannon's measure.

Theorem 11.1. For any q-symbol lexicon,

$$E\{\ell\} \geqslant -\sum_{i=1}^{m} P_i \log P_i \,/\, \log q = H(P_\eta) \,/\, \log q.$$

Proof. Define g_i to be the product of the reciprocals of the degrees of branch points between M_i and the base. Suppose the branches had thickness, beginning with a unit thick trunk and uniformly thinning out at each branching point. The branches have a width which is a fraction, the reciprocal of the degree, of that of the branch below. The thickness of the peripheral branch is g_i (see fig. 11.2). Clearly $g_i > 0$ and since width is conserved,

$$\sum_{i=1}^{m} g_i = 1.$$

By Gibb's lemma (see Chapter 9):

$$-\sum_{i=1}^{m} P_i \log g_i \geqslant -\sum_{i=1}^{m} P_i \log P_i.$$

Since the degree of each branching point is less than or equal to q, it must be true that

$$g_i \geqslant \frac{1}{q}^{\ell_i} = q^{-\ell_i}.$$

The function $-\log$ is monotonic decreasing, so

$$-\log g_i \leqslant -\log q^{-\ell_i} = \ell_i \log q.$$

Multiplying by P_i and summing over i gives

$$-\sum_{i=1}^{m} P_i \log g_i \leqslant \log q \sum_{i=1}^{m} P_i \ell_i.$$

Combining this with the result from Gibb's lemma gives the inequality desired. ■

Theorem 11.1 states that when q symbols are used, the expected number of symbols in a message must exceed Shannon's measure when logarithms are base q. Shannon's measure equals the rate of transmission of information when words are coded noiselessly:

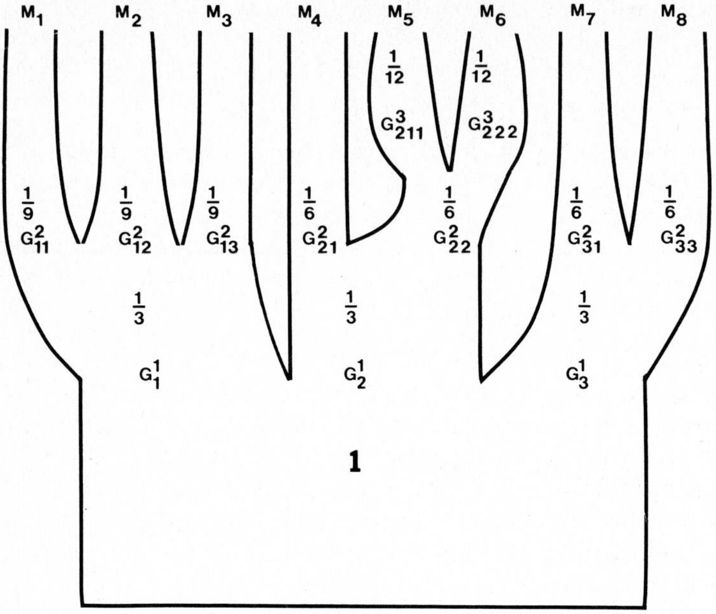

Figure 11.2

$$
\begin{aligned}
H(P_\eta) &= H(P_{s\eta}) - H(P_{s\,|\,\eta}) \\
&= H(P_{s\,|\,\eta}) - H(P_s) + T(s\,|\,\eta) \\
&= H(P_{\eta\,|\,s}) + T(s\,|\,\eta) \\
&= T(s\,|\,\eta).
\end{aligned}
$$

This lower bound can be reached only when $g_i = P_i$, due to Gibb's lemma, and it is not clear that a communication system with only q symbols can be constructed to accomplish this.

A related question is: "Can we construct a tree with no more than q branches at each branch point such that the ranks of the peripheral branches are $\ell_1, \ell_2, \ldots, \ell_m$?" The following gives a necessary and sufficient condition for the feasibility of these ranks.

Theorem 11.2. A set of ranks $\ell_1, \ell_2, \ldots, \ell_m$ is feasible for a given q if and only if

$$\sum_{i=1}^{m} q^{-\ell_i} \leqslant 1.$$

Proof. Assuming such a tree exists it must be that

$$g_i \geqslant q^{-\ell_i}$$

and

$$\sum_{i=1}^{m} g_i = 1,$$

which clearly implies the stated inequality. Assume the inequality and construct a tree by grouping messages in $\mathcal{S}$ according to their ranks and letting m_k equal the number of messages with rank k. Clearly, $\Sigma_k\, m_k = m$. Connect m_1 messages directly to the first branching point; to ensure that this can be done we must have $0 \leqslant m_1 \leqslant q$. Only $q - m_1$ branches remain available out of the first branching point, each of which is connected to a new branching point. There are $(q - m_1) \cdot q$ new branches made available at this higher level, and if m_2 are to be peripheral branches then

$$0 \leqslant m_2 \leqslant (q - m_1)q.$$

Repeating this process out to $L = \max[\ell_1, ..., \ell_m]$, the inequality

$$0 \leqslant m_L \leqslant q^L - m_1\, q^{L-1} - m_2\, q^{L-2} - ... - m_{L-1}q$$

is needed to guarantee that a tree can be constructed. This condition may be re-expressed as

$$0 \leqslant q^L - \sum_{k=1}^{L} m_k\, q^{L-k} = q^L \left(1 - \sum_{k=1}^{L} m_k\, q^{-k}\right) .$$

We can conclude that $\ell \leqslant L$ implies

$$\sum_{k=1}^{\ell} m_k\, q^{-k} \leqslant \sum_{k=1}^{L} m_k\, q^{-k} \leqslant 1.$$

From the definition of m_k we can see that

$$m_k\, q^{-k} = \sum_{i \in \{i \mid \ell_i = k\}} q^{-\ell_i},$$

and this implies that

$$\sum_{k=1}^{\ell} m_k q^{-k} = \sum_{i=1}^{m} q^{-\ell_i} \leqslant 1,$$

which was to be shown. ■

We would like to choose an optimally short lexicon by setting word lengths $\ell_1, \ell_2, \ldots, \ell_m$ to minimize the expected length of the word communicated subject to the feasibility of the lexicon with only q available symbols. That is, we want to

$$\text{minimize } \sum_{i=1}^{m} P_i \ell_i$$

$$\text{subject to } \sum_{i=1}^{m} q^{-\ell_i} \leqslant 1$$

$$\text{and } \ell_i \in \{1, 2, 3, \ldots\}, \quad \text{for all } i = 1, \ldots, m.$$

The solution of this integer program depends in a very important way on the probabilities and the number of symbols. From theorem 11.1 we have a lower bound on the solution, but how close can we get to this limit?

Theorem 11.3. The optimal lexicon with q symbols will have an expected word length in the interval

$$[H(P_\eta) / \log q, H(P_\eta) / \log q + 1].$$

Proof. Let the word length of message i be the smallest integer greater than or equal to

$$-\log P_i / \log q.$$

Hence,

$$\ell_i \geqslant -\log_q P_i.$$

As a direct consequence of this choice we have

$$q^{\ell_i} \geqslant q^{-\log_q P_i} = 1 / P_i.$$

Cross multiplying and summing across i gives:

$$\sum_{i=1}^{m} P_i = 1 \geqslant \sum_{i=1}^{m} q^{-\ell_i},$$

which by theorem 11.2 implies that this choice of word length is feasible. By definition of ℓ_i the next smallest integer is less than $-\log P_i/\log q$,

$$\ell_i - 1 < -\log P_i / \log q.$$

Multiply this by P_i and sum with respect to i to get

$$\mathrm{E}\{\ell\} - 1 \leqslant -\sum_i P_i \log P_i / \log q = H(P_\eta)/\log q.$$

From this we have the desired upper bound. ■

The cost of sending a message depends on the language chosen and in this model that requires the determination of the number of symbols which can be distinguished and the lexicon which codes the messages into words using the recognized symbols. The expected word length is proportional to the rate of transmission, as measured by Shannon, and inversely proportional to the logarithm of the number of symbols. The cost of the communication system will generally depend on the expected word length and the number of symbols to be recognized:

$$C(\mathrm{E}\{\ell\}, q).$$

For example, suppose that the cost of transmitting each symbol rises as a power of the number of symbols which must be distinguished

$$C = \mathrm{E}\{\ell\}\, q^{\nu}.$$

The choice of symbols which minimize cost can be approximated by assuming that the amount of information transmitted is so large that the expected word length equals its minimum. The cost,

$$C = \frac{H(P_\eta)}{\log q}\, q^{\nu},$$

is minimized when

$$q = 10^{1/\nu}.$$

When cost rises with the square root of the number of symbols, 100 symbols should be used.

Oniki (1974) used Shannon's measure of information to approximate the cost of communicating knowledge of production technologies. How costly is it to send a message which describes in a finite number of symbols a production function $y = f(x)$, where y is the output available, if x units of input are used? If the technology is easily represented by parameters or technical drawings, communication costs would be modest, but when the technology is more complicated, the description becomes more costly.

Suppose that the scalar input space is approximated by the set of points $\{x_1, ..., x_m\}$, where $x_i < x_{i+1}$. Furthermore, assume that the rate of change of output with respect to input takes on values in a set of marginal productivities $\{0, 1/n, 2/n, ..., (n-1)/n, 1\}$, so that outputs are approximated in the set $\{y_1, y_2, ..., y_{nm+1}\}$, where $y_i < y_{i+1}$, a typical y_i created by computing $x_k + (j/n)(x_k - x_{k-1})$ for some $j = 1, ..., n$, $k = 1, ..., m$. For any production function f an approximate production function g is defined as a mapping of $\{x_1, ..., x_m\}$ into $\{y_1, ..., y_{nm+1}\}$ by

$$g(x_i) = y_{k_i},$$

for each $i = 1, ..., m$, such that

$$y_{k_i} \geqslant f(x_i) > y_{k_i - 1}.$$

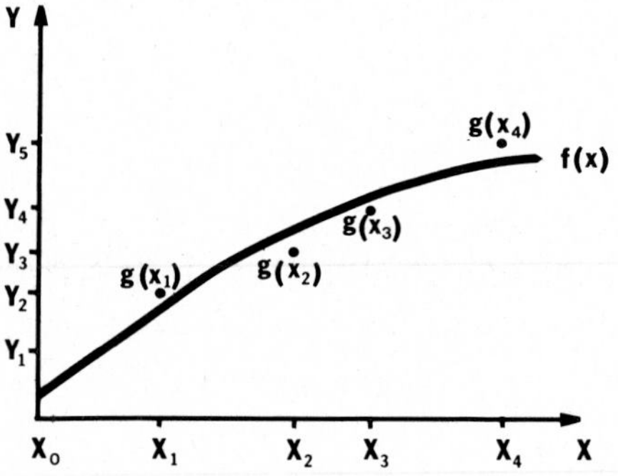

Figure 11.3

See fig. 11.3 for an example. g is a finite collection of points in $\{x_1, \ldots, x_m\} \times \{y_1, \ldots, y_{nm+1}\}$. Define a set

$$G = \{g \mid g \text{ approximates a function } f \text{ which is continuous, non-decreasing, concave, } 0 \leqslant f(x_0) \leqslant y_1 \text{ and } 0 \leqslant f'(x_0) \leqslant 1\}.$$

How costly would it be for one member of the organization to communicate a production function to another member? From our previous analysis we know that the expected message length depends on the prior probabilities of the functions in G. However, a worst-case analysis will be used in which each approximating function is equally likely. The expected number of symbols used is then proportional to

$$\log |G|,$$

where $|G|$ is the cardinality of G, the number of distinct functions g in the class G.

As Oniki (1974) pointed out, the cardinality of the set G cannot be calculated directly. However, by ingenious selection of sub- and supersets of G, Oniki was able to find upper and lower bounds on $|G|$. To this end, define the sets G_* and G^* by

$$G_* = \left\{ g: \{x_1, \ldots, x_m\} \to \{y_1, \ldots, y_{nm+1}\} \mid g(x_{i+1}) \geqslant g(x_i) \text{ and } \frac{g(x_i) - g(x_{i-1})}{x_i - x_{i-1}} \geqslant \frac{g(x_{i+1}) - g(x_i)}{x_{i+1} - x_i} \right\},$$

$$G^* = \left\{ g: \{x_1, \ldots, x_m\} \to \{y_1, \ldots, y_{nm+1}\} \mid g(x_{i+1}) \geqslant g(x_i) \text{ and } \frac{g(x_i) - g(x_{i-1})}{x_i - x_{i-1}} \geqslant \frac{g(x_{i+1}) - g(x_i)}{x_{i+1} - x_i} + \frac{1}{m} \right\}.$$

If an element of G_* is extended outside of $\{x_1, \ldots, x_m\}$ by connecting the points by line segments, the resulting function is a piecewise linear, non-decreasing, concave function. If an element of G^* is extended similarly, it will result in a piecewise linear function whose slope is decreasing or at most increasing by $1/m$.

It is easily shown that

$$G_* \subseteq G \subseteq G^*.$$

This implies that $|G_*| \leqslant |G| \leqslant |G^*|$. These bounds are of interest because they can be expressed as explicit functions of m and n.

Theorem 11.4. (Oniki).

$$|G_*| = \frac{(m+n)!}{m!n!}, \qquad |G^*| = \frac{(2m+n-1)!}{m!(m+n-1)!}.$$

Proof. For a given $g \in G_*$ define a function

$$h(x_i) = \frac{g(x_i) - g(x_{i-1})}{x_i - x_{i-1}} - \frac{i-1}{m}.$$

Since the function g has a non-increasing difference quotient and $(i-1)/n$ is increasing, the function h is a decreasing function from $\{x_1, ..., x_m\}$ into:

$$Z \equiv \left\{\frac{-(m-1)}{n}, \frac{-(m-z)}{n}, ..., \frac{-1}{n}, 0, \frac{1}{n}, ..., \frac{n}{n}\right\}.$$

On the other hand, if h is a decreasing function form $\{x_1, ..., x_m\}$ into Z, then the function g defined by

$$g(x_i) = y_1 + \sum_{j=1}^{i} \left(h(x_j) + \frac{j-1}{n}\right) (x_j - x_{j-1})$$

is an element of G_*. This follows since

$$(g(x_i) - g(x_{i-1}))/(x_i - x_{i-1}) = h(x_j) + \frac{j-1}{n},$$

which is at worst a non-increasing function of j. Therefore $|G_*|$ equals the number of strictly decreasing functions h which map $\{x_1, ..., x_m\}$ into Z. How can the functions h be counted? To create an h, draw m numbers from Z without replacement, order them in a decreasing sequence, and assign them to $h(x_i)$, $i = 1, ..., m$. There are $(m+n)!/(m!n!)$ ways to draw the numbers without replacement.

To get $|G^*|$ define a function

$$h(x_i) = (g(x_i) - g(x_{i-1}))/(x_i - x_{i-1}) - 2((i-1)/n).$$

This is a decreasing function from $\{x_1, ..., x_m\}$ into

$$W = \left\{ \frac{-2(m-1)}{n}, \frac{-2(m-2)}{n}, \ldots, \frac{-1}{n}, 0, \frac{1}{n}, \ldots, \frac{n}{n} \right\}$$

by the properties of G^* and $2(i - 1)/n$. To find h by drawing from W without replacement, there are

$$\frac{(2(m-1)+n+1)!}{m!\,(m+n-1)!}$$

possibilities which is the cardinality of $|G^*|$. ∎

Clearly, the cost of communication is generally an increasing function of the number of points in the approximation. The change in log $|G_*|$ when m is increased by one is

$$\Delta_m \log |G_*| = \log \left(1 + \frac{n}{m+1}\right),$$

which is positive for all m and n. If the number of possible values of the slope, n, equals the number of points in the x grid, m, then the change in the cost of communication for adding one to m is

$$\Delta_{m=n} \log |G_*| = (\log 4) \cdot \frac{m^2 + \frac{3}{2}m + \frac{1}{2}}{m^2 + 2m + 1}.$$

For large $m = n$ the cost is bounded below by a function which is approximately linear with a slope log 4.

The cost of communication does not accelerate rapidly, however. It is bounded above by log $|G^*|$ and the change in log $|G^*|$ when m is increased by one is

$$\Delta_m \log |G^*| = \log \left[\frac{(2m+n+1)(2m+n)}{(m+1)(m+n)} \right],$$

which achieves its minimum when $m = 1$ and approaches a limit of log 4 monotonically from below. Similarly, if we restrict m to be equal to n, then the increase in log $|G^*|$ when m is increased by one is

$$\Delta_{m=n} \log |G^*| = \log \left[\frac{(3m+2)(3m+1)(3m)}{(m+1)(2m+1)(2m)} \right].$$

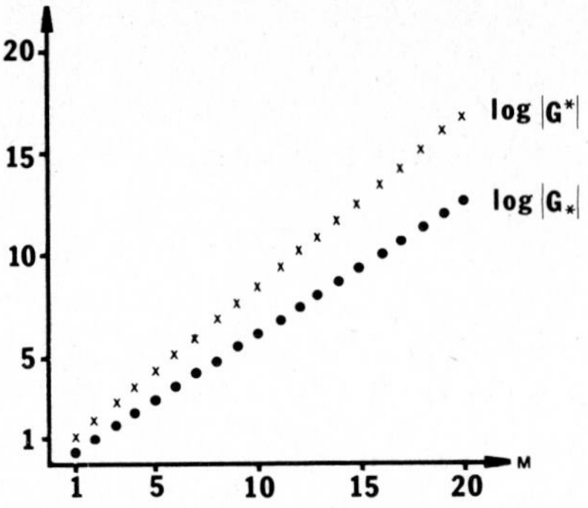

Figure 11.4

This monotonically increases from log 5 to log (27/4). For large $m = n$, the cost is bounded above by a function which is approximately linear with a slope log 6.75. Fig. 11.4 graphs log $|G_*|$ and log $|G^*|$ for $m = n$ running from 1 to 20.

The upper and lower bounds on the worst-case Shannon measure of communicating an approximating function, log $|G^*|$ and log $|G_*|$, have been used by Oniki to compare the costs of communication in centralized organizations and in decentralized organizations. The organizational problem is modelled as follows. There are k divisions which produce revenue from the use of organizational capital according to revenue functions

$$y^i = f_i(x^i), \qquad i = 1, 2, ..., k,$$

where y^i is revenue of the ith division and x^i is organizational capital used in the production process of division i. The organization has a fixed amount of capital, $\bar{x}$, to allocate between the divisions. The organization must solve the problem:

$$\text{maximize} \quad \sum_{i=1}^{k} f_i(x^i)$$

$$\text{subject to} \quad \sum_{i=1}^{k} x^i \leqslant \bar{x},$$

$$x^i \geqslant 0, \qquad i = 1, 2, ..., k.$$

A centralized organization would ask each division to communicate an approximation of its revenue function to the top management. The management would then solve the approximated problem and order divisions to use only prescribed amounts of organizational capital. If the management has a uniform prior probability over the set of possible revenue functions, the expected cost of the communication of revenue functions is

$$k \log |G|.$$

If the allocations to divisions can take on any one of m values with equal likelihood, the cost of communicating the capital allocation to all divisions is

$$k \cdot \log m.$$

Oniki modelled the decentralized organization by assuming that transfer prices for the organization's capital would be sought using an iterative technique. An extensive discussion of such processes will be found in Chapter 12. At each stage of the process the management sends a price quote to each division (at total cost of $k \cdot \log n$) and receives a pair of bids for organizational capital in return (at total cost $2k \cdot \log m$). The pair of bids are the point in the grid $\{x_1, ..., x_m\}$ which gives the interval in which the profit maximizing choice of x is to be found. In order to find the price which balances supply and demand, a q-polychotomic search of prices would be used. The largest number of steps needed is then $\log_q n$. The total cost of this procedure would therefore be

$$\log_q n \cdot (k \log n + 2k \log m).$$

If $m = n$ and $q = 2$ (bisectioning search for prices equilibrium), then the total cost of decentralized transfer pricing procedure is

$$3k \cdot (\log m)^2 / \log 2.$$

Table 11.1

m	$\log \lvert G_* \rvert + \log m$	$\log \lvert G^* \rvert + \log m$	$3(\log m)^2/\log 2$
4	2.44	3.12	3.61
10	7	8.4	10
100	62	85	40
1000	605	832.5	89.5
10000	6024.5	8297	159.5

Centralized organization is less costly in terms of communication if

$$\log |G| + \log m \leqslant 3 \quad (\log m)^2 / \log 2.$$

The upper and lower bound on log $|G|$ can be used to have a rough idea of when this is true (see table 11.1). This table indicates that when the organization is interested only in crude approximations of the production technology (m is small) it is less costly to use a centralized communication system. However, if accurate solution is desirable, the decentralization by transfer prices may be less costly.

CHAPTER 12

BUDGET PLANNING: TRANSFER PRICES OR QUOTAS

Organizations periodically plan their activities for the coming year by constructing budgets that outline the use of capital, labor, and other organizational resources. The process of constructing the budget requires drawing together from a wide range of sources information on technological capabilities, marketing opportunities, and resource availability. The sales department has obvious advantages in keeping track of market developments but cannot compete with the engineering staff in developing new production processes. The coordination of the activities of the many subunits of the organization is achieved through the budget planning process. The planning process, which is the focus of this chapter, is modelled as an iterative exchange of information between the subunits, possessors of detailed knowledge of potential activities, and an accounting office which is responsible for producing the budgetary allocation of organizational resources.

The information dispersion in the organization is modelled as follows. Each division i performs activities, α_i, which is a general production plan specifying outputs of goods and inputs of factors. The activities of this division lead to rewards for the organization according to the functional relationship

$$r_i = \rho_i(\alpha_i).$$

The activities of the division may be executed only when the division knows that they are feasible in their environment and technological situation. This will be symbolized by membership in a set, A_i, of feasible activities; the activity α_i is feasible if and only if

$$\alpha_i \in A_i.$$

The activity of the division requires or produces resources which are available only within the organization. If we think of these resources as organizational capital, it will be convenient to denote the resource so used as

$$\kappa_i(\alpha_i).$$

When the organization is considering a short-term plan, this organization capital is fixed and we will denote the total available capital by κ. The joint activities of the divisions must satisfy the organizational capital restriction,

$$\sum_i \kappa_i(\alpha_i) \leqslant \kappa.$$

An omniscient accounting office would need to determine divisional activities to maximize total rewards:

$$\sum_i \rho_i(\alpha_i)$$

subject to

$$\sum_i \kappa_i(\alpha_i) \leqslant \kappa$$

and

$$\alpha_i \in A_i, \quad \text{for all } i.$$

The dispersion of information prevents such a centralized choice. The set A_i and functions ρ_i and κ_i may only be implicitly known, even by the division, and the cost of introspection to fill in details, coding the knowledge and then transmitting it en masse might be too large to even contemplate. Instead, the accounting office would like to sequentially question each division only about activities which are in the realm of possible choices and build up an approximation of the relevant regions of the sets and functions. For example, when r_i is the revenue of a division which monopolizes its market, standard economic theory implies that only that part of the demand curve in the elastic region is relevant to the accounting office. The profit maximizing choice cannot occur where demand is inelastic.

We will begin our studies of budget planning processes by looking at a price guided mechanism. In this process transfer prices, P, are established for the organizational capital. These transfer prices (sometimes called shadow prices) reflect the value of the resources to the organization, not the fair market value or replacement costs. Such accounting prices are used solely to guide the budget process toward the most profitable use of organizational capital and will be changed throughout the iterative process as the accounting office builds successively better approximations of the decision elements.

The general stage of the process is a positive integer t. At stage t the accounting office announces that organization capital will be evaluated at transfer prices P^t. Each division chooses an activity to maximize its reward net of the transfer value of organizational capital

$$\rho_i(\alpha_i) - P^t \kappa_i(\alpha_i),$$

subject to

$$\alpha_i \in A_i$$

Denote the optimal activity at stage t by α_i^t; the optimal demand for organizational capital is designated $\kappa_i^t = \kappa_i(\alpha_i^t)$ and the optimal (gross) reward is $r_i^t = \rho_i(\alpha_i^t)$. The division reports this triple $(\alpha_i^t, \kappa_i^t, r_i^t)$ to the accounting office.

The accounting office constructs an approximation to the organization problem by taking convex combinations. If the accounting office knows that $\alpha_i^1, \alpha_i^2, ..., \alpha_i^t$ are feasible for division i, then the convex hull of these,

$$A_i^t = \left\{ \alpha_i \mid \alpha_i = \sum_{\tau=1}^{t} \mu_i^\tau \alpha_i^\tau, \text{ for some } \mu_i^1, ..., \mu_i^t \text{ such that } \mu_i^\tau \geqslant 0 \text{ and } \sum_{\tau=1}^{t} \mu_i^\tau = 1 \right\},$$

provides an approximation to the unknown feasible set A_i. When A_i is convex, this approximation is entirely contained within the feasible set, as in fig. 12.1, so any point which the accounting office considers will be feasible for the division.

The functions $\rho_i(\cdot)$ and $\kappa_i(\cdot)$ may also be approximated by the use of the convex combination of known points, as in fig. 12.2.

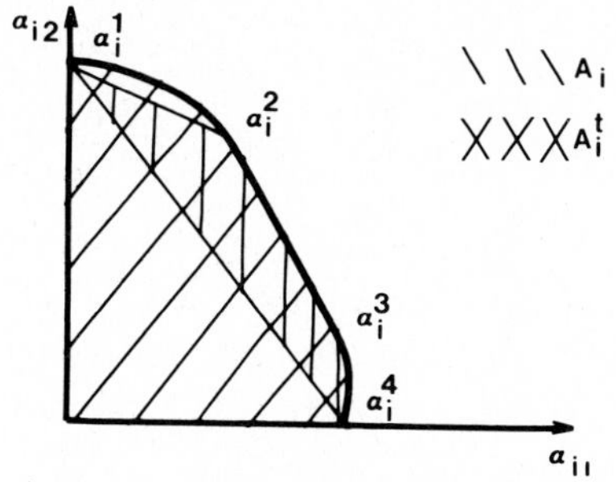

Figure 12.1

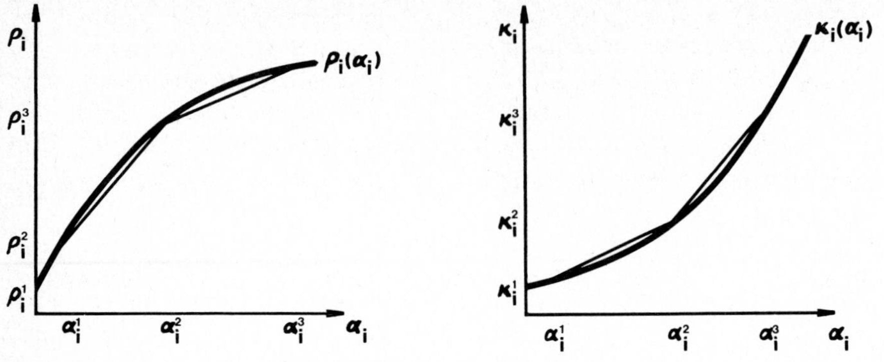

Figure 12.2

When ρ_i is concave, the function

$$\rho_i^t(\alpha_i) = \sum_{\tau=1}^{t} \mu_i^\tau \rho_i^\tau, \quad \text{where } \alpha_i = \sum_{\tau=1}^{t} \mu_i^\tau \alpha_i^\tau,$$

provides an understated approximation of the rewards produced by division i. Similarly the capital-use equation

$$\kappa_i^t(\alpha_i) = \sum_{\tau=1}^{t} \mu_i^\tau \kappa_i^\tau, \quad \text{where } \alpha_i = \sum_{\tau=1}^{t} \mu_i^\tau \alpha_i^\tau,$$

provides an exaggerated approximation of the convex demand for organizational capital.

The accounting office uses these approximations to choose a tentative budget. The formal statement of the problem is to choose weighting coefficients μ_i^1, ..., μ_i^t to maximize

$$\sum_i \left(\sum_{\tau=1}^{t} \mu_i^\tau \rho_i^\tau \right)$$

subject to

$$\sum_i \left(\sum_{\tau=1}^{t} \mu_i^\tau \kappa_i^\tau \right) \leqslant \kappa$$

and

$$\mu_i^\tau \geqslant 0, \qquad \sum_{\tau=1}^{t} \mu_i^\tau = 1, \quad \text{for all } i, \tau.$$

The organizational capital constraint has a Lagrange multiplier which at the optimum measures the marginal value of the capital to the organization and will be denoted P^{t+1}. If the anticipated total profit has not increased sufficiently from stage $t-1$, then the budget planning process ceases. Otherwise the transfer price P^{t+1} is announced to the divisions and a new stage $t+1$ is entered. When the process stops, the capital is allocated to the divisions according to the most recent choice of the accounting office.

Example. Consider a two-division firm where each division uses organizational capital to produce revenue according to the functions

$$\rho_1(\alpha_1) = \alpha_1 - \tfrac{1}{2}(\alpha_1)^2$$

and

$$\rho_2(\alpha_2) = 1 + 2\alpha_2 - \tfrac{1}{2}(\alpha_2)^2 .$$

For simplicity, assume that the accounting office knows that the capital demand for each division equals

$$\kappa_i(\alpha_i) = \alpha_i,$$

and that the feasible set A_i is just the non-negative reals. If there are two units of organizational capital available to budget between the divisions, the omniscient planner would choose

$$\alpha_1 = \tfrac{1}{2}, \qquad \alpha_2 = \tfrac{3}{2}.$$

If the accounting office begins the process by making capital free, $P^1 = 0$, the divisions will respond by reporting the net reward maximizing choices $\alpha_1^1 = 1$ and $\alpha_2^1 = 2$, and rewards $\rho_1^1 = 0.5$ and $\rho_2^1 = 3$. The accounting office chooses μ_1^1, μ_2^1 to solve the problem

$$\begin{array}{ll}
\text{maximize} & \mu_1^1\, 0.5 + \mu_2^1\, 3. \\
\text{subject to} & \mu_1^1\, 1.0 + \mu_2^1\, 2.0 \leqslant 2, \\
 & \mu_1^1 \qquad\qquad\quad\;\; \leqslant 1, \\
 & \qquad\quad\;\; \mu_2^1 \qquad \leqslant 1, \\
 & \mu_1^1 \geqslant 0,\; \mu_2^1 \geqslant 0.
\end{array}$$

The Lagrange multiplier of the capital constraint is $P^2 = 1.5$ and anticipated profit equals 3.

At stage 2 the net reward maximizing choices with transfer price $P^2 = 1.5$ are $\alpha_1^2 = 0$ and $\alpha_2^2 = 0.5$ and reported rewards are $\rho_1^2 = 0$ and $\rho_2^2 = 1.875$. The accounting office chooses weights to

$$\begin{aligned}
\text{maximize} \quad & \mu_1^1\, 0.5 + \mu_1^2\, 0.0 + \mu_2^1\, 3 + \mu_2^2\, 1.875 \\
\text{subject to} \quad & \mu_1^1\, 1.0 + \mu_1^2\, 0.0 + \mu_2^1\, 2 + \mu_2^2\, 0.5 \leqslant 2, \\
& \mu_1^1 + \mu_1^2 \leqslant 1, \\
& \mu_2^1 + \mu_2^2 \leqslant 1, \\
& \mu_1^1 \geqslant 0,\ \mu_1^2 \geqslant 0,\ \mu_2^1 \geqslant 0,\ \mu_2^2 \geqslant 0.
\end{aligned}$$

The multiplier of the capital constraint equals $P^3 = 0.75$, and the anticipated profit is again 3. Table 12.1 provides summary data for additional stages of the

Table 12.1

t	P^t	α_1^t	α_2^t	ρ_1^t	ρ_2^t	*Anticipated profit*
1	0.0	1.0	2.0	0.5	3.0	3.00
2	1.5	0.0	0.5	0.0	1.875	3.00
3	0.75	0.25	1.25	0.219	2.719	3.125
4	0.375	0.625	1.625	0.429	2.929	3.187
5	0.688	0.312	1.312	0.263	2.763	3.23

budget planning process. Within three iterations the accounting office has achieved 96% of the sales that are possible with the given organizational capital. If the process is stopped after three stages, then 0.25 units of capital are budgeted to division 1 and 1.75 units to division 2 (See fig. 12.3).

The transfer price guided budget process does not mirror exactly the traditional "tatonnement" process of price adjustment in which prices change in proportion to excess demand. The tatonnement process uses only the most recent information to determine the price adjustment, while the budget process cumulates information about the organization's decision problem. At any particular stage the tatonnement process makes no guarantee that the allocation is feasible, since the most recent price announced might produce excess demand. On the other hand, the transfer price guided budget process preserves feasibility in a convex environment since the accounting office can always ask the division to execute the activity which is the optimal convex combination of accumulated feasible activities. This last point brings into relief another distinction: the plan-

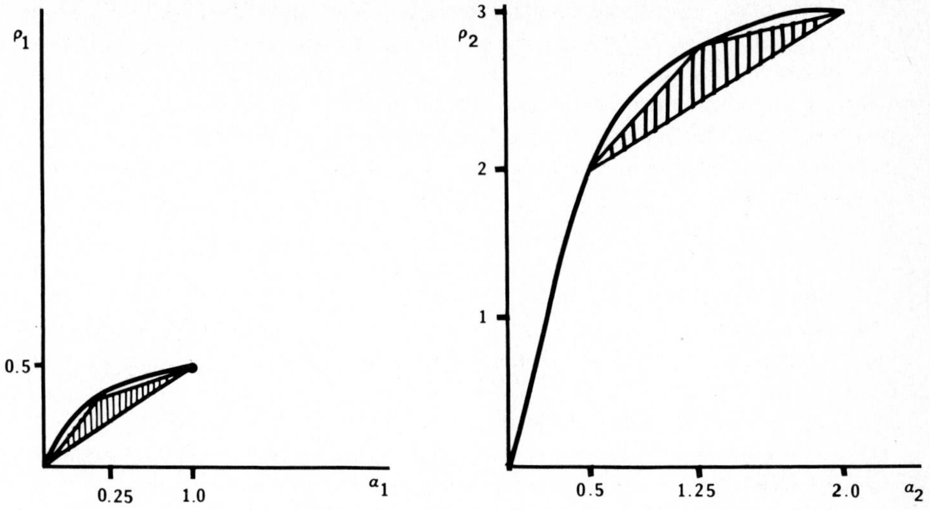

Figure 12.3

ning process is not one which decentralizes the power completely. The divisions do not have complete freedom to choose the amount of organizational capital and activities to pursue at the given transfer price. The transfer price has been used to guide the organization to a suitable decision matrix and may be used to simplify the evaluation of divisional performance, but the allocation of organizational capital and the performance of activities is dictated from the accounting office. A final point to be made about the process is that with suitable convex curvature and continuity of sets and functions, Dantzig and Wolfe (1960) (in the linear programming problem) and Malinvaud (1967) (in the non-linear programming problem) have shown that such planning processes will converge to the global optimum of the organization's resource allocation problem.

While many accounting systems do in fact use transfer prices to evaluate the performance of those divisions whose outputs are not sold directly on a market, this does not mean that such transfer prices are the instruments for directing the budgeting process. Weitzman (1970) argued that a more representative process would be one that is guided by targets or quotas in physical goods and services, and he constructed a model which allows the accounting office to use commands about resource use as the tool for guilding resource allocation.

Consider the same organizational resource allocation as before but with a quota guided budget process. At stage t of the budget process the accounting office provided each division with a two-part quota; the first part dictates the activity quota q_i^t and the second part specifies the organizational capital allocated to the division, Q_i^t. Division i must choose its activity to maximize its reward without exceeding the activity quota or underusing the organizational capital allocation. This prevents the division from following its rewards function to its uncoordinated maximum. Notice that the division is asked not to exceed output targets or underutilize input quotas. If the quota is feasible from the division perspective, then it should be executed. The division's must choose activity α_i to

$$\begin{array}{ll} \text{maximize} & \rho_i(\alpha_i) \\ \text{subject to} & \alpha_i \in A_i, \\ & \alpha_i \leqslant q_i^t, \ \text{ and } \ \kappa_i(\alpha_i) \geqslant Q_i^t. \end{array}$$

See figs. 12.4 and 12.5 for an illustration. In fig. 12.4 the feasible set A_i consists of the points within the region *OBC*. Given the quota, the division cannot choose the optimal point in A_i at the tangency point of the isoreward curve $\overline{\rho}_i$ and the production possibility frontier *BC*. The division is restricted to choose from the region *ODFGE*, which satisfies the first two constraints above. The division's optimal activity, α_i^t, in this region is the point *G* where the isoreward curve ρ_i^t is tangent to the choice set. Corresponding to this activity, point *I* of fig. 12.5 specifies the capital needed and since this lies to the northwest of point (q_i^t, Q_i^t), the final constraint is also satisfied.

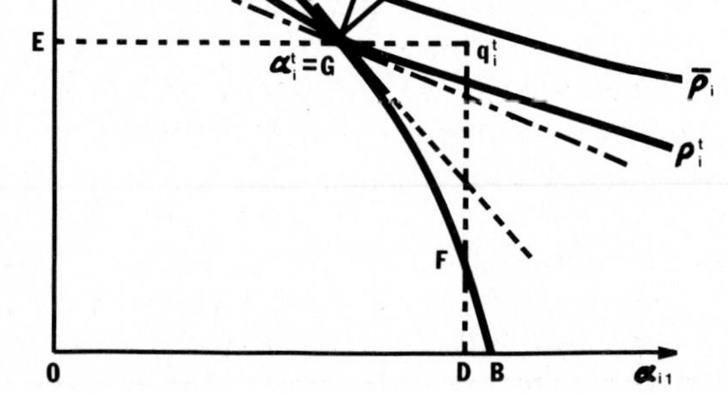

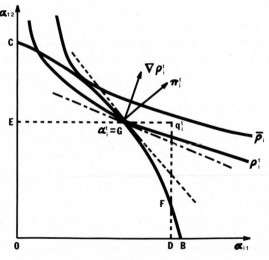

Figure 12.4

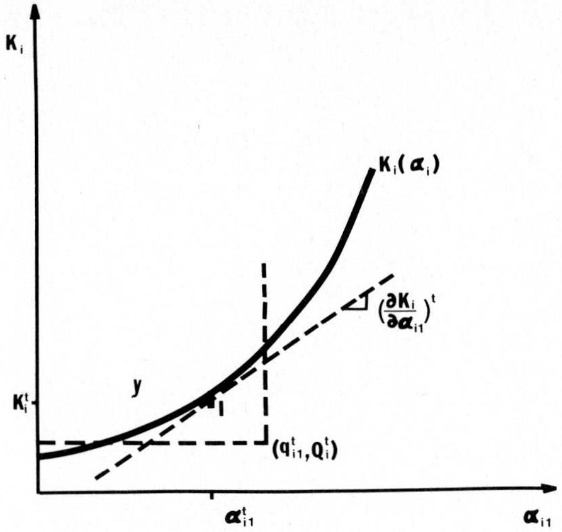

Figure 12.5

The division may be unable to achieve the output targets assigned to them, as in fig. 12.4 where q_i^t lies outside *OBC*. The solution of the division problem presents a second-best attempt at reaching the quota. The budget process requires that the division not only communicate this alternative activity, its corresponding reward, and capital requirement, but also some sense of the shape of the feasible sets and reward functions in the vicinity of the second best. For the set A_i the normal at the second best indicates the rate at which one component of the activity can be exchanged for another component. If we denote this normal vector π_i^t as in fig. 12.4, a convex set A_i would be bounded above by a hyperplane:

$$A_i \subseteq \{\alpha_i \mid \pi_i^t \alpha_i \leqslant \pi_i^t \alpha_i^t\}.$$

The gradient of the reward function at the second-best activity, $\nabla \rho_i^t = (\partial \rho_i / \partial \alpha_{ij})$, allows us to approximate the reward function (from above if it is concave) by the linear function

$$\rho_i(\alpha_i) \cong \rho_i^t + \nabla \rho_i^t (\alpha_i - \alpha_i^t).$$

The slope of the capital use equation at the second-best point provides a linear (lower bound if convex) approximation:

$$\kappa_i(\alpha_i) \cong \kappa_i^t + \left(\frac{\partial \kappa_i}{\partial \alpha_i}\right)^t (\alpha_i - \alpha_i^t).$$

The accounting office uses these linear approximations to improve the accuracy of its estimate of divisional productivity. At stage t the accounting office can use the envelope of accumulated information to construct the following approximations:

$$\rho_i^t(\alpha_i) = \min\,[\rho_i^1 + \nabla\rho_i^1(\alpha_i - \alpha_i^1), ..., \rho_i^t + \nabla\rho_i^t(\alpha_i - \alpha_i^t)],$$

$$A_i^t = \{\alpha_i \mid \pi_i^\tau \alpha_i \leqslant \pi_i^\tau \alpha_i^\tau, \tau = 1, 2, ..., t\},$$

$$\kappa_i^t(\alpha_i) = \max\left[\kappa_i^t + \left(\frac{\partial \kappa_i}{\partial \alpha_i}\right)^1 (\alpha_i - \alpha_i^1), ..., \kappa_i^t + \left(\frac{\partial \kappa_i}{\partial \alpha_i}\right)^t (\alpha_i - \alpha_i^t)\right].$$

The accounting office constructs new quotas from these approximations by solving the problem of choosing $q_1, ..., q_n$ to maximize

$$\sum_i \rho_i^t(q_i)$$

subject to

$$\sum_i \kappa_i^t(q_i) \leqslant \kappa,$$

$$q_i \in A_i^t, \quad \text{for all } i.$$

Denoting the solution to this q_i^{t+1} and defining Q_i^{t+1} to be $\kappa_i^t(q_i^{t+1})$, the target quotas are established for the next stage. If total rewards have not decreased sufficiently from the previous stage then the budget planning process is terminated and the most recent feasible activities are executed.

Example. The organizational problem of the previous illustration will be solved using a quota guided system. At stage 1 suppose that the accounting office proposes a quota $q_1^1 = 1, q_2^1 = 1$. The capital demands are not restricted since the accounting office knows that $\rho_i(\alpha_i) = \alpha_i$. The first division's second-best solution is $\alpha_1^1 = 1$ and will earn a reward $\rho_1^1 = 0.5$. The gradient of the reward is $\nabla\rho_1^1 = 0$, so the approximating equation is simply

$$\rho_1(\alpha_1) \cong 0.5.$$

The second division finds that $\alpha_2^1 = 1$ is optimal given the quota and it will earn a reward $\rho_2^1 = 2.5$ with gradient $\nabla\rho_2^1 = 1.0$; the approximating function equals

$$\rho_2(\alpha_2) \cong 2.5 + 1.0(\alpha_2 - 1) = 1.5 + \alpha_2 .$$

The solution lies in the interior of the feasible set (non-negative reals) so the normal is zero. The accounting office must solve the following linear program.

At *stage 1*, choose non-negative ρ_1, ρ_2, q_1, q_2 to

$$\begin{array}{ll} \text{maximize} & \rho_1 + \rho_2 \\ \text{subject to} & q_1 + q_2 \leqslant 2, \\ & \rho_1 \leqslant 0.5, \\ & \rho_2 \leqslant 1.5 + q_2 . \end{array}$$

The solution to this, $q_1^2 = 0$ and $q_2^2 = 2$, becomes the new quota. The sales estimate is $\rho_1 + \rho_2 = 4.0$.

At *stage 2* the first division's second-best solution is

$$\alpha_1^2 = 0, \quad \rho_1^2 = 0, \quad \nabla\rho_1^2 = 1,$$

and the second division's solution equals

$$\alpha_2^2 = 2, \quad \rho_2^2 = 3, \quad \nabla\rho_2^2 = 0.$$

The piecewise linear approximation to the reward functions are illustrated in fig. 12.6.

The linear programming problem of the accounting office is now

$$\begin{array}{ll} \text{maximize} & \rho_1 + \rho_2 \\ \text{subject to} & q_1 + q_2 \leqslant 2, \\ & \rho_1 \leqslant 0.5, \\ & \rho_1 \leqslant q_1, \\ & \rho_2 \leqslant 1.5 + q_2, \\ & \rho_2 \leqslant 3. \end{array}$$

The solution to this provides the new quota, $q_1^3 = 0.5, q_2^3 = 1.5$, which is in fact the optimal activity for the organization. The exaggerated sales estimate now equals $\rho_1 + \rho_2 = 0.5 + 3.0 = 3.5$; the decrease occurs because the quota guided budget process approximates the reward function and constraint regions from above.

Additional stages of the budget process are summarized in Table 12.2. The budget planning process has reached a fairly accurate estimation of the optimal choice after just a few iterations of the budget. If the process is stopped at stage

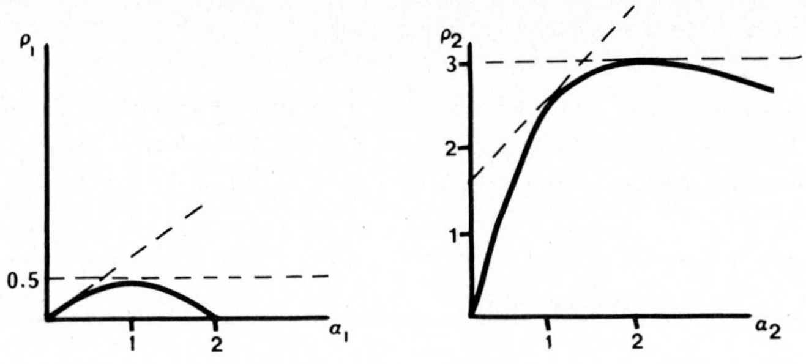

Figure 12.6

Table 12.2

t	q_1^t	q_2^t	α_1^t	ρ_1^t	$\nabla\rho_1^t$	α_2^t	ρ_2^t	$\nabla\rho_2^t$	$\rho_1 + \rho_2$
1	1.0	1.0	1.0	0.5	0.0	1.0	2.5	1.0	4.0
2	0.0	2.0	0.0	0.0	1.0	2.0	3.0	0.0	3.5
3	0.5	1.5	0.5	0.375	0.5	1.5	2.875	0.5	3.25
4	0.25	1.75	0.25	0.219	0.75	1.75	2.969	0.25	3.25
5	0.375	1.625	0.375	0.305	0.625	1.625	2.929	0.375	–

4 after the lack of change in $\rho_1 + \rho_2$, among those activities known precisely the allocation from stage 3 gives the highest actual sales of $\rho_1^3 + \rho_2^3 = 0.375 + 2.875 = 3.25$, and hence would be budgeted. This is the global optimum as it turns out. ■

The quota guided budget process has many of the desirable properties of the transfer price process. For instance, the process may be stopped at any time and a feasible allocation of organizational resources may be executed. The process converges (shown by Weitzman, 1970) and monotonically decreases the overestimates of organizational profit. The process takes relatively large steps toward the optimum and therefore converges to a near optimum within a reasonable number of stages. In fact, Weitzman also showed that if the original problem was a linear programming problem, the process will converge in a finite number of steps since each stage picks up a new flat of a polyhedral set. See also Hurwicz (1973) and Heal (1973).

The quota guided budget process is obviously not meant to decentralize power greatly. The accounting office continually challenges the divisions by proposing exaggerated targets and finally imposes unilaterally its final choice. The quota guided system seems to entail much more communication than the transfer price guided system at each stage, because the quotas are tailored specifically to each division and the division must respond with not only activity vectors but also information about the tradeoffs along boundaries of sets or functions. This is somewhat exaggerated in the above process because there are alternative formulations which attenuate such problems. The following provides one such alternative.

The accounting office need not know all the details of the reward functions and feasible activity sets as long as it knows the "indirect" reward functions defined as follows:

$$\phi_i(\kappa_i) \equiv \text{maximum } \rho_i(\alpha_i) \text{ subject to } \kappa_i(\alpha_i) \leqslant \kappa_i, \qquad \alpha_i \in A_i.$$

The function $\phi_i(\kappa_i)$ dictates the largest reward which division i can generate when given access to organizational capital κ_i. The optimal allocation of organizational capital maximizes

$$\sum_i \phi_i(\kappa_i)$$

subject to

$$\sum_i \kappa_i \leqslant \kappa.$$

Benders (1962) and Geoffrion (1972) have shown that when $\kappa_1^*, ..., \kappa_n^*$ solves this problem and $\alpha_1^*, ..., \alpha_n^*$ achieves the maximum in the definition of indirect reward then $\alpha_1^*, ..., \alpha_n^*$ solves the organizational decision problem. Conversely, the solution of the organizational problem and corresponding capital allocation solve the above problem.

Either the transfer price guided or quota guided budget process can be used to iteratively solve the allocation of capital to indirect rewards. Geoffrion (1972) showed that the quota guided budget process will converge when the original problem is suitably convex. The accounting office announces a tentative capital allocation κ_i^t and asks the division to respond by telling the maximum reward generated from this allocation, $\phi_i(\kappa_i^t)$, as well as the marginal value of more capital, $\nabla\phi_i(\kappa_i^t)$. From these the accounting office builds an envelope approximation of

$$\phi_i^t(\kappa_i) = \min\,[\phi_i(\kappa_i^1) + \nabla\phi_i(\kappa_i^t)\,(\kappa_i - \kappa_i^1), ..., \phi_i(\kappa_i^t) + \nabla\phi_i(\kappa_i^t)\,(\kappa_i - \kappa_i^t)].$$

The next capital allocation announced is the one which maximizes

$$\sum_i \phi_i^t(\kappa_i)$$

subject to

$$\sum_i \kappa_i \leqslant \kappa .$$

In a transfer guided process the accounting office announces prices P^t and the division i responds with the capital demand, κ_i^t, which maximizes $\phi_i(\kappa_i) - P^t\kappa_i$ along with the indirect payoff $\phi_i^t = \phi_i(\kappa_i^t)$. The accounting office then takes convex combinations to maximize

$$\sum_i \sum_{\tau=1}^{t} \mu_i^\tau \phi_i^\tau$$

subject to

$$\sum_i \sum_{\tau=1}^{t} \mu_i^\tau \kappa_i^\tau \leqslant \kappa .$$

The marginal value of capital from this constraint is used for the succeeding transfer price.

The point to be made here is that the transfer price budget process does not inherently conserve on communication relative to a property formulated quota guided budget process. The price guided process requires that a price be communicated to each division while the quota guided process requires that a capital quota be communicated. It would be hard to argue that prices are less costly to code, communicate, and decode than quotas. It should also be mentioned that even though the price is identical for all divisions, it must still be communicated to all divisions. The division communicates the value of ϕ_i and the capital demand κ_i in the price guided system while in the quota guided system the value of ϕ_i and its gradient $\nabla\phi_i$ are communicated. Again, these are highly comparable in terms of communication costs.

If one cannot judge the two processes on their respective communication costs, how could we compare the advantages and disadvantages of transfer price guided and quota guided budget planning processes? Weitzman (1974) initiated a line of analysis which Laffont (1977), Yohe (1978), and Ireland (1977) have extended. Weitzman considers an organization which produces identical goods in several different divisions. The total output of all divisions,

$$\alpha = \sum_i \alpha_i ,$$

is marketed jointly and brings in revenue according to a function

$$\rho(\alpha).$$

The cost of producing output α_i in division i is related not only to α_i but also a parameter, s_i, in the cost function

$$C(\alpha_i, s_i).$$

Were the accounting office able to observe the parameters s_i for each division it would choose the production plan which maximized total profit

$$\rho(\alpha) - \sum_i C(\alpha_i, s_i).$$

However, when acquiring knowledge of s_i is very costly, the accounting office must be satisfied with a budget that does not depend directly on the cost parameters. Assume that the beliefs about the cost parameter can be quantified in a subjective probability distribution.

A simple quantity oriented budget would instruct each division to produce the quantity $\tilde{\alpha}_i$ which maximizes the expected profit:

$$\rho(\alpha) - \sum_i \mathrm{E}\,\{C(\alpha_i, s_i)\}.$$

On the other hand, a transfer price P might be announced and each division allowed to choose the output which maximizes its accounting profit:

$$P\alpha_i - C_i(\alpha_i, s_i).$$

If the optimal choice is denoted $\alpha_i(P, s_i)$ the accounting office would choose that transfer price $\hat{P}$ which maximizes the resulting expected profit,

$$\mathrm{E}\left\{\rho\left(\sum_i \alpha_i(P, s_i)\right)\right\} - \sum_i \mathrm{E}\,\{C(\alpha_i(P, s_i), s_i)\}.$$

Denoting the optimal output at this transfer price as

$$\hat{\alpha}_i(s_i) \equiv \alpha_i(\hat{P}, s_i),$$

the two budget systems were compared by Weitzman (1974) by computing a coefficient of comparative advantage of prices over quantities:

$$\Delta = \mathrm{E}\left\{\rho\left(\sum_i \hat{\alpha}_i(s_i)\right)\right\} - \sum_i \mathrm{E}\,\{C(\hat{\alpha}_i(s_i), s_i)\} - \rho(\hat{\alpha}) + \sum_i \mathrm{E}\,\{C(\hat{\alpha}_i, s_i)\}.$$

Weitzman's analysis continues by making quadratic approximations of the revenue and cost functions:

$$\rho(\alpha) \cong \rho'\alpha + \tfrac{1}{2}\rho''\alpha^2,$$

$$C(\alpha_i, s_i) \cong (c' + s_i)\,\alpha_i + \tfrac{1}{2}c''\alpha_i^2.$$

Notice that the cost parameter is assumed to appear only in the linear coefficient. It will be assumed that revenue is concave, costs convex, and $\rho' > c'$. It is also convenient to assume that s_i has an identical independent distribution for each division with mean zero and variance $v = \mathrm{E}\{s_i^2\}$.

With these approximations, the optimal outputs in the quantity specified budget system must satisfy the first-order conditions:

$$\rho' - \rho'' \sum_i \tilde{\alpha}_i = c' + c''\tilde{\alpha}_i.$$

Simple algebra allows the expected profit to be expressed as

$$\rho(\tilde{\alpha}) - \sum_i \mathrm{E}\{\rho(\tilde{\alpha}_i, s_i)\} = \tfrac{1}{2}\,\frac{(\rho' - c')^2}{c''/n - \rho''}.$$

The optimal outputs at transfer price P must satisfy the first-order conditions

$$P = c' + s_i + c''\alpha_i(P, s_i).$$

Hence, expected profit equals

$$\left[\frac{nv}{c''} + \frac{\rho'}{2}\,\frac{n^2 v}{c''} - \frac{n}{2}\,\frac{v}{c''}\right] + \frac{n(\rho' - c')}{c''}\,(P - c') - \frac{(n - n^2\rho'')}{2c''}\,(P - c')^2.$$

The optimal transfer price is easily calculated to be

$$\hat{P} = c' + \frac{\rho' - c'}{1 - n\rho''}.$$

The coefficient of comparative advantage equals

$$\Delta = \frac{n\,(\rho'' + c'')\,v}{2\,(c'')^2},$$

given the above approximations. The larger the variance of cost parameters, the larger the magnitude of the coefficient of advantage. In an environment where the accounting office has great uncertainties about the divisional cost functions, the advantage of one system over the other is magnified, but this does not bias the advantage toward price or quantity oriented budgets. The determination of which process holds the advantage hinges on whether the revenue function has greater curvature than the cost functions. When marginal cost is almost constant and marginal revenue is very sensitive to output sold, profit is most easily acquired by fixing quantities. If the marginal cost is not forecast accurately and is very flat, the transfer price might lead to huge over- or underproduction. On the other hand, when marginal costs rise rapidly with output and marginal revenue is almost constant, the optimal output will not vary much with the cost parameter s_i. Allowing each firm to choose its own output captures the benefits of scale.

Weitzman notes that the only way for the coefficient of comparative advantage Δ to be infinitely large is for both c'' and ρ'' to be almost zero and $c'' + \rho'' > 0$, while Δ might be infinitely small if either ρ'' equals minus infinity, c'' equals zero or both. One might thus argue that when c'' and ρ'' are unknown, the quantity budget system prevents disasters better. To formalize this last result, Weitzman generalizes his approximate cost function slightly:

$$C = (c' + s_i)\alpha_i + \tfrac{1}{2} \frac{a''}{a(s_i)} \alpha_i^2$$

where $\mathrm{E}\,\{a(s_i)\} = 1$ and $\mathrm{var}\,(a) = v_a = \mathrm{E}\,\{a(s_i) - 1)^2\}$. In this case the coefficient of comparative advantage equals

$$\Delta = \frac{n\,v\,(c'' + \rho''\,(1 + v_a))}{2\,(c'')^2} .$$

An increase in the uncertainty of the cost's quadratic coefficient, v_a, increases the advantage of the quantity budget relative to the transfer price system

CHAPTER 13

PRINCIPALS AND AGENTS

An agency relationship between two individuals exists when the agent is authorized by the principal to make, modify, or cancel contracts with a third party in the principal's name. A movie star hires an agent to arrange for her appearance in films. A sharecropper is the agent for the principal who owns the land which is farmed. A salesman acts as an agent for the manufacture of the commodity being sold. A foreman is employed by a construction company and given the power to decide the hiring and firing of workers.

An agent differs from an employee by the fact that the activities of the agent are not monitored in detail. The principal does not give his agent contingency orders on how to handle each possible decision situation as he does to supervised employees. Some guidlines may be spelled out and the agent may be monitored to some extent, but the essential feature of the agency relationship is the freedom of the agent to determine activities and contracts independently.

The power to act independently for the principal might be used by the agent for his own benefit. Why should the principal grant the individual the authority to act in his name when there is the possibility that the activities of the agent are undesirable? To answer this, one must look at the alternative relationships, each of which has its shortcomings.

The principal could do the work himself, but this may be too costly, preventing the principal from participating in other profitable ventures. He may lack the time (or value it too highly) to enter into this potentially valuable activity. The operation may require resources or knowledge which are too costly to acquire, or the principal may simply lack the skills necessary to accomplish a task which he knows can be done by a trained individual. He may be forced, therefore, to hire another individual to do the job. But why an agent?

Why not, instead, an independent contractor who promises delivery of a specified product or service? Obviously this requires that the independent contractor have the technical and institutional knowledge to produce the good or service. Often the principal has unique and specific requirements which are hard to describe without moment-by-moment renegotiations of the contract. Moreover, when uncertainties are important there may be circumstances in which the independent contractor finds it impossible to execute the contract without large losses. A breach of contract makes the contractor liable for damages, but the legally determined financial compensation may not be a satisfactory alternative to specific performance. The contract could spell out the principal's desires for performance in each possible contingency, but this detailed negotiation may use just those resources which the principal wants to conserve. Moreover, the principal may find it difficult to acquire enough information about the environment to enforce such a contingent contract.

Another alternative for the principal is to hire a subordinant employee whose job is to perform exactly those tasks the principal mandates. While this may increase the available physical resources of the principal, it does not really economize on the time and effort the principal puts into decision-making. Moreover, the employee must be monitored to ensure that orders are carried out, adding to the principal's costs. There are many tasks that subordinate employees perform which impart idiosyncratic knowledge which is valuable but unobservable to even a close supervisor. In addition, the subservient nature of such a personal relationship between principal and employee may be so distasteful to the employee that high wages must be paid in compensation for the loss of independence.

As a result of the shortcomings of these alternative relationships, the principal enters into a principal–agent contract with another person. This contract should specify the venture for which the agent is hired. For example, the contract might specify how the actions of the agents and the state of nature determine the outcome which is of interest to the principal. The contract will also have to specify how the agent is rewarded. The literature on these contracts has focused on the reward systems found in agencies. In what follows we explore how reward systems can be designed to entice the agent to make efficient risk-bearing decisions and to expend an optimal amount of effort. The emphasis will be on the information used to determine reward levels.

Before developing the general problem of the principal and agent, two specific examples will be considered which illustrate the variety of agency relations. In the first the agent sells several goods for a manufacturer who uses the commission rates to motivate the appropriate time allocation of the salesperson. The second illustration explores the issue of equity finance. An entrepreneur sells stock in his enterprise to finance a project. The funds raised by the stock sales depend on how many perquisities the entrepreneur-agent consumes. In both cases inability to verify the actions of the agent result in a loss to the agency.

Example. The sales commission rate on good i, b_i, specifies the fraction of the dollar sales volume, r_i, which is paid to the salesperson as a commission. The salesperson's total commission from all product lines equals

$$\sum_i b_i r_i.$$

Sales volume depends on the time dedicated to promoting the good, α_i, and the state of nature, s, the dependence given by a function

$$r_i = \rho_i(\alpha_i, s).$$

When the salesperson has allocated a total of T days to sales promotion,

$$\sum_i \alpha_i = T,$$

the expected sales commission is

$$\sum_i b_i R_i(\alpha_i),$$

where $R_i(\alpha_i) = \mathrm{E}\,\{\rho_i(\alpha_i, s)\}$ is the expected revenue raised by spending α_i days promoting good i. The salesperson, assumed to be risk neutral and to dislike sales promotion, obtains an expected utility from this job of

$$\mathrm{E}\,U = \sum_i b_i R_i(\alpha_i) - D(T).$$

The disutility of time spent promoting sales, $D(T)$, increases with T and with growing marginal disutility, $D' > 0$, $D'' \geqslant 0$. The salesperson has an alternative occupation which places a floor, $\bar{U}$, under that acceptable expected utility.

The efficient commission rates and sales promotion are found by solving:

$$\begin{array}{ll} \text{maximize} & \sum_i (1 - b_i)\, R_i(\alpha_i) \\ \text{subject to} & \sum_i \alpha_i = T, \\ \text{and} & \sum_i b_i R_i(\alpha_i) - D(T) = \bar{U}. \end{array}$$

That is, the manufacturer maximizes net sales revenue subject to the floor on the salesperson's utility. Substituting from the constraints, the objective function equals

$$\sum_i R_i(\alpha_i) - D\left(\sum_i \alpha_i\right) - \bar{U}.$$

The manufacturer cannot hope to entice the salesperson to exert as much effort as would be efficient without monitoring sales promotion since EU has the same disutility as this objective function but has smaller expected revenue. Efficiency requires that α_i satisfy

$$R_i' = D',$$

while utility maximization requires

$$R_i' = D'/b_i > D', \quad \text{if } b_i < 1.$$

If the distribution of promotion effort cannot be observed in detail but the total promotion time can be verified, the manufacturer must choose α_i, b_i, and T to

$$\begin{array}{ll} \text{maximize} & \sum_i (1 - b_i) R_i(\alpha_i) \\ \text{subject to} & \alpha_i \text{ is the solution to} \\ & \begin{array}{ll} \text{maximize} & \sum_i b_i R_i(\alpha_i) - D(T) \\ \text{subject to} & \sum_i \alpha_i = T, \end{array} \\ \text{and} & \sum_i b_i R_i(\alpha_i) - D(T) = \bar{U}. \end{array}$$

That is, the manufacturer cannot directly control α_i but can set the commission rates and the total time requirement to maximize net revenue subject to the behavior of the salesperson and the utility floor. Srinivasan (1981) shows that a uniform commission rate solves the manufacturer's problem. For uniform commission rates, $b_i = b$, the expected utility of the salesperson,

$$b \sum_i R_i(\alpha_i) - D(T)$$

is equivalent to an objective function

$$\sum_i R_i(\alpha_i)$$

because the total time T is not controlled by the salesperson. Substituting the utility floor constraint into net revenue, the manufacturer maximizes

$$\sum_i R_i(\alpha_i) - \bar{U} - D(T).$$

Considering sequentially the optimal time allocation and then the optimal total time, the manufacture has the same desire to maximize $\Sigma_i R_i(\alpha_i)$ that the salesperson has. By dictating T and a uniform sales commission rate the manufacture can provide incentives for the salesperson to maximize net revenue. Therefore, when T can be observed there is no need to supervise the exact allocation of time. The allocation of resources will be efficient.

When the manufacturer can monitor neither the total nor the allocation of time to various sales promotion, the best it can do is maximize net revenue subject to the utility floor constraint given the choice made by the salesperson,

$$\underset{\alpha_i, T}{\text{maximize}} \quad \sum_i b_i R_i(\alpha_i) - D(T)$$

$$\text{subject to} \quad \sum_i \alpha_i = T.$$

The second-best commission rates will not necessarily be uniform. Srinivasan illustrated this fact by assuming that expected revenue has a constant elasticity with respect to promotion effort:

$$R_i(\alpha_i) = \alpha_i^{\gamma_i}, \qquad 0 < \gamma_i < 1,$$

and disutility is linear:

$$D(T) = \delta T.$$

The optimal commission rates,

$$b_i = \gamma_i,$$

depend on the elasticities and therefore are not uniform or efficient. The salesperson will promote sales by working

$$\alpha_i = (\gamma_i^2/\delta)^{1/(1-\gamma_i)}$$

days, but efficiency demands a larger promotion of sales,

$$\alpha_i = (\gamma_i/\delta)^{1/(1-\gamma_i)}. \quad \blacksquare$$

Example. The second principal–agent relationship exemplifies financing investments by issuing stocks. Consider an entrepreneur who has an idea for a profitable project but who has no wealth to finance the enterprise. The project requires capital in an amount κ and generates gross profit π. The entrepreneur can use these profits for perquisites such as plush carpeting, three-Martini lunches, or junkets. Letting α denote the monetary value of the perquisites, only the net profit, $\pi - \alpha$, will be distributed to the stockholders. The fraction of the stock held by the entrepreneur is chosen, along with the perks, to maximize the entrepreneur's income, consisting of dividends and the value of the equity sold to the investors. If a price P were paid for a share $1 - b$, then the income, r, of the entrepreneur is

$$r = P + b(\pi - \alpha).$$

As Jensen and Meckling (1976) have made clear, the price that investors pay for the shares depends upon their anticipations of the perquisites consumed by the entrepreneur. In fig. 13.1 the behavior of the entrepreneur is analyzed. (The following is based upon Jensen and Meckling's insightful study.) The dotted indifference curves labelled $U_1 - U_4$ indicate the willingness of the entrepreneur to trade income for perks according to a utility function

$$U(r, \alpha).$$

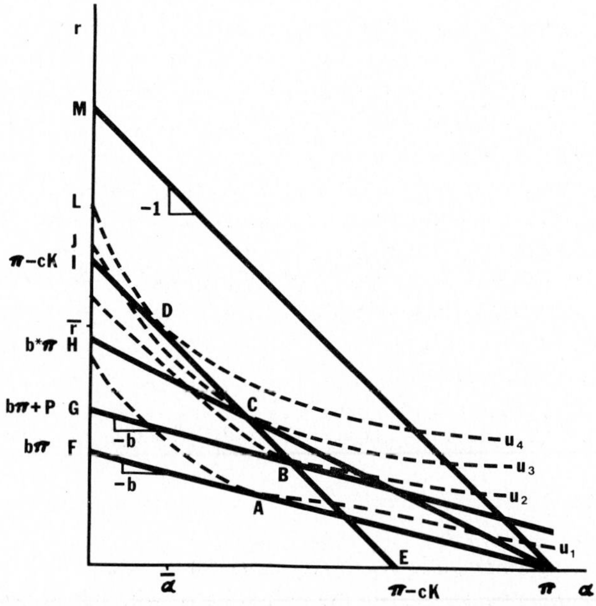

Figure 13.1

If the entrepreneur exchanges a portion $1 - b$ of the equity in his enterprise for access to the capital, the income and perks which are feasible lie on the line $F\pi$. The optimal choice, point A, lies below the line IE that delineates the income and perks available after the opportunity cost of capital, $c\kappa$, is deducted from gross profit. The investors will receive dividends exceeding their opportunity cost of capital and will therefore bid $P > 0$ for the equity. For a fixed b, equilibrium occurs at point B which is characterized by:

(a) α and r maximize $U(\alpha, r)$ subject to

$$r = P + b(\pi - \alpha);$$

(b) $P + c\kappa = (1 - b)(\pi - \alpha)$.

Condition (a) states that the entrepreneur chooses an optimal amount of perquisities and income. Condition (b) balances the costs that investors incur in acquiring equity and the dividends paid. The equilibrium depends on the stock held by the entrepreneur:

$$\alpha(b), r(b), P(b).$$

The entrepreneur, controlling the equity sold to finance the enterprise, chooses b to maximize his equilibrium utility subject to $P(b) \geqslant 0$. The payment must be non-negative because the entrepreneur lacks the credit to finance capital rental or purchase. The optimum equity b^*, point C, is such that the investors make no payment. In fact, without the non-negativity restriction on $P(b)$ the entrepreneur would choose to keep all equity and rent the capital, achieving the allocation D. The inability to finance the project with current wealth forces the entrepreneur to issue stock. The unmonitored consumption of perquisites results in such a large exchange of equity for capital that the entrepreneur's expected utility is decreased by an amount given by the distance between the indifference curves U_3 and U_4. In money terms, the entrepreneur loses JL dollars because of his inability to finance the capital by debt rather than equity and the investors' inability to monitor the expenditure on perquisites. If the perquisites could be monitored, the entrepreneur would contract with the investors to consume only those perquisites, $\bar{\alpha}$, associated with point D and to accept a salary of $\bar{r}$ in exchange for all equity, and thereby achieve the highest possible utility. ■

The salesman and entrepreneur both act on the behalf of principals who, having a stake in the outcome, want to design payment schemes that motivate efficient decisions. We will now explore a general model of principal and agents which permits a theoretical investigation of the organization of the decision-making in the enterprise. The principal and agent participate in the achievement of outcomes which will be interpreted as monetary rewards, r. The value of the outcome may depend upon the resources supplied by the principal, the activities of the agent, and the state of nature. The principal's contributions will be invariable, so the reward is attributed to the agent's action α, and the state, s:

$$r = \rho(\alpha, s).$$

The principal derives utility only from income while the agent, having to expend effort to carry out his activities, obtains utility from both income and action:

$$U_P = U_P(r); \qquad U_A = U_A(r, \alpha).$$

The payment of the agent must be based on verifiable information and this requires us to specify what the principal and agent can observe. Throughout it will be presumed that the outcome r is common knowledge. The agent may observe an information variable, η, which improves his knowledge of the state of nature and obviously knows the action implemented. The principal may be unable to monitor the agent's activities. The state of nature is revealed to the agent *ex post*, but the principal often does not have the ability to verify s. The agency constructs a contract specifying the payment to the agent, P, as a function of the mutually confirmable information. For example, when only outcome is common knowledge the payment contract would be written

$$P = P(r).$$

The agent chooses a decision rule $\alpha(\eta)$ to maximize the utility he expects to derive from his payment and action:

$$\mathrm{E}U_{\mathrm{A}} = \mathrm{E}\,\{U_{\mathrm{A}}\,[P(\rho(\alpha(\eta), s)), \alpha(\eta)]\}.$$

The principal chooses a payment contract to guide the agent toward actions which he, the principal, most desires:

$$\mathrm{E}U_{\mathrm{P}} = \mathrm{E}\,\{U_{\mathrm{P}}\,[\rho(\alpha(\eta), s) - P(\rho(\alpha(\eta), s))]\}.$$

Employment opportunities exist for the agent beyond the agency, so unless expected utility exceeds or equals a utility floor, $\bar{U}_{\mathrm{A}}$, the agent will reject the agent contract.

The optimal agency relationship consists of a payment contract and a decision rule which

$$\begin{array}{ll} \text{maximizes} & \mathrm{E}\,U_{\mathrm{P}} \\ \text{subject to } \alpha \text{ maximizes } \mathrm{E}\,U_{\mathrm{A}} & \\ \text{and} & \mathrm{E}\,U_{\mathrm{A}} \geqslant \bar{U}_{\mathrm{A}}. \end{array}$$

This is a second-best solution because of the behavioral restriction that α maximizes $\mathrm{E}\,U_{\mathrm{A}}$. If the principal could use any contract and decision rule without fear of malfeasance, this requirement could be avoided and the contract would be (Pareto) efficient. However, in many cases the principal cannot count on the agent following instructions; if α does not maximize $\mathrm{E}\,U_{\mathrm{A}}$ and there is no way to oversee the decision rule, the agent will choose personally desirable but inefficient actions.

Must the optimal agency relation be inefficient? There clearly are some cases where it need not be. First, consider a situation where the agent's preferences exhibit risk neutrality in income, and where no information, η, is available to improve decisions. Let (P^+, α^+) denote an efficient contract:

$$(P^+, \alpha^+) \text{ maximizes } \mathrm{E}\,U_{\mathrm{P}} \text{ subject to } \mathrm{E}\,U_{\mathrm{A}} \geqslant \bar{U}_{\mathrm{A}}.$$

The principal expects to receive an income of the amount

$$\bar{r}_{\mathrm{P}} = \mathrm{E}\,\{\rho(\alpha^+, s) - P^+(\rho(\alpha^+, s))\}.$$

Suppose that we define a new contract where

$$P^* = r - \bar{r}_{\mathrm{P}}$$

and

$$\alpha^* \text{ maximizes } \mathrm{E}\,\{U_{\mathrm{A}}\,[P^*(\rho(\alpha, s)), \alpha]\}.$$

Assuming that the principal is risk averse, the expected utility for P^* exceeds or equal that for P^+ since

$$\rho - P^* = \bar{r}_{\rho}.$$

That is, the principal receives the income he expected to receive in the efficient contract but with no risk attached. On the other hand, by the optimality of α^*,

$$\mathrm{E}\,U_{\mathrm{A}}^* = \mathrm{E}\,\{U_{\mathrm{A}}\,[P^*(\rho(\alpha^*, s)), \alpha^*]\} \geqslant \mathrm{E}\,\{U_{\mathrm{A}}\,[P^*(\rho(\alpha, s)), \alpha]\},$$

for all actions α. In particular, for $\alpha = \alpha^+$ we get (using the definition of P^*),

$$\begin{aligned} \mathrm{E}U_{\mathrm{A}}^{*} &\geqslant \mathrm{E}\{U_{\mathrm{A}}[\rho(\alpha^{+}, s) - \bar{r}_{\mathrm{P}}, \alpha^{+}]\} \\ &= \mathrm{E}\{U_{\mathrm{A}}[\mathrm{E}\{P^{+}(\rho(\alpha^{+}, s))\} + \rho(\alpha^{+}, s) - \mathrm{E}\{\rho(\alpha^{+}, s)\}, \alpha^{+}]\}. \end{aligned}$$

By risk neutrality we can pass expectations through the utility function which implies that

$$\begin{aligned} \mathrm{E}U_{\mathrm{A}}^{*} &\geqslant U_{\mathrm{A}}[\mathrm{E}\{P^{+}(\rho(\alpha^{+}, s))\} + \mathrm{E}\{\rho(\alpha^{+}, s)\} - \mathrm{E}\{\rho(\alpha^{+}, s)\}, \alpha^{+}] \\ &= U_{\mathrm{A}}[\mathrm{E}\{P^{+}(\rho(\alpha^{+}, s))\}, \alpha^{+}] \\ &= \mathrm{E}\{U_{\mathrm{A}}[P^{+}(\rho(\alpha^{+}, s)), \alpha^{+}]\} \\ &\geqslant \bar{U}_{\mathrm{A}}. \end{aligned}$$

The last inequality follows from the definition of the efficient contract.

It had been shown that (P^*, α^*) gives the principal at least as much utility and the agent finds that the instruction α^* is his best activity and that he receives enough benefits from the agency to justify continued participation. In fact, the agent must receive exactly utility $\mathrm{E}U_{\mathrm{A}}^* = \bar{U}_{\mathrm{A}}$, for otherwise the principal could lower P^* slightly without the risk of losing the agent, and such a contract would contradict the efficiency of (P^+, α^+). Similarly, the principal cannot really be better off with (P^*, α^*). In fact, the efficient contract must be of the form where the principal is paid a fixed fee and the agent is given 100 percent of the equity. Risk neutrality demands that the agent bear all the risk. Since the principal's fee is paid regardless of outcome or action, there is no fear of malfeasance and it would be unnecessary for the principal to monitor the agent or even to verify the outcome.

It should be pointed out that when the decisions are based on information, η, the above argument does not hold without additional restrictions on the agent's utility function. Risk neutrality of the agent implies that the utility function is of the form

$$U_{\mathrm{A}}(r, \alpha) = v(\alpha) r + \bar{w}(\alpha).$$

If $\alpha(\eta)$ is a random variable, then so are $v(\alpha)$ and $w(\alpha)$. It would not be permissible to pass expectations through the agent's utility function unless $v(\alpha)$ is a constant function. Only if the agent's utility is additively separable in income and action will efficiency result from risk neutrality when decisions are based on uncertain information.

A second situation where second-best contracts are efficient occurs when the state of nature is verifiable *ex post*. (The following is based on Harris and Raviv,

1978). Suppose the contract $(P^+(r, \alpha), \alpha^+)$ is efficient. Define an alternative payment system by

$$P^*(r, s) = r - \rho(\alpha^+, s) + P^+(\rho(\alpha^+, s), s),$$

and let α^* be the action which maximizes

$$\mathrm{E}\{U_{\mathrm{A}}[P^*(\rho(\alpha, s), s), \alpha]\}.$$

From the definition of P^*, the income of the principal equals

$$r - P^*(r, s) = \rho(\alpha^+, s) - P^+(\rho(\alpha^+, s), s).$$

The income of the principal is independent of the actual action of the agent but is based instead on the efficient action. The principal therefore obtains the same expected utility with (P^*, α^*) as with (P^+, α^+). The optimality of α^* implies

$$\begin{aligned} \mathrm{E}\{U_{\mathrm{A}}[P^*(\rho(\alpha^*, s), s), \alpha^*]\} &\geqslant \mathrm{E}\{U_{\mathrm{A}}[P^*(\rho(\alpha^+, s), s), \alpha^+]\} \\ &= \mathrm{E}\{U_{\mathrm{A}}[\rho(\alpha^+, s) - \rho(\alpha^+, s) + P^+(\rho(\alpha^+, s), s), \alpha^+]\} \\ &= \mathrm{E}\{U_{\mathrm{A}}[P^+(\rho(\alpha^+, s), s), \alpha^+]\} \\ &\geqslant \bar{U}_{\mathrm{A}}. \end{aligned}$$

Again a strict inequality would contradict the definition of (P^+, α^+), so the agent must receive the same expected utility with (P^*, α^*) as with (P^+, α^+). In conclusion, when the state of nature is verifiable, the principal may take a fee equal to the income he would have if the efficient contract was used and the agent receives 100 percent of the equity. The malfeasance is eliminated and the principal does not need to monitor outcome or action.

As before, this conclusion must be modified if the agent bases his action on uncertain information. Knowledge of s does not imply that η is verified. If the principal is to receive the payment due under the efficient decision rule,

$$\rho(\alpha^+(\eta), s) - P^+(\rho(\alpha^+(\eta), s), s),$$

then either the action or the information η must be verifiable. If η is verifiable along with s, then the agent should be given 100 percent of the equity.

Might the principal use the observed reward to infer the state of nature? Indeed, when $\rho(\alpha, s)$ is one-to-one in s for all α the principal can calculate s exactly from the efficient action and the observed outcome. However, if the agent realizes that the state is not directly verified but is only inferred, it will be in his self-interest to choose an (inefficient) action that exploits the principal to the agent's advantage.

A third circumstance where efficiency does not conflict with the independent decision-making of the agent was explored by Wilson (1968) and Ross (1974). They considered an agent whose utility was independent of the magnitude of the action:

$$U_A(r, \alpha) = U_A(r).$$

For example, a financial trustee of the principal would not be directly interested in a change in portfolio but would care how such a change influenced the portfolio's yield. The agent will not shirk but may choose too risky or too conservative a portfolio for the principal's tastes. The agency must contractually share risks for the mutual benefit of principal and agent. If the principal can design a payment rule that induces a similarity in preferences, then the agent will choose actions which are in the principal's interest. Suppose that the payment rule can be chosen so the agent's utility is an affine transformation of the principal's:

$$U_P(r - P(r)) = c + d\,U_A(P(r)), \quad \text{for all } r.$$

The action that maximizes the agent's expected utility also maximizes the principal's expected utility.

When malfeasance can be eliminated by inducing similarity the only remaining difficulty is efficiency. Wilson and Ross found that a particularly simple sharing rule will be able to transform similarity into efficiency – a linear payment function:

$$P(r) = a + br.$$

In fact, any two of three conditions imply the third.

Theorem 13.1. If any two of the conditions (a) efficiency, (b) similarity, and (c) linearity are satisfied by the payment rule, then so is the third.

Proof. (Efficiency and similarity imply linearity). For a fixed action α, the efficient payment rule must render the Lagrangian

$$L = \mathrm{E}\{U_P[\rho(\alpha, s) - P(\rho(\alpha, s))]\} + \lambda(\mathrm{E}\{U_A[P(\rho(\alpha, s))]\} - \bar{U}_A)$$

extreme. Consider adding a small multiple of an arbitrary payment rule $P(r)$ to the efficient rule, $P^+ + \epsilon P$. If P^+ renders L extreme, then

$$0 = \left.\frac{\partial L}{\partial \epsilon}\right|_{\epsilon=0} = \mathrm{E}\{(-U'_{\mathrm{P}} + \lambda U'_{\mathrm{A}}) \cdot P(\rho(\alpha, s))\},$$

for all arbitrary functions P. Since P may be positive or negative this implies that

$$U'_{\mathrm{P}}(r - P^+(r)) = \lambda U'_{\mathrm{A}}(P^+(r)), \quad \text{for all } r.$$

Since the efficient payment also induces similarity,

$$U_{\mathrm{P}}(r - P^+(r)) = c + d U_{\mathrm{A}}(P^+(r)), \quad \text{for all } r.$$

Differentiating this with respect to r and substituting from the efficiency condition above gives:

$$U'_{\mathrm{P}}(r - P^+(r)) \left(1 - \frac{\mathrm{d}P^+}{\mathrm{d}r}\right) = d \cdot U'_{\mathrm{A}}(P^+(r)) \frac{\mathrm{d}P^+}{\mathrm{d}r}$$

$$= \frac{d}{\lambda} U'_{\mathrm{P}}(r - P^+(r)) \frac{\mathrm{d}P^+}{\mathrm{d}r} .$$

Cancelling marginal utilities and rearranging, this implies

$$\frac{\mathrm{d}P^+}{\mathrm{d}r} = \frac{\lambda}{\lambda + d}, \quad \text{for all } r.$$

This ordinary differential equation has the general solution

$$P^+(r) = a + \frac{\lambda}{\lambda + d} r,$$

which was to be shown.

(Efficiency and linearity imply similarity). From the condition characterizing efficiency and linearity we have

$$U'_{\mathrm{P}}(r - a - br) = \lambda U'_{\mathrm{A}}(a + br), \quad \text{for all } r.$$

Integrate both sides with respect to r to get:

$$U_{\mathrm{P}}(r - a - br)/(1 - b) = \lambda U_{\mathrm{A}}(a + br)/b + k,$$

where k is a constant of integration. Rearranging this gives

$$U_P(r - a - br) = k(1 - b) + \frac{\lambda(1 - b)}{b} U_A(a + br),$$

which was to be shown.

(Linearity and similarity imply efficiency). Differentiating the similarity condition after substituting the linear sharing gives

$$U_P' \cdot (1 - b) = d \cdot U_A' \cdot b.$$

For $\lambda = d \cdot b/(1 - b)$ this is the efficiency condition for the payment function. The efficient action renders the Lagrangian L extreme:

$$\mathrm{E}\left\{U_P' \cdot \left(1 - \frac{\mathrm{d}P}{\mathrm{d}r}\right) \cdot \rho_\alpha\right\} + \lambda \mathrm{E}\left\{U_A' \cdot \frac{\mathrm{d}P}{\mathrm{d}r} \rho_\alpha\right\} = 0.$$

However, similarity and linearity imply that

$$\mathrm{E}\left\{U_P' \cdot \left(1 - \frac{\mathrm{d}P}{\mathrm{d}r}\right) \cdot \rho_\alpha\right\} = d \cdot \mathrm{E}\left\{U_A' \cdot \frac{\mathrm{d}P}{\mathrm{d}r} \cdot \rho_\alpha\right\},$$

and since the agent will choose α so that the right-hand side equals zero, the Lagrangian is rendered extreme. ■

This result is very convenient, but how practicable is it? Is it possible that preferences can be made similar by using only linear payment contracts? Ross (1974) found that this can be guaranteed only for an interesting but narrow class of utility functions.

Theorem 13.2. If efficiency may be obtained with linear payment contracts for a range of values of $\bar{U}_A$, then both principal and agent have utilities with linear risk tolerance and identical cautiousness:

$$\tau_A(P) \equiv -U_A'/U_A'' = \epsilon_A + \kappa P$$

and

$$\tau_P(r - P) \equiv -U_P'/U_P'' = \epsilon_P + \kappa(r - P).$$

Proof. Efficiency and linearity imply

$$U_P'(r - (a + br)) = \lambda U_A'(a + br), \quad \text{for all } r.$$

Differentiate this with respect to r to obtain:

$$U''_P(r - (a + br)) \cdot (1 - b) = \lambda U''_A(a + br) \cdot b.$$

A change in $\bar{U}_A$ changes the value of a, b, and λ, so let us denote the derivative of these with respect to $\bar{U}_A$ by a', b', and λ'. Differentiating the efficiency condition with respect to $\bar{U}_A$ results in:

$$-U''_P(r - (a + br)) \cdot (a' + b'r) = \lambda' U'_A(a + br) + \lambda U''_A(a + br) \cdot (a' + b'r).$$

Substitution from the previous equation gives:

$$-\lambda b/(1 - b) \cdot U''_A(a + br) \cdot (a' + b'r)$$
$$= \lambda' U'_A(a + br) + \lambda U''_A(a + br) \cdot (a' + b'r).$$

Rearranging this gives:

$$\tau_A = \frac{-U'_A}{U''_A} = \left(\frac{\lambda}{\lambda'}\ \frac{1}{1 - b}\ \frac{ab' + a'b}{b}\right) + \left(\frac{\lambda}{\lambda'}\ \frac{1}{1 - b}\ \frac{b'}{b}\right)(a + br)$$
$$= \epsilon_A + \kappa P,$$

which was to be shown. From the efficiency condition and its derivative with respect r we have

$$\frac{-U'_P}{U''_P} = \frac{-U'_A}{U''_A} \cdot \frac{1 - b}{b}$$

or

$$\tau_P = \frac{1 - b}{b}\, \tau_A.$$

Differentiating this with respect to r gives:

$$\frac{\partial \tau_P}{\partial (r - P)} \cdot \frac{\partial (r - P)}{\partial r} = \frac{1 - b}{b}\ \frac{\partial \tau_A}{\partial P}\ \frac{\partial P}{\partial r},$$

$$\frac{\partial \tau_P}{\partial (r - P)} \cdot (1 - b) = \frac{1 - b}{b}\ \frac{\partial \tau_A}{\partial P}\, b,$$

or

$$\frac{\partial \tau_P}{\partial (r - P)} = \frac{\partial \tau_A}{\partial P}.$$

That is to say, the slope of the risk tolerance, called the cautiousness, must be identical for both principal and agent. From the above, the agent's cautiousness is a constant, so integration of the equation

$$\frac{\partial \tau_P}{\partial (r - P)} = \kappa$$

gives

$$\tau_P = \epsilon_P + \kappa (r - P). \quad \blacksquare$$

Treating the restrictions on the utility functions found in theorem 13.2 as second-order differential equations, the class of utility functions which can induce efficiency for a range of $\bar{U}_A$ using only linear payment contracts is

$$U_A(P) = \frac{1}{\lambda} (\delta_A + P)^\gamma, \quad \text{where } \tau_A = \frac{\delta_A}{1-\gamma} + \frac{1}{1-\gamma} P.$$

Limiting cases where $\gamma = 0$ and $\gamma = 1 - \delta_A/\nu = -\infty$ are:

$$U_A(P) = \log (\delta_A + P), \quad \text{where } \tau_A = \delta_A + P,$$

and

$$U_A(P) = -e^{-P/\nu}, \quad \text{where } \tau_A = \nu.$$

These functions are quite popular for theoretical reasons, but it would be surprising if the principal and agent both had preferences in this class. In conclusion, if similarity is to be induced to eliminate malfeasance, and if efficiency is to be maintained, then the agent's preference must not be directly influenced by this action, and both principal and agent must have linear risk tolerance with identical cautiousness.

The previous three situations suggest that a second-best contract will seldom be efficient. In fact we can prove a theorem to that effect.

Theorem 13.3. Suppose that the utility of the agent is additively decomposable:

$$U_A = V_A(r) - D(\alpha),$$

where V_A is a risk averse utility indicator and $D(\alpha)$ is an increasing disutility function. If the principal is not a risk seeker and neither s nor α is verifiable, then the second-best contract is inefficient.

Proof. To prove this result, Holmstrom (1979) made a change of variables first suggested by Mirrlees (1976). For a given reward function $\rho(\alpha, s)$ and probability distribution of the state s, an implied distribution of outcomes, given the action, can be calculated. Let $F(r, \alpha)$ denote the probability that the outcome is smaller than or equal to r, given an action α was used with the reward function $\rho(\alpha, s)$. If $\rho(\alpha, s)$ is a non-decreasing function of α, then it can be shown that

$$F_\alpha(r, \alpha) \leqslant 0, \quad \text{for all } r.$$

That is, increasing α makes it less likely that the observed outcome lies below r. It will also be assumed that α has some impact on the reward: $F_\alpha(r, \alpha) < 0$ for some non-trival set of r's.

With this change of variables the second-best agency contract is characterized as follows:

$$\begin{array}{ll} P, \alpha \text{ maximize} & \int_R U_\text{P}(r - P(r))\,\mathrm{d}F(r, \alpha) \\ \text{subject to} & \int_R U_\text{A}(P(r))\,\mathrm{d}F(r, \alpha) - D(\alpha) = \bar{U}_\text{A} \\ \text{and } \alpha \text{ maximizes} & \int_R U_\text{A}(P(r))\,\mathrm{d}F(r, \alpha) - D(\alpha). \end{array}$$

It will be convenient to treat the agent's behavior as though it satisfied the first-order condition:

$$\frac{\partial \mathrm{E} U_\text{A}}{\partial \alpha} = \int_R U_\text{A}(P(r))\,\mathrm{d}F_\alpha(r, \alpha) - D'(\alpha) = 0.$$

Letting λ be the Lagrange multiplier of the utility constraint and μ be the multiplier of the behavior equation of the agent, the first-order condition for the sharing rule is

$$\frac{U'_\text{P}(r - P(r))}{U'_\text{A}(P(r))} = \lambda + \mu \frac{f_\alpha(r, \alpha)}{f(r, \alpha)},$$

where f is the density function of the probability distribution, $f(r, \alpha) = F_r(r, \alpha)$. The second-best action satisfies the first-order condition:

$$0 = \int_R U_\text{P}(r - P(r))\,\mathrm{d}F_\alpha(r, \alpha) + \lambda \frac{\partial \mathrm{E} U_\text{A}}{\partial \alpha} + \mu \frac{\partial^2 \mathrm{E} U_\text{A}}{\partial \alpha^2}.$$

The behavior of the agent implies that the second term above is zero. If the multiplier μ equals zero, then the first-order conditions are

$$\frac{U'_P(r - P(r))}{U'_A(P(r))} = \lambda$$

and

$$0 = \int_R U_P(r - P(r))\, dF_\alpha(r, \alpha).$$

Differentiating the first equation with respect to r and rearranging gives:

$$1 - P'(r) = \frac{-U''_A/U'_A}{-U''_A/U'_A - U''_P/U'_P} > 0,$$

which is positive since the agent is risk averse. Integrating the second equation by parts gives:

$$0 = U_P(r - P(r))\, F_\alpha(r, \alpha)\,|_{-\infty}^{\infty} - \int_R U'_P(r - P(r))\,(1 - P'(r))\, F_\alpha(r, \alpha)\, dr.$$

The fact that F is a cumulative distribution implies that $F(\infty, \alpha) = 1$, $F(-\infty, \alpha) = 0$, so the first term vanishes. Monotonicity of the principal's utility, and the fact that $F_\alpha(r, \alpha) \leqslant 0$ with strict inequality over a non-trivial region, implies the integral is negative, contradicting the equality. We must conclude that $\mu > 0$ and hence the principal would like the agent to increase α. The agent's first-order condition implies that this does not influence his expected utility and hence would be an improvement on the second-best policy. ■

The inability to monitor the action of the agent gives him the freedom to choose the action which suits his preferences. Since his tastes for risk may differ from those of his principal, and since he must exert the effort to carry out the activities, it would be naive for the principal to anticipate that the agent follows orders blindly. The loss of control decreases the total effectiveness of the agency. If no costs were involved in monitoring the agent it would seem worth while. What if the monitoring was imperfect? Might not the uncertainty and errors of monitoring impose a loss that exceeds the benefits of improved control? Holmstrom (1979) and Shavell (1979) have addressed this question, to which we now turn.

Suppose that the principal and agent can observe a variable e which provides information about the agent's action. Should this estimated effort e be included in the contractual payment terms? Let $F(r, e, \alpha)$ be the cumulative distribution on r and e given the action α; that is, $F(r, e, \alpha)$ is the probability that the outcome will not exceed r and the estimated effort will not exceed e when the agent has in fact exerted the effort α. Consider the case where the density derived from F, denoted $f(r, e, \alpha)$, factors in the following fashion:

$$f(r, e, \alpha) = g(r, e) \cdot h(r, \alpha).$$

In such a case the estimated effort does not provide information about α. To see this, treat α as a random variable with density $k(\alpha)$ and calculate the posterior density of α, given r and e, using Bayes formula:

$$\begin{aligned} k(\alpha|r, e) &= \frac{f(r, e, \alpha)\, k(\alpha)}{\int f(r, e, \alpha)\, k(\alpha)\, \mathrm{d}\alpha} \\ &= \frac{g(r, e)\, h(r, \alpha)\, k(\alpha)}{\int g(r, e)\, h(r, \alpha)\, k(\alpha)\, \mathrm{d}\alpha} \\ &= \frac{g(r, e)\, h(r, \alpha)\, k(\alpha)}{g(r, e) \int h(r, \alpha)\, k(\alpha)\, \mathrm{d}\alpha} \\ &= \frac{h(r, \alpha)\, k(\alpha)}{\int h(r, \alpha | k(\alpha)\, \mathrm{d}\alpha} \\ &= k(\alpha|r). \end{aligned}$$

That is to say, when the density f factors this way the knowledge of the outcome contains all the information contained in the estimated effort, e. The efficient sharing would then require

$$\begin{aligned} \frac{U'_{\mathrm{P}}(r - P(r, e))}{U'_{\mathrm{A}}(P(r, e))} &= \lambda + \mu \frac{f_\alpha(r, e, \alpha)}{f(r, e, \alpha)} \\ &= \lambda + \mu \frac{h_\alpha(r, \alpha)}{h(r, \alpha)}, \end{aligned}$$

so the second-best payment will not depend on the estimated effort, e.

On the other hand, if $f(r, e, \alpha)$ does not factor into $g(r, e)\, h(r, e)$, then e is informative about α. Will the benefits of monitoring e be positive?

Theorem 13.4 (Holmstrom and Shavell). If e is an informative, observable, and costless predictor of α, the agency benefits from making payment contingent upon e.

Proof. Since e is informative there must be a non-trival set Y and its complemement Y^{c} such that:

$$\frac{\int_Y f_\alpha(r, e, \alpha)\, \mathrm{d}e}{\int_Y f(r, e, \alpha)\, \mathrm{d}e} > \frac{\int_{Y^{\mathrm{c}}} f_\alpha(r, e, \alpha)\, \mathrm{d}e}{\int_{Y^{\mathrm{c}}} f(r, e, \alpha)\, \mathrm{d}e}, \text{ for all } r, \alpha.$$

Otherwise we could choose $Y = (e, e + \mathrm{d}e)$ and this would imply that f_α/f is constant for all e. Choose two functions, $\nu(r)$ and $\xi(r)$, such that

$$\nu(r) > 0, \quad \xi(r) < 0,$$

and

$$\nu(r) \int_Y f(r, e, \alpha)\, \mathrm{d}e + \xi(r) \int_{Y^c} f(r, e, \alpha)\, \mathrm{d}e = 0, \quad \text{for all } r \text{ and } \alpha.$$

Consider adding to any payment contract $P(r)$, which only uses the outcome, a small multiple of the function

$$\hat{P}(e, r) = \begin{cases} \nu(r), & \text{for } e \in Y, \\ \xi(r), & \text{for } e \in Y^c. \end{cases}$$

This new payment contract, $P(r, e) = P(r) + \epsilon\hat{P}(e, r)$ has the same expected value for each r as $P(r)$ by the construction of ν and ξ. Take the derivative of the agent's expected utility with respect to ϵ and evaluate at $\epsilon = 0$;

$$\left.\frac{\partial \mathrm{E} U_\mathrm{A}}{\partial \epsilon}\right|_{\epsilon=0} = \int\int U'_\mathrm{A}(P(r))\, \hat{P}(e, r) f(r, e, \alpha)\, \mathrm{d}e\, \mathrm{d}r$$
$$= \int U'_\mathrm{A}(P(r)) \int \hat{P}(e, r) f(r, e, \alpha)\, \mathrm{d}e\, \mathrm{d}r$$
$$= 0.$$

That is to say, the agent's expected utility does not change if a small payment based on $P(e)$ is incorporated into the contract. Take the derivative of the principal's Lagrangian with respect to ϵ;

$$\left.\frac{\partial L}{\partial \epsilon}\right|_{\epsilon=0} = \int\int - U'_\mathrm{P}(r - P(r))\, \hat{P}(e, r)\, \mathrm{d}F(r, e, \alpha) + \lambda \int\int U'_\mathrm{A}(P(r))\, \hat{P}(e, r)\, \mathrm{d}F(r, e,$$
$$+ \mu \int\int U'_\mathrm{A}(P(r))\, \hat{P}(e, r) f_\alpha(r, e, \alpha)\, \mathrm{d}e\, \mathrm{d}r$$
$$= \int (- U'_\mathrm{P}(r - P(r)) + \lambda U'_\mathrm{A}(P(r))\, \mathrm{E}\{\hat{P}(e, r)\}\, \mathrm{d}F(r, \alpha)$$
$$+ \mu \int U'_\mathrm{A}(P(r)) \left(\int_Y \nu(r) f_\alpha(r, e, \alpha)\, \mathrm{d}e + \int_{Y^c} \xi(r) f_\alpha(r, e, \alpha)\, \mathrm{d}e \right) \mathrm{d}r$$
$$= \mu \int U'_\mathrm{A}(P(r)) \left[\nu(r) \int_Y f_\alpha(r, e, \alpha)\, \mathrm{d}e + \xi(r) \int_{Y^c} f_\alpha(r, e, \alpha)\, \mathrm{d}e \right] \mathrm{d}r.$$

From the definition of $\nu(r)$ and $\xi(r)$ we know that

$$\xi(r)/\nu(r) = - \int_Y f(r, e, \alpha)\, \mathrm{d}e \Big/ \int_{Y^c} f(r, e, \alpha)\, \mathrm{d}e.$$

Substituting this into the above derivative gives:

$$\left.\frac{\partial L}{\partial \epsilon}\right|_{\epsilon=0} = \mu \int U'_{\mathrm{A}}(P(r))\, \nu(r) \left(\int_Y f(r, e, \alpha)\, \mathrm{d}e\right)$$

$$\times \left[\frac{\int_Y f_\alpha(r, e, \alpha)\, \mathrm{d}e}{\int_Y f(r, e, \alpha)\, \mathrm{d}e} - \frac{\int_{Y^{\mathrm{c}}} f_\alpha(r, e, \alpha)\, \mathrm{d}e}{\int_{Y^{\mathrm{c}}} f(r, e, \alpha)\, \mathrm{d}e} \right] \mathrm{d}r.$$

Since $\mu > 0$ by theorem 13.3, $U'_{\mathrm{A}} > 0$, $\nu(r) > 0$, and the term in square brackets is positive by the construction of the sets Y and Y^{c}, we have

$$\left.\frac{\partial L}{\partial \epsilon}\right|_{\epsilon=0} > 0.$$

The principal is made better-off when a small multiple of $\hat{P}(e, r)$ is added to any payment contract which is not contingent on estimated effort e. Since the agent was unaffected, the second-best contract must have e-contingent terms. ∎

This result should not be interpreted as saying that the principal always monitors the agent, because the cost of monitoring may exceed the benefits. The shareholders of the firm may find day-to-day monitoring of the management too costly but may find that an external audit, checking for excessive perquisites, has a low enough cost and high enough value to be worth while. The entrepreneur's problem discussed above indicates that there is a cost to the agent for his inability to warranty his behavior.

The second-best payment contract when the principal monitors the agent is characterized by the condition:

$$\frac{U'_{\mathrm{P}}(r - P(e, r))}{U'_{\mathrm{A}}(P(e, r))} = \lambda + \mu \frac{f_\alpha(r, e, \alpha)}{f(r, e, \alpha)}, \quad \text{for all } r, e.$$

The marginal share of the outcome paid to the agent is found by differentiating this condition with respect to r and solving for $\partial P/\partial r$:

$$\frac{\partial P}{\partial r} = \frac{\tau_{\mathrm{A}}}{\tau_{\mathrm{A}} + \tau_{\mathrm{P}}} \left(1 + \mu \frac{U'_{\mathrm{A}}}{U'_{\mathrm{P}}} \cdot \frac{\partial}{\partial r}\left(\frac{f_\alpha}{f}\right) \tau_{\mathrm{P}}\right),$$

where τ_{A} is the agent's measure of tolerance of risk, $\tau_{\mathrm{A}} = -U'_{\mathrm{A}}/U''_{\mathrm{A}}$, the reciprocal of his measure of absolute risk aversion. The marginal payment is related directly to the proportion of the agent's risk tolerance in the total agency risk tolerance. From theorem 13.1 we know that a risk neutral agent, $\tau_A = \infty$, has no problem of malfeasance, $\mu = 0$, so the marginal share is 1. On the other hand, if the principal is risk neutral, this does not imply that the marginal share of the agent is zero; $\tau_P = \infty$ implies that the marginal share equals

$$\frac{\partial P}{\partial r} = \mu \frac{U'_A}{U'_P} \frac{\partial}{\partial r}\left(\frac{f_\alpha}{f}\right) \neq 0.$$

The Lagrange multiplier μ might be interpreted as the expected marginal cost of malfeasance. The larger is this malfeasance cost, the more sensitive is payment to reward. The term f_α/f equals the derivative of $\ln f(r, e, \alpha)$ with respect to the agent's action. Holmstrom (1979) interpreted $\ln f$ as a log-likelihood function, indicating the probability that this r would be observed if the action had been α. If its derivative with respect to α is positive, this gives evidence that a more likely explanation would be that the agent took a larger action. When larger outcomes increase the evidence that the agent has been working hard, the payment should increase to provide motivation.

The second-best payment depends on the estimated effort and its sensitivity can be found just as above:

$$\frac{\partial P}{\partial e} = \mu \frac{U'_A}{U'_P} \frac{\partial}{\partial e}\left(\frac{f_\alpha}{f}\right) \frac{\tau_A \tau_P}{\tau_A + \tau_P}.$$

Again interpreting f_α/f as the degree of evidence for harder work, if larger e makes it seem more likely that α was large, then payment increases with estimated effort.

CHAPTER 14

HIERARCHICAL SUPERVISION AND LOSS OF CONTROL

The single proprietor firm is limited by the capacity of the owner-manager to organize production activities, monitor the random fluctuations in technological characteristics, and supervise the workers who must carry out the physical operations involved in production. If there was no way for the owner to supplement his own endowment of management energy, the size of the firm would be limited by the diminishing returns of the variable inputs. Therefore one should expect classical entrepreneural-run firms to be relatively small in comparison to total output of the entire industry (see Robinson, 1934; Kaldor, 1934; and Williamson, 1967).

However, the job of managing a production process is as open to specialization of labor as is the actual physical operations which the technology requires for production. The owner may hire managers to supervise various parts of the production and may concentrate his efforts on monitoring only these managers. If the technology requires many disparate activities, then the owner may decide to add more and more layers to a management hierarchy. It is not clear that management-supervision continues to be reasonable explanation for eventual diseconomies of scale.

However, the transmission of information is commonly thought to produce severe distortions if the information must pass through several individuals. Moreover, even the most energetic supervisor cannot monitor all the actions of his subordinates. Therefore the informational difficulties of supervision in a multi-tiered hierarchy are thought to lead to a "loss of control". That is, there appears to be a cumulative inability to get workers to perform those tasks which would be thought most desirable from the owner's viewpoint.

In this chapter we develop models of hierarchical supervision which allow us to theorize about the economic and technical conditions which might limit the size of an organization. The models are based on work done by Beckmann (1960, 1977), Williamson (1967), and Calvo and Wellisz (1978). Beckmann has formulated the theory of management production functions and used these to explore the limits of firm size. Williamson has a particularly simple specification of management's contribution which sheds light on the optimal number of management tiers in a firm. However, he assumes that there is an exogenous loss of control at each level. Calvo and Wellisz give explanations of the underlying informational situations which may or may not lead to limited firm size through loss of management control.

Beckmann (1977) looks at a business firm as consisting of H administration levels, $h = 1, 2, ..., H$, plus a production tier, $h = 0$. The top level $h = H$ will be referred to as the entrepreneur. At each hierarchical level h it is postulated that supervision of lower level $h - 1$ personnel is accomplished by combining the labor of managers and the supervision from above. Let y_h be the units of supervision produced at level h, and let there be x_h supervisors at this level who each contribute 1 unit of labor. The supervision from above and the effort of management at hierarchical level h combine to produce supervision of subordinates according to a production function,

$$y_h = f_h(x_h, y_{h+1}).$$

At the production level $h = 0, x_0$ is interpreted as production labor and the resulting output, y_0, is sold at a price P. It will be assumed that the entrepreneur at the top of the hierarchy is unsupervised and always contributes 1 unit of effort:

$$y_H = x_H = 1.$$

The technology of supervision will exhibit constant returns to scale if the production function can be written as

$$y_h = x_h f_h(1, y_{h+1}/x_h) = x_h g_h(y_{h+1}/x_h).$$

It will be assumed that constant returns to supervision hold; any limitations in the size of the firm will not be attributed to limitations in the supervision at some hierarchical level.

The output of the hierarchical firm can be found by composition of the supervision production functions

$$y_0 = x_0 g_0 \left(\frac{x_1}{x_0} g_1 \left(\frac{x_2}{x_1} g_2 \left(\frac{x_3}{x_2} \cdots g_{H-1} \left(\frac{1}{x_{H-1}} \right) \cdots \right) \right) \right).$$

The term x_h/x_{h-1} tells as the fraction of a supervisor's time at level h spent monitoring each of his subordinates. Its reciprocal, x_{h-1}/x_h, is called the span of control and will be denoted σ_h. The larger the span of control, the more subordinates a manager must supervise. Since the entrepreneur's labor is fixed, the aggregate production does not exhibit constant returns to scale. The span of control of the entrepreneur rises when the size of the work force doubles.

Following Beckmann (1977), we will now specify the technology of supervision using Cobb–Douglas production functions:

$$f_h(x_h, y_{h+1}) = x_h^{1-\beta} y_{h+1}^{\beta}, \qquad 0 \leqslant \beta \leqslant 1.$$

The elasticity of supervision at level h with respect to supervision from above, β, is assumed to be constant for all hierarchical levels; as Beckmann says, "administration is administration no matter at what level". The overall productivity of management and production labor is given by the above composite function:

$$y_0 = x_0 \left(\frac{x_1}{x_0}\left(\frac{x_2}{x_1} \cdots \left(\frac{1}{x_{H-1}}\right)^{\beta} \cdots\right)^{\beta}\right)^{\beta}$$

$$= \prod_{h=0}^{H-1} x_h^{(1-\beta)\beta^h}.$$

That the technology exhibits decreasing returns to scale follows from

$$\sum_{h=0}^{H-1} (1-\beta)\beta^h = 1 - \beta^H < 1.$$

If production of supervision depends little on monitoring from above, $\beta \cong 0$, then for very small number of hierarchical levels the firm exhibits almost constant returns.

If supervisors and workers can be hired in labor markets at wages w_h, $h = 0, \ldots, H-1$, then the organization's reward, profit to the entrepreneur, with H hierarchical tiers, is:

$$r = P \prod_{h=0}^{H-1} \left(x_h^{(1-\beta)\beta^h}\right) - \sum_{h=0}^{H-1} w_h x_h.$$

The entrepreneur maximizes profit by choosing the structure of the hierarchy so that the marginal revenue product of each supervisor and worker equals their wage:

$$\frac{\partial r}{\partial x_h} = P \prod_{j=0}^{H-1} x_j^{(1-\beta)\beta^j} \cdot (1-\beta)\beta^h x_h^{-1} - w_h = 0.$$

This requires the span of control to satisfy

$$\sigma_h = \frac{x_{h-1}}{x_h} = \frac{1}{\beta}\frac{w_h}{w_{h-1}}.$$

The span of control will increase if the productivity of direct supervision, $1-\beta$, increases. The span of control must adjust so that the total wage bill of a management level is a fraction β of the wage bill of those they supervise. This does not say that higher level management has lower salaries, but does imply that if wages are approximately equal, the span of control will be greater than 1. When management's salaries increase relative to their subordinates, their span of control will increase as fewer managers are hired relative to subordinates.

Solving the marginal conditions for $x_0, x_1, ..., x_{H-1}$ gives

$$x_h^* = \frac{\beta^h}{w_h} P^{\beta} \prod_{j=0}^{H-1} (w_j^{-(1-\beta)\beta^{j-H}})\, \beta^{(\beta^{-H}-1)\beta/(1-\beta)^{-H}}.$$

Substituting this into the definition of profit and simplifying, the maximum profit equals

$$r^* = P^{\beta^{-H}}(1-\beta)^{\beta^{-H}-1}\, \beta^{(\beta^{-H}-1)\beta/(1-\beta)} \prod_{h=0}^{H-1} (w_h^{-(1-\beta)\beta^{h-H}}).$$

It is convenient to take the logarithm of maximum profits for an organization with H hierarchical levels:

$$\log r^*(H) = \beta^{-H}\left(\log P + \log(1-\beta) + \frac{\beta}{1-\beta}\log\beta - (1-\beta)\sum_{h=0}^{H-1}\beta^h \log w_h\right)$$
$$-\left(\log(1-\beta) + \frac{\beta}{1-\beta}\log\beta\right).$$

Does maximum profit go up when hierarchy is extended? Taking the difference in logarithms of profits we find:

$$\log r^*(H+1) - \log r^*(H) = \beta^{-H}\,\frac{1-\beta}{\beta}\left[\log P + \log(1-\beta) + \frac{\beta}{1-\beta}\log\beta - (1-\beta)\sum_{h=0}^{H-1}\beta^h\log w_h\right]$$
$$-\frac{1-\beta}{\beta}\log w_H.$$

This is non-negative when

$$\log P - \log w_0 + \log (1 - \beta) + \frac{\beta}{1-\beta} \log \beta \geqslant \sum_{h=1}^{H} \beta^h \log \left(\frac{w_h}{w_{h-1}}\right).$$

Notice that a unit increase in H increases the right-hand side by

$$\beta^{H+1} \log \left(\frac{w_{H+1}}{w_H}\right).$$

Unless wages rise very rapidly with hierarchical level, this term will not be very large. In fact it is quite possible that although the firm's technology exhibits decreasing returns to scale, no finite optimal H exists. The entrepreneur will find it optimal to expand his hierarchy until this inequality is reversed. If we ignore the integer nature of H, the optimal number of hierarchical levels, H^*, if it exists, must satisfy

$$\log P - \log w_0 + \log (1 - \beta) + \frac{\beta}{1-\beta} \log \beta = \sum_{h=1}^{H^*} \beta^h \log \left(\frac{w_h}{w_{h-1}}\right).$$

When supervisors' wages exceed those of subordinates at all levels, $w_h > w_{h-1}$, the right-hand side of this equation increases with H^*. This allows us to make the following comparative static statements. First, when the price of output rises or the wages of production workers fall, the degree of hierarchy increases. The reasoning is that large outputs are optimal and the larger resulting production force requires more supervisors. Since the span of control is optimally fixed independent of these factors, the height of the hierarchical pyramid must increase. Second, an increase in the salary of a level h manager impacts the right-hand side in two terms:

$$\beta^h \log \frac{w_h}{w_{h-1}} + \beta^{h+1} \log \frac{w_{h+1}}{w_h} = \beta^h \log w_h^{1-\beta} + \beta^h \log \frac{w_{h+1}^{\beta}}{w_{h-1}},$$

and when simplified clearly increases the right-hand side. The entrepreneur's optimal response is to decrease the extent of the hierarchy, reasoning that the decrease in employment at any level, given the span of control already determined for superordinates, will make fewer levels necessary. Third, the productivity of direct supervision, β, enters both sides of the optimality equation but nonetheless has a unique impact on H. Taking the derivative of the left-hand side and treating logarithms as natural logarithms gives:

$$\frac{\partial}{\partial \beta}\left(\log (1-\beta) + \frac{\beta}{1-\beta} \log \beta\right) = \frac{-1}{1-\beta} + \left(\frac{\beta}{1-\beta} + \frac{\beta}{(1-\beta)^2}\right) \log \beta + \frac{\beta}{1-\beta}$$

$$= \frac{1}{(1-\beta)^2} \log \beta.$$

The assumption that $\beta < 1$ implies that the left-hand side decreases as β increases. Taking the partial derivative of the right-hand side gives:

$$\sum_{h=1}^{H^*} h\beta^{h-1} \log\left(\frac{w_h}{w_{h-1}}\right),$$

and assuming wages increase with hierarchical level, this implies the right-hand side increases with β. In order to preserve the equality, H^* must decrease as β increases. Mathematics aside, an increase in β signifies an increase in productivity of supervision by superordinates and a decrease in the productivity of direct management. As seen above, the span of control, σ_h, must fall at all hierarchical levels, making each hierarchical level less productive and decreasing the optimal number of hierarchical levels. Thes results are summarized in table 14.1

Table 14.1

Parameter	P	w_0	w_h	β
Response of H^* to increase in the parameter	+	–	–	–

Williamson (1967) developed a model to characterize the optimal number of tiers in a hierarchy by specifying a different technology than Beckmann's. The span of control is constant at all levels so employment is determined by the formula

$$x_h = \sigma^{H-h}.$$

Each worker spends only a fraction t of each work day pursuing supervision or production, so total output is given by

$$y_0 = (t\sigma)^H.$$

For convenience it is assumed that each manager is paid a constant multiple of his employee's wage:

$$w_h = w_0 w^h, \quad h \geqslant 0, \quad w > 1.$$

The profit which becomes the entrepreneur's reward equals:

$$r = P(t\sigma)^H - \sum_{h=0}^{H-1} w_0 w^h \sigma^{H-h}$$

$$= P(t\sigma)^H - w_0 \sigma^H \sum_{h=0}^{H-1} \left(\frac{w}{\sigma}\right)^h$$

$$= P(t\sigma)^H - w_0 \sigma^H \frac{(w/\sigma)^H - 1}{w/\sigma - 1} .$$

Treating H as a continuous variable, the derivative of profit with respect to the number of hierarchical levels can be calculated as:

$$\frac{\partial r}{\partial H} = P(t\sigma)^H \ln(t\sigma) - \frac{w_0 \sigma^{H+1}}{\sigma - w} \left(\ln \sigma - \left(\frac{w}{\sigma}\right)^H \ln w\right) .$$

For small H it is not always true that this derivative is positive, but for sufficiently large P/w_0 a positive H seems desirable. Unlike the technology used by Beckmann, here the firm always has an optimal finite chain of command; the limit of $\partial r/\partial H$ is a positive multiple of

$$\frac{-w_0 \sigma}{\sigma - w} \ln \sigma,$$

and hence an infinite H is undesirable. Since typically the span of control is in the neighborhood of 5 and the wage markup factor w is around 1 or 2, the term $(w/\sigma)^H \ln w$ is negligible for H of moderate size. Treating that term as zero allows us to set the derivative equal to zero and find the approximate optimal hierarchical size:

$$H^* = \left[\ln\left(\frac{w_0}{P}\right) + \ln\left(\frac{\sigma}{\sigma - w}\right) + \ln\left(\frac{\ln \sigma}{\ln(t\sigma)}\right)\right] \Big/ \ln t.$$

Many of the comparative static results of Beckmann's model carry over to Williamson's solution. Of some significance is the fact that an increase in worker's diligence, t, causes a definite increase in the length of the chain of command. Recall that a change in β, the effectiveness of supervision per subordinate in Beckmann's formulation, had a similar effect on H^*. It is possible to deduce that an increase in the proportional growth factor of wages in the hierarchy, w, causes the number of levels of supervision to decrease. As the span of control increases, the hierarchy will increase and the organization will have a longer chain of command as well as a larger number of supervisors at each level. This somewhat surprising result follows because the diligence of workers is unaffected by the intensity of supervision. More generally, t will decreases as σ increases and, depending on its elasticity, we may have a less surprising result.

The above analysis of the limits on hierarchical size is based on the assumption that at each stage there is a loss of control and that this cumulates down the organization pyramid until final output is proportional to $(t\sigma)^H$. Beckmann's formulation makes this loss of control more flexible, but also does not really explain why all labor inputs into the supervision process do not fully succeed in controlling subordinates. Williamson argues that the informational imperfection of supervision is the reason for this loss of control. However, Mirrlees (1976) and Calvo and Wellisz (1978) present models which seem to indicate that informational difficulties alone cannot lead to this loss of control. It appears that the loss of control depends on exactly how the informational difficulties arise when supervisors try to prevent shirking.

In order to explore effort, shirking, and supervision, we must introduce preferences for labor and income. In the Beckmann–Williamson models labor supply was assumed to be inelastic. Suppose that all individuals, whether manager or production workers, have preferences represented by the utility function

$$U = U(r) - D(\alpha),$$

where α represents effort and takes on values between zero and one.

The monitoring system proposed by Calvo and Wellisz (1978) is very simple. Workers are spot-checked by their supervisors, and when checked are paid in proportion to the level of effort. If they are not checked then the supervisor gives them credit for complete effort. A worker monitored with probability q expects a utility equal to

$$q(U(w\alpha) - D(\alpha)) + (1 - q)(U(w) - D(\alpha)).$$

The optimal effort from the worker's perspective is denoted

$$\alpha = \alpha(q, w),$$

and the maximum expected utility is designated

$$\mathrm{E}U(q, w).$$

The organization consists of H supervisory hierarchical levels plus a production unit. The probability of being monitored at level h is presumed to be some function of the degree of supervision or span of control:

$$q_h = q\left(\frac{\alpha_h x_h}{x_{h-1}}\right),$$

where x_{h-1} is the number of workers at level $h - 1$ and $\alpha_h x_h$ is the number of effective supervisors at level h. The effective span of control equals $x_{h-1}/\alpha_h x_h$. The effort of the workers at level $h - 1$ is thus:

$$\alpha_{h-1} = \alpha\left(q\left(\frac{\alpha_h x_h}{x_{h-1}}\right), w_{h-1}\right)$$
$$= \bar{\alpha}\left(\frac{\alpha_h x_h}{x_{h-1}}, w_{h-1}\right).$$

The workers have alternative employment opportunities, so not just any supervision scheme and wage will attract them to the organization. The firm faces a utility floor constraint:

$$\mathrm{E}U\left(q\left(\frac{\alpha_h x_h}{x_{h-1}}\right), w_{h-1}\right) \geqslant \bar{U}, \qquad h = 1, 2, ..., H.$$

The top level supervisor receives the residual profit.

The firm produces output from effective production workers with a linear technology that generated profits of

$$r(H) = \beta x_0 \alpha - \sum_{h=0}^{H-1} w_h x_h (q_h \alpha_h + (1 - q_h) \cdot 1).$$

The organization determines its supervision–production schedule, $x_0, x_1, ..., x_H$, and wage schedule, $w_0, w_1, ..., w_H$, to maximize profits subject to the constraints on expected utility.

Calvo and Wellisz (1978) show that this system of organization cannot lead to a finite positive size hierarchy. In particular, if it pays to hire any workers then it pays to increase the layers of the administration without bound. This proposition is verified under the assumption that $x_H = 1$. Let $r^*(H)$ be the maximum profits of a firm with H tiers in the hierarchy. Suppose that profit with 1 tier exceeds self-produced income:

$$\beta < r^*(1) = \beta x_0^* \bar{\alpha}\left(\frac{1}{x_0^*}, w_0^*\right) -$$
$$- w_0^* x_0^* \left[1 - q\left(\frac{1}{x_0^*}\right)\left(1 - \bar{\alpha}\left(\frac{1}{x_0^*}, w_0^*\right)\right)\right].$$

Let $\gamma^* = 1/x_0^*$, $\alpha^* = \bar{\alpha}(1/x_0^*, w_0^*)$, $q^* = q(1/x_0^*)$, and write this constraint as

$$\beta\gamma^* < \beta\alpha^* - w_0^*[1 - q^*(1 - \alpha^*)].$$

Now suppose that for $h > 1$ we set $w_h = w_0^*$, $\alpha_h = \alpha^*$, $\alpha_h x_h / x_{h-1} = \gamma^*$, with $1/x_{H-1} = \gamma^*$, and $q_h = q^*$. This implies

$$x_h = \frac{\gamma^{*2}}{\alpha^*} \left(\frac{\alpha^*}{\gamma^*}\right)^{H-h}, \quad h = 0, \ldots, H-1.$$

This supervision–production scheme and wage schedule will not be profit maximizing in general but it does satisfy the expected utility constraint since by definition of optimality of

$$\mathrm{E}U\left(q\left(\frac{\alpha_h x_h}{x_{h-1}}\right), w_{h-1}\right) = \mathrm{E}U(q(\gamma^*), w_0^*) \geqslant \bar{U}.$$

The change in profits when H is increased by 1 layer using the above rules is:

$$r(H) - r(H-1) =$$

$$= \beta \frac{\gamma^{*2}}{\alpha^*} \left(\frac{\alpha^*}{\gamma^*}\right)^H \alpha^* - \sum_{h=0}^{H-1} w_0^* \frac{\gamma^{*2}}{\alpha^*} \left(\frac{\alpha^*}{\gamma^*}\right)^{H-h} (1 - \alpha^*))$$

$$- \gamma \frac{\gamma^{*2}}{\alpha^*} \left(\frac{\alpha^*}{\gamma^*}\right)^{H-1} \alpha^* - \sum_{h=0}^{H-2} w_0^* \frac{\gamma^{*2}}{\alpha^*} \left(\frac{\alpha^*}{\gamma^*}\right)^{H-1-h} (1 - q^*(1 - \alpha^*))$$

$$= \beta \gamma^{*2} \left(\frac{\alpha^*}{\gamma^*}\right)^H \left(1 - \frac{\gamma^*}{\alpha^*}\right) - w_0^* \frac{\gamma^{*2}}{\alpha^*} \left(\frac{\alpha^*}{\gamma^*}\right)^H (1 - q^*(1 - \alpha^*))$$

$$= \frac{\gamma^{*2}}{\alpha^*} \left(\frac{\alpha^*}{\gamma^*}\right)^H [\beta\alpha^* - \beta\gamma^* - w_0^*(1 - q^*(1 - e^*))].$$

The term in square brackets is positive by the above assumption that $\beta < r^*(1)$. The term α^*/γ^* is greater than unity because otherwise the term is square brackets would be negative. We conclude that

$$\lim_{H \to \infty} (r(H) - r(H-1)) = \infty,$$

and $r(H) - r(H-1) > 0$ for all H. Since maximum profit for hierarchical level H must exceed $r(H)$, and since $r(H)$ grows to ∞, it must be that maximum profit is an unbounded function of administration staff levels.

By this argument Calvo and Wellisz show that loss of control due to shirking by employees cannot by itself put a lid on the hierarchy. Something further must be said about the monitoring techniques if we are to be sure that information losses lead to scale diseconomies of administration.

In order to develop sufficient conditions for finite hierarchical size Calvo and Wellisz modify the above by assuming that employees can identify some periods of time during which they are not monitored. Suppose that employees at level h can observe their supervisor leaving for a coffee break. During this period they too can relax without fear of losing pay for shirking. Let us assume that during that period of time with length $1 - \alpha_{h+1}$, where α_{h+1} is the effort of the supervisor, the employees at level h can stop working entirely without financial repercussions. The worker puts in effort $\tilde{\alpha}_h$ for the remainder of the work shift but the total effort is only

$$\alpha_h = \alpha_{h+1}\,\tilde{\alpha}_h.$$

The expected utility from this is

$$q_h\,U(\alpha_{h+1}w_h + (1 - \alpha_{h+1})w_h\tilde{\alpha}_h) + (1 - q_h)\,U(w_h) - D(\alpha_{h+1}\,\tilde{\alpha}_h).$$

Let the optimal effort be denoted

$$\tilde{\alpha}_h = \tilde{\alpha}(q_h, w_h, \alpha_{h+1}),$$

and the maximum expected utility

$$\widetilde{EU}(q_h, w_h, \alpha_{h+1}).$$

Again we shall assume that the probability of detection depends on $\alpha_h x_h/x_{h-1}$, the inverse of the effective span of control, and write the composition of probability and effort function as

$$\tilde{\alpha}_h = \tilde{\tilde{\alpha}}(\alpha_{h+1}x_{h+1}/x_h, w_h, \alpha_{h+1}).$$

The output of the firm is determined by the supervised effort of workers, which is given by

$$\alpha_h = \alpha_{h+1}\,\tilde{\alpha}_h$$

and

$$\alpha_H = \tilde{\alpha}_H = 1.$$

This difference equation has a solution

$$\alpha_0 = \tilde{\alpha}_0\,\tilde{\alpha}_1\,\dots\,\tilde{\alpha}_{H-1}.$$

The firm wants to select $x_0, ..., x_{H-1}$ and $w_0, ..., w_{H-1}$ to maximize

$$r(H) = \beta\tilde{\alpha}_0\, \tilde{\alpha}_1 \,...\, \tilde{\alpha}_{H-1} x_0 - \sum_{h=0}^{H-1} w_h x_h (1 + q_h(\alpha_h - 1)).$$

In order that profit be unlimited as layers are added to the administration hierarchy, it is necessary that

$$\lim_{H\to\infty} \tilde{\tilde{\alpha}}(x_H^*/x_{H-1}^*, w_H^*, 1) \geqslant 1.$$

Otherwise, revenue would decline until profits are negative. Turning this argument around, if

$$\tilde{\tilde{\alpha}}(x_H/x_{H-1}, w_H, 1) < 1, \quad \text{for all } x_H/x_{H-1}, w_H,$$

then the most desirable size hierarchy cannot be infinitely large. This condition says that it is impossible to completely prevent shirking by adjusting the probability of detection and wage. This is exactly the type of restriction which Williamson uses to limit the size of the hierarchy.

CHAPTER 15

FORMAL ORGANIZATION OF DECISION-MAKING

The previous chapters explained why there may be roles for administration, management, judgement, and supervision in the allocation of resources in an economy. In a nutshell, authority replaces contractual exchanges because of the difficulties that occur in an environment with uncertainty and differing information. Since activities of employees are more productive when they are selected after natural circumstances have been observed, the employment relationship involves adjustments to the evolving situation. One way to create this flexibility is to introduce hierarchy in the decision-making process; a group of workers grant an individual the authority to direct their actions in the workplace. Because projects involve many workers the production process is subdivided and a nesting of authority associations is created where supervisors themselves have supervisors.

Authority necessarily gives the controlling individual freedom to choose the activities of the supervised individual, but this does not mean that unlimited power is placed in the hands of the supervisor. In fact, the specification of the job is nothing other than a description of the tasks that might be performed and the frequency with which they must be executed. The worker enters a subordinate position with an understanding of the nature of the activities, although the exact sequence of tasks is left undetermined until the supervisor has observed the environment and determined the most appropriate response.

To be in a subordinate position in an organization's hierarchy is not to be in a position of disesteem. The subordinates' activities may be extremely complicated, requiring great skill and training. The subordinate position may in fact have a higher attractiveness to most individuals. In institutions of higher education the position of departmental chairman is not attractive to most professors, although it is a position of authority. The director of a hospital is not always a more admired individual than the brain surgeon who works under him. The music directorship of a symphony orchestra is not necessarily a position that musicians in the orchestra want to hold. The objective of these examples is to take some of the derogation out of the term "subordinate" and make the word "authority" seem less pejorative.

Moreover, subordinates are not powerless to influence their work conditions. In non-coercive economies individuals are free to choose their profession as well as employer. When an individual has very strong distaste for working indoors, jobs which do not involve enough exposure to the elements may be rejected. This freedom of job choice may not lead a particular individual to a satisfying job because his desires do not match the offers presently being made by the collection of employers. However, the aggregate effect is to force employers to modify the work conditions until the job is acceptable. The entry and exit of individuals into particular job types has an influence on the work conditions; this is sometimes underrated in the face of the obvious influence that the employer holds over job offers. The presence of a rich list of attractive alternatives available to workers may be more important in determining the job characteristics than the employer's wishes.

Hirschman (1970) has pointed out that most members of organizations have an alternative to "exiting" when faced with undesirable job characteristics – they can "voice" their complaints and attempt to restructure the demands placed upon them. The typical worker renews his contract with the employer on a recurring, regular basis. While he grants the employer authority during the execution of the employment, the renegotiation of the contract is not done in a coercive fashion. The worker at this junction can propose modifications to the job description just as easily as the employer. The worker may want to add or subtract particular activities from the job description or may want to increase or reduce the frequency which current activities are required.

The employee's proposed modifications may require alteration in the job characteristics of fellow employees. For example, a worker might suggest that he spend less time performing preventive maintenance and therefore the repair-person will have to spend more time fixing inoperative machines. As a second example, when a salesperson suggests that he offer a product to a new group of customers, this may lead to increased sales and thus to more effort from the production workers. The interdependence of the activities of many employees makes the negotiation of suitable job descriptions necessarily a complex and costly procedure. If there is no uniform structure to the procedure of formulating the goals and job descriptions of employees, the members of the organization may have to invest a large amount of time in negotiation.

In order to simplify the process of determining the goals and resulting plans for adjusting tasks to changing circumstances, a formal organization is created. The formal organization consists of a set of roles or positions in the organization along with a constitution which specifies how the beliefs and desires of the individuals who hold those positions are reconciled to produce a group decision.

For example, suppose that a firm consists of an owner, a foreman, and several workers. The individual who fills the owner position might have the unilateral right to determine the output, the manager might have the unilateral right to determine the capital stock and total hours of labor service, and the workers by majority voting determine how they will divide the labor among them.

Formal organizations exist to help groups of individuals coordinate the desires, ambitions, and resources of the members in such a way as to achieve successful group activities. The choice of such formal organizations may be based on the relative desirability of various aspects of the organization's structure, such as the immunity from dishonest manipulation, the efficiency of group decisions, the rights guaranteed individual members, and the coherency of the organization's choices. The following sections provide a series of results which are basically negative. The desirable aspects of formal organizations seem to be in conflict more often than not. The choice of a formal organization will typically involve the rejection of one or more basic attributes that are attractive. This situation signals the fact that internal organization of resource allocation will not be the solution to all types of problems.

Organizations must decide between alternative group activities. Because an organization is nothing but a collection of natural agents, the actual decision must reflect a compromise of conflicting views within the membership of the organization. Since the alternatives and membership of an organization vary from time to time, the formal organization is partially defined by the method of resolving conflicting attitudes about the group activities. Political economists have investigated in great detail the properties of many methods of group decision-making in their studies of collective choice rules (Arrow, 1951a; Sen, 1970a; Fishburn, 1973). This chapter will precisely define the concept of collective choice rules used for constitutionally aggregating the views, judgements, or interests of a group of individuals. An organization may want its collective choice rule to perform well in varied circumstances. A set of apparently reasonable restrictions on the collective choice rule are postulated, but it is then discovered that only one class of collective choice rules (dictatorial) can satisfy these restrictions. It is shown that such a result does not disappear when the problem is modified in various fashions.

Let $\mathscr{A}$ be a fixed set of alternatives from which the group must make a collective choice. The generic element of $\mathscr{A}$, denoted $a \in \mathscr{A}$, is a complete specification of the activities to be performed by all the members of the organization. This may include productive as well as distributive aspects of group activities. The membership of the organization consists of n positions indexed by $i \in N =$

$\{1, 2, ..., n\}$. The index i not only represents a different natural agent but also may represent the position the natural agent holds in the decision-making structure of the organization. Hence, two indices i and j, $i \neq j$, might represent the same natural agent playing dual roles in the decision-making process. For example, the president of a firm may also be the chairman of the board, or the chairman of a committee may also be a member of the committee.

It will be assumed that the members of the organization have well-defined preferences over the alternatives faced by the group. By this we mean that to each member has a binary relation, $a \succsim_i b$, between two alternatives $a, b \in \mathscr{A}$. The symbols "$a \succsim_i b$" is to be read as "member i desires a at least as much as b". In order to guarantee coherent decisions in simple choice problems it is usually assumed that these preferences satisfy the following.

Assumption. The preferences of member $i \in N, \succsim_i$, satisfy the following:

(a) For all $a \in \mathscr{A}, a \succsim_i a$ (reflexivity).
(b) For all $a, b, c, \in \mathscr{A}$ if $a \succsim_i b$ and $b \succsim_i c$, then $a \succsim_i c$ (transitivity).
(c) For all $a, b \in \mathscr{A}$, if $a \neq b$, then either $a \succsim_i b$ or $b \succsim_i a$ (complete).
Such binary relations are referred to as preference orderings

If member i was given a free hand to choose any element from a subset A of the set of alternatives, which we might call the *agenda*, it is assumed that he would choose the "best" alternative with respect to his preference relation.

Definition. An element $a \in A \subseteq \mathscr{A}$ is the *best* element of agenda A with respect to the preference ordering $\succsim_i$ if and only if for all $b \in A, a \succsim_i b$. The set of best elements in A for member i is called his choice set and is denoted $C_i(A, \succsim_i)$.

The choice set of a member i may be empty because the agenda includes an infinite number of alternatives. If any positive number of dollars is possible the member may be unable to choose because each number is not largest. However, with a finite agenda a member whose preferences are an ordering will be able to choose a best alternative.

It might appear that an individual i's choice of a best element from an agenda represents selfish behavior. This is not true. The alternatives may include differences in factors related to other members and member i may take positive pleasure (or displeasure) in these factors. He may choose an alternative to help his fellow members. Choice by member i may therefore involve altruistic motives.

Organizations are not expected to induce a "single collective mind" among its members. The choice of member i among the alternatives might be distinctly different from the choice of member j. In general

$$C_i(A, \succsim_i) \neq C_j(A, \succsim_j), \quad \text{when } i \neq j.$$

The organization is faced with the problem of making decisions when there are conflicting views about the desirability of various cooperative alternatives. If the organization is unable to reconcile the differences of opinion, interests, or judgments, then the group activity may revert to a *status quo* alternative which is undesirable to all members. Hence, most organizations explicitly or implicitly have a constitutional method for aggregating preference orderings or resolving differences in choices. A committee might have an implied constitution of majority voting; a business enterprise might have a ruling elite or even a dictator, depending on the ownership structure. What do we mean by a constitutional aggregation method and what properties would we like it to possess?

A *collective choice rule* (CCR) is a mapping which produces one organizational preference relation $\succsim_O$ from a preference profile $\succsim = (\succsim_1, ..., \succsim_n)$ of preference orderings of members. (The index $i = O$ denotes the organization.) The organization's preference relation $\succsim_O$ is not necessarily a preference ordering (reflexive, transitive, and complete), although this may well be a desirable situation. The organization's collective choice rule should be able to resolve conflicting opinions even if the members change their preferences over alternatives. When a committee uses majority voting, the choice may differ over time as members vary their beliefs, but the mechanism itself (majority voting) does not change as the preference profile changes.

It would be highly desirable for a collective choice rule, like majority voting, to be operable irrespective of the opinions held by the organization's membership. The collective choice rule may be used over and over again to help select group activities. Since the actual members of the organization may change from time to time, or the preference orderings of given members may change, it would be unattractive if the collective choice rule was not adaptable to the changing circumstances. This is crystallized in the following assumption.

Assumption U. The collective choice rule has as its domain the set of all logically possible n-tuples of individual preference orderings defined on $\mathscr{A}$ (Unrestricted preference profiles).

The collective choice rule produces a preference relation which represents the compromises and conciliations of the differing opinions of individual members. It would be useful if the relation $\succsim_O$ was also a preference ordering. If it violated reflexivity, then a choice could not be made even when the agenda had but one alternative. Without completeness the organization might be unable to choose when the agenda had but two alternatives. Finally, transitivity guarantees that choices from finite collections of activities can be made by the organization. This rationality on the part of the organization is formalized by the following restriction on the CCR.

Assumption O. The collective choice rule has a range which consists of reflexive, transitive, and complete binary relations (Organizational preference ordering).

If all members of the organization strictly prefer an alternative a to b ($a \succ_i b$, $i \in N$, where $a \succ_i b$ means $a \succsim_i b$ and not $b \succsim_i a$), then the organizational preferences should reasonably reflect a preference for a over b, strictly ($a \succ_O b$). This is a very old and distinguished assumption in economics, referred to as the Pareto principle.

Assumption P. If $a, b \in \mathscr{A}$ and $a \succ_i b$ for all $i \in N$, then $a \succ_O b$ (Pareto principle).

When the organization is faced with a choice from an agenda A it seems reasonable to focus attention only on the alternatives that can be chosen. If the organization's members change their attitudes about alternatives that are not under consideration, but not their attitudes about items on the agenda, the group choice should not change. For example, if the organization must decide whether to grow corn or potatoes the choice should not be dependent upon whether or not individuals would rather fish than farm. Such an assumption forces the group decision between two alternatives to depend only on the individual members' ordering of these two items and not on irrelevant alternatives.

Assumption IIA. Let $\succsim$ and $\succsim^*$ be two preference profiles which are identical on an agenda A but which may differ on the alternatives not on the agenda. Let $C_O(A, \succsim_O)$ and $C_O(A, \succsim_O^*)$ be the organizational choice sets corresponding to the organizational preferences determined by profiles $\succsim$ and $\succsim^*$, respectively. Then $C_O(A, \succsim_O) = C_O(A, \succsim_O^*)$ (Independence of irrelevant alternatives).

Finally, most individuals, even if they are willing to submit to a certain amount of authority, would like to have some say, however minute, in the determination of the goals or preferences of the organizations to which they belong. Limiting the organizational constitution to the class of collective choice rules which are dictatorial would be unacceptable for most organizations. Even the tight-fisted entrepreneur permits his employees to determine some aspects of the organizational activities.

Assumption ND. There is no $i \in N$ such that for all $a, b \in \mathscr{A}$, if $a \succ_i b$ then $a \succ_O b$, no matter what the preferences are between a, b for other members (Non-dictatorship).

We began by assuming that an organization has a collective choice rule which mapped profiles of preference orderings into preference relations defined on $\mathscr{A}$. By adding, successively, restrictions on CCR we have narrowed down the set of possible collective choice rules which the organization might use. Each restriction on its own seems reasonable, but in combination they turn out to be quite stringent. No collective choice rule exists which satisfies all of the above restrictions.

Impossibility theorem 1. There is no collective choice rule which satisfies all the assumptions U, O, P, IIA, and ND.

This theorem will not be proved in detail here. The reader is referred to the original proof in Arrow (1951a). However, the general idea can be illuminated by two lemmas. A set of individuals $V \subseteq N$ is determinant for a against b, $a, b \in \mathscr{A}$, if $a \succ_O$ when $a \succ_i$ for every $i \in V$, no matter what the preferences of individuals in N-V.

Lemma 1. If V is determinant for a against b, then V is decisive for any pair $c, d \in \mathscr{A}$.

The lemma is proved as follows. By assumption U it is possible that the preference orderings of the membership among three alternatives, a, b, and c, are

$$a \succ_i b \succ_i c, \quad \text{for } i \in V,$$

and

$$b \succ_j c \succ_j a, \quad \text{for } j \notin V.$$

Since V is determinant for a against b, the organization must rank a better than b:

$$a \succ_O b.$$

Assumption P applied to b and c must give

$$b \succ_O c.$$

By assumption O these two combine to imply

$$a \succ_O c.$$

However, in the preferences constructed above only members of group V like a better than c. By assumption IIA, this result cannot depend on the relative rankings *vis-à-vis* b, so V is also decisive for a against c.

Let us construct a second possible preference profile for the organization. Let

$$d \succ_i a \succ_i c, \quad \text{for } i \in V,$$

and

$$c \succ_j d \succ_j a, \quad \text{for } j \notin V.$$

By an exactly analogous argument as that above, it is shown that V is determinant for d against c, which was to be shown. ■

Lemma 2. If V is a determining group containing two or more members, a proper subgroup of V is also determinant.

To prove this, let A, B, and C be subsets of the membership M defined so that $A \subseteq V$, $A \neq V$, $B = V - A$, and $C = N - V$ (see fig. 15.1). Obviously the union of the disjoint sets A, B, and C is exactly the membership of the organization. By assumption U it is possible that the organization has the following preference profile for alternatives a, b, and c:

$$a \succ_i b \succ_i c, \quad \text{for } i \in A,$$

$$b \succ_j c \succ_j a, \quad \text{for } j \in B,$$

$$c \succ_k a \succ_k b, \quad \text{for } k \in C.$$

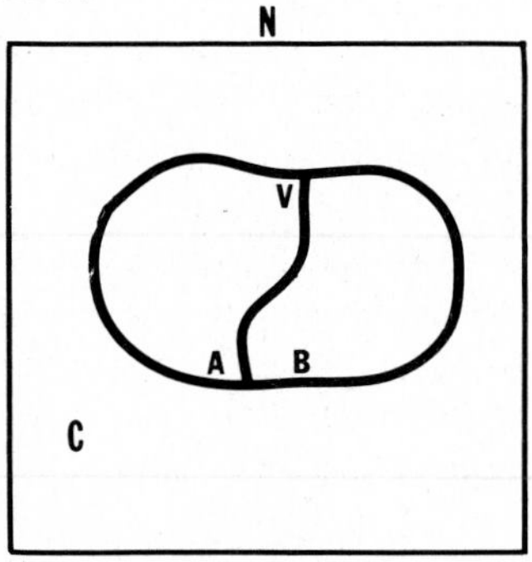

Figure 15.1

Since $V = A \cup B$ is determinant for b against c, the organizational ordering must be $b \succ_O c$. Suppose first that $b \succ_O a$; the members of group B are the only ones whose preferences correspond to the organization's preferences. Therefore B is determinant for b against a. Similarly, suppose $a \succsim_O b$; this makes group A determinant for a against c. In either case a proper subgroup of V is itself determinant, which was to be shown. ■

The above two lemmas require the use of assumptions U, O, P, and IIR. Nothing has been said about non-dictatorship, ND. There must be a determinant group V since at least the full membership must be determinant according to assumptions P and O. The second lemma says that any determinant group (containing at least two members) can be split and a proper subgroup will also be determinant. Since there are only a finite number of members in the organization, after at most n-1 such splits we are left with a determinant group consisting of one member. This member is determinant over all alternatives, by lemma 1, and hence is a dictator. The constitution must be dictatorial.

The above formulation is based on the supposition that a collective choice rule produces a preference relation on the set of alternatives $\mathscr{A}$. The set of alternatives should probably be viewed as "potential alternatives". At any given time the organization may be faced with a restricted subset of potential alternatives, $A \subseteq \mathscr{A}$, which represents the actual alternatives that may be selected. Since $\succsim_O$ is defined over $\mathscr{A}$, it is also defined over any agenda like A. As this agenda A varies, the organizational preferences, $\succsim_O$, determined by the CCR may be used to select best alternatives. However, if the objective of aggregation is the actual organizational decision, not the preference relation, it might seem reasonable to reformulate the problem so that the constitution produces decisions, not preference relations. Since the impossibility theorem is a negative result, perhaps its conclusion can be evaded by such a reformulation.

A *collective decision functional* (CDF) is a mapping which produces a choice function for the organization, $C_O(A)$, from a preference profile $\succsim = (\succsim_1, ..., \succsim_n)$ of the membership such that $C_O(A)$ is non-empty for all $A \subseteq \mathscr{A}$. That is to say, if the membership holds preferences, $\succsim$, the organization has a choice function C_O which is capable of making a decision no matter what alternatives are actually faced. A CDF concentrates directly on the decision-making not on the underlying preference structure of the organization.

To a limited degree this reformulation does help circumvent the above impossibility result. The CDF defined by $C_O(A) = \{a \in A \mid \text{for all } b \in A \text{ either } a \succ_i b$ for some $i \in N$ or $a \succsim_i b$ for all $i \in N\}$ satisfies assumptions U, IIA, P, and ND, and is non-empty for all agendas. However, the aid is only limited. Suppose we make a stronger restriction than non-dictatorship.

Assumption NO. There is no unique group of members of the organization $\mathrm{O} \subseteq N$ such that

(a) If $a \succ_i b$ for all $i \in \mathrm{O}$, then $a \in C_{\mathrm{O}}(\{a, b\})$ and $b \notin C_{\mathrm{O}}(\{a, b\})$.

(b) If $a \succ_i b$ for some $i \in \mathrm{O}$, then $a \in C_{\mathrm{O}}(\{a, b\})$. (Non-oligarchy.)

Thus, we would like to choose a CDF such that no oligarchy exists in the organization. If there is no oligarchy, then there can be no dictator since a dictator is a one-person oligarchy. Let us define a binary relation $\succsim_{\mathrm{OC}}$ from the organization's choice function as follows:

$$a \succsim_{\mathrm{OC}} b, \quad \text{if and only if } a \in C_{\mathrm{O}}(\{a, b\}).$$

And the binary relation, $\succsim_i$, is quasi-transitive if $a \succ_i b$, $b \succ_i c$ imply $a \succ_i c$. Quasi-transitivity is implied by transitivity but not conversely, since indifference, $\sim_i$, may lack transitivity. Given these definitions the following impossibility result holds (see Sen, 1977).

Impossibility theorem 2. There is no CDF such that $\succsim_{\mathrm{OC}}$ is quasi-transitive and satisfies assumptions U, IIA, P, and NO.

This theorem forces us to conclude that while a collective decision functional may be found which avoids a dictatorship, it cannot avoid an oligarchy. This is a mild improvement.

Suppose that another reasonable restriction is added to the collective decision functional. If $a \in C_{\mathrm{O}}(\{a, b\})$ and one member changes his preferences so that a is now more desirable (in relation to b), then not only should a continue to belong to the choice set of $\{a, b\}$ but it must be that b is not in this choice set (if ever it was). The CDF must be responsive in a positive fashion.

Assumption PR. If (1) $\succsim_i = \succsim_i^*$ for all $i \in N$ except $j \in N$; (2) either ($b \succ_j a$ and $a \sim_j^* b$) or ($a \sim_j b$ and $a \succ_j^* b$); and (3) $a \in C_{\mathrm{O}}(\{a, b\})$, then $a \in C_{\mathrm{O}}^*(\{a, b\})$ and $b \notin C_{\mathrm{O}}^*(\{a, b\})$.

This additional restriction brings back the dictator (see Mas-Colell and Sonnenschein, 1972).

Impossibility theorem 3. If $\mathscr{A}$ contains at least three alternatives, then there is no CDF such that $\succsim_{\mathrm{OC}}$ is quasi-transitive and satisfies assumptions U, IIA, P, PR, and ND.

It appears that an impossibility theorem of the above variety cannot be evaded by reformulation of the aggregation procedure itself. One or more of the assumptions U, O, IIA, P, ND, NO, and PR must be dropped as unrealistic if the organization is to find a collective choice rule or collective decision functional which performs satisfactorily. The following chapter discusses the strengths and weaknesses of each of these assumptions.

Alternatives may be distinguished not only by what physical goods or services are involved but also by the natural circumstances which occur. The members of an organization may differ in their opinions about alternatives, not only in their preferences for the commodities but also in their beliefs about the likelihood of the uncertain natural events. In what follows the problem of aggregating opinions will be studied with emphasis on differing beliefs about uncertainty.

Let the state of nature be specified by an element of a set

$$S = \{s_1, s_2, ..., s_m\}.$$

A collection of states from S, $E \subseteq S$, is called an event. If the true state of nature lies in E, then the event E occurs. Beliefs about the relative likelihood of events may be specified by a binary relation on the collection of all events. If individual i feels that event E_1 is at least as likely to occur as event E_2, this will be expressed as

$$E_1 \succsim_i^{\mathcal{L}} E_2.$$

The qualitative likelihood of events may be expressed in a quantitative fashion using probabilities. Let P_j^i be a non-negative number representing the ith individual's view of the probability of state s_j. These probabilities are assumed to be normalized so that $\Sigma_{j=1}^m P_j^i = 1$. The probability of an event E occurring is computed as the sum of the probability of the states in E:

$$P^i(E) = \sum_{j \in (s_j \in E)} P_j^i.$$

The probability vector $P^i = (P_1^i, ..., P_m^i)$ and the qualitative likelihood ordering of events are compatible with each other when

$$E_1 \succsim_i^{\mathcal{L}} E_2, \quad \text{if and only if } P^i(E_1) \geqslant P^i(E_2).$$

For example, for $S = \{1, 2, 3\}$ the probability vector

$$P^i = (1/6, 1/3, 1/2)$$

is compatible with the likelihood ordering given in table 15.1

Table 15.1

E_1 \ E_2	{1}	{2}	{3}	{1, 2}	{1, 3}	{2, 3}	{1, 2, 3}
{1}	$\sim_i^{\mathcal{L}}$						
{2}	$\succ_i^{\mathcal{L}}$	$\sim_i^{\mathcal{L}}$					
{3}	$\succ_i^{\mathcal{L}}$	$\succ_i^{\mathcal{L}}$	$\sim_i^{\mathcal{L}}$				
{1, 2}	$\succ_i^{\mathcal{L}}$	$\succ_i^{\mathcal{L}}$	$\sim_i^{\mathcal{L}}$	$\sim_i^{\mathcal{L}}$			
{1, 3}	$\succ_i^{\mathcal{L}}$	$\succ_i^{\mathcal{L}}$	$\succ_i^{\mathcal{L}}$	$\succ_i^{\mathcal{L}}$	$\sim_i^{\mathcal{L}}$		
{2, 3}	$\succ_i^{\mathcal{L}}$	$\succ_i^{\mathcal{L}}$	$\succ_i^{\mathcal{L}}$	$\succ_i^{\mathcal{L}}$	$\succ_i^{\mathcal{L}}$	$\sim_i^{\mathcal{L}}$	
{1, 2, 3}	$\succ_i^{\mathcal{L}}$	$\succ_i^{\mathcal{L}}$	$\succ_i^{\mathcal{L}}$	$\succ_i^{\mathcal{L}}$	$\succ_i^{\mathcal{L}}$	$\succ_i^{\mathcal{L}}$	$\sim_i^{\mathcal{L}}$

The probability vector is not always unique. $\overline{P}^i = (1/8, 3/8, 1/2)$ and $\overline{\overline{P}}^i = (1/10, 4/10, 1/2)$ also are compatible with the likelihoods given in table 15.1. In Chapter 6 above, the conditions on the qualitative beliefs that imply a unique representation were given.

Suppose that all the organization's members agree on the desirability of the physical commodities involved in the resource allocation problem, but have differing views on the qualitative likelihood of events. The organization must reach some consensus on the likelihood based upon its members' beliefs. The assumptions that one finds reasonable about aggregation of preferences may not be so reasonable when interpreted in this uncertainty situation. For example, if one individual is a recognized expert in forecasting the state of nature, the imposition of his beliefs on the organization may not be viewed as ethically unattractive. The assumption of independence of irrelevant alternatives is based upon a choice function which does not really make sense in this context. $C(S, \succsim^{\mathcal{L}})$ contains the most likely states of nature, not the chosen states of nature.

As a result there are many aggregation procedures which seem reasonable if there is agreement on preferences and disagreement of probabilistic beliefs. One such procedure is called opinion pooling and has an interpretation as a dialogue between members (see DeGroot, 1974). Suppose each person has opinions about the capabilities of the other individuals as probability assessors. Let c_{ij} be the ith person's view of the capability of person j as a probability assessor, $0 \leqslant c_{ij} \leqslant 1$, $\Sigma_{j \in N} c_{ij} = 1$. Let P^i_k be the ith person's belief about the probability of state s_k, $0 \leqslant P^i_k \leqslant 1$, $\Sigma^m_{k=1} P^i_k = 1$. The beliefs of the group are stored in a matrix P

whose ith row is the probability distribution of person i. When individual i observes the matrix P, he modifies his own beliefs according to the probabilities of others and the relative capability of others as evaluators. This is done simultaneously by all members so that the resulting probabilistic beliefs are CP. The dialogue between probability evaluators can be represented by a simple system of difference equations relating last stages evaluation to the current probability assessment:

$$P_s = CP_{s-1}$$

If the original probabilistic beliefs were P, then the solution of the dialogue is

$$P_s = C \dots CP = C^s P.$$

When at least one person is respected by all others as a probability evaluator ($c_{ij} > 0$ for all $i \in N$) the dialogue converges to a consensus.

Theorem 15.1. If $(c_{1k}, c_{2k}, \dots, c_{nk}) > 0$ for some k, then P_s converges to a matrix P^* whose rows are identical and equal to wP, where w is a unique vector of non-negative weights which satisfies

$$w = wC$$

and

$$\sum_{i \in N} w_i = 1.$$

Proof. The consensus will be achieved if C^s converges to a matrix whose rows all equal w. Let $\max_s$ and $\min_s$ be the maximum and minimum elements of the jth column of C^s, denoted $C^s(j)$. Let $0 \leqslant \epsilon \leqslant \frac{1}{2}$ be the minimum element of C. The objective is to show that

$$\max_s \geqslant \max_{s+1}, \tag{15.1}$$

$$\min_s \leqslant \min_{s+1}, \tag{15.2}$$

$$\max_{s+1} - \min_{s+1} \leqslant (1 - 2\epsilon)(\max_s - \min_s). \tag{15.3}$$

This clearly implies that the elements in the jth column of C^s converge to identical values, say w_j.

Let x be a vector obtained from $C^s(j)$ by replacing all elements by $\max_s$ except one element whose value is $\min_s$. Clearly,

$$C^s(j) \leqslant x.$$

Each component of Cx is of the form

$$a_i \min_s + (1 - a_i) \max_s,$$

where $a_i \geqslant \epsilon$. Since C is non-negative,

$$C\,C^s(j) = C^{s+1}(j) \leqslant Cx.$$

Therefore it must be true that

$$\max_{s+1} \leqslant \epsilon \min_s + (1 - \epsilon) \max_s. \tag{15.4}$$

Let y be a vector obtained from $C^s(j)$ by replacing all elements by $\min_s$ except one element whose value is $\max_s$. By analogous reasoning to the above

$$\min_{s+1} \geqslant \epsilon \max_s + (1 - \epsilon) \min_s. \tag{15.5}$$

Clearly, (15.4) and (15.5) imply (15.1) and (15.2). Combining (15.4) and (15.5) gives (15.3). One can conclude that C^s converges to a matrix of the form

$$\begin{bmatrix} 1 \\ \vdots \\ 1 \end{bmatrix} w,$$

where w is non-negative and positive in at least its kth component, and C^sP converges to $[1...1]'\ wP = P^*$. Since C^s approached $[1...1]'w$, so does $C^{s+1} = C^sC$. Hence $[1...1]'w = [1...1]'wC$. Pre-multiplying by $(1/n)\,[1 ... 1]$ gives $w = wC$. ■

This proposition implies that the dialogue is equivalent to an opinion pool whose weights are determined by the eigenvector of the evaluation matrix C. The group comes to a consensus on weights by solving for w and then uses this to average out the beliefs of the members.

Having established a consensus on probabilities, the group selects an activity which maximizes the expected utility using the common utility and consensus probabilities. The action selected will be efficient for the following reason. Suppose that a is chosen using the consensus probability, but a' is an alternative with higher expected utility for all the members,

$$\sum_{s \in S} U(a', s)P^i_s > \sum_{s \in S} U(a, s)P^i_s.$$

Multiplying these inequalities by w_i and summing across i gives:

$$\sum_{s \in S} U(a', s)\left(\sum_{i \in N} w_i P^i_s\right) > \sum_{s \in S} U(a, s)\left(\sum_{i \in N} w_i P^i_s\right).$$

But this contradicts the optimality of a for the consensus probability distribution $(\Sigma_i w_i P^i_s)_{s \in S}$.

The opinion pooling does not have to deal with conflicting preferences. Hylland and Zeckhauser (1979) have shown that the simultaneous aggregation of utilities and probabilities will not always lead to efficient group decisions. Before stating a general result, let us explore an example developed by Zeckhauser. Suppose there are two states so that the probability distribution is defined by the probability of state 1, P^i_1. In fig. 15.2 the ith member's utility for an action a is exhibited by connecting the points $(0, U^i(a, s_2))$ and $(1, U^i(a, s_1))$ by a straight line. If the probability of state 1 is P^i_1, then expected utility is $P^i_1(U^i(a, s_1) - U^i(a, s_2)) + U^i(a, s_2)$ which is the height of the line above the value P^i_1. Suppose that the organization must choose between a and an alternative which has zero utility for all members. Fig. 15.3 indicates the tastes and beliefs of two members. Both individuals find that activity a has positive expected utility, at points A and B, and would both prefer this alternative to the zero utility activity. However, if opinion pooling was used, as discussed above, the consensus probability of state 1 would be a weighted average of P^1_1 and P^2_1. If the weights were such that the con-

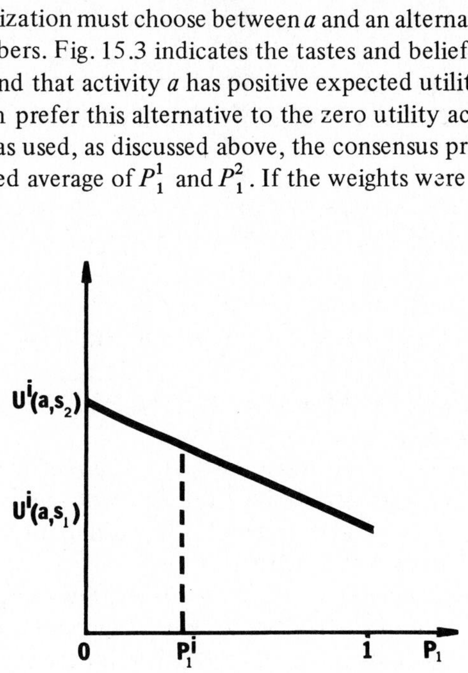

Figure 15.2

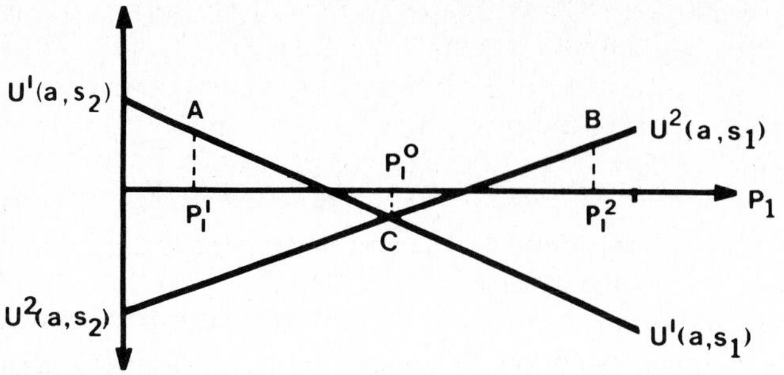

Figure 15.3

sensus was P_1^0, then both individuals would feel that activity *a* has negative utility and would choose the alternative which is inefficient. This type of inefficiency is possible even when the aggregation procedure is not an opinion pool.

Zeckhauser makes the following assumptions about the procedure in which the group makes decisions.

Assumption U. There exists a non-empty choice set for all probability and utility profiles $(P^1, ..., P^n, U^1, ..., U^n)$.

Assumption AP. There exists an aggregated probability distribution, P^0, which is a function only of individual probability distributions: $P^0 = f(P^1, ..., P^n)$.

Assumption AU. There exists an aggregated utility function, $U^0(a, s)$, which is a function only of individual utility functions: $U^0 = g(U^1, ..., U^n)$.

Assumption BGD. The choice set is a function only of P^0 and $U^0(a, s)$ and is a subset of the optimal Bayesian group decision,

$$B(P^0, U^0) = \{a \in \mathscr{A} \mid \sum_{s \in S} U^0(a, s)P^0_s \geqslant \sum_{s \in S} U^0(a', s)P^0_s \text{ for all } a' \in \mathscr{A}\}.$$

Assumption P. Elements in the choice set are efficient: if for some $a' \in \mathscr{A}$,

$$\sum_{s \in S} U^i(a, s)P^i_s < \sum_{s \in S} U^i(a', s)P^i_s, \quad \text{for all } i,$$

then *a* cannot be chosen.

Assumption UnB. If every individual has the same probability distribution, then the group probability is identical to this: $P = f(P, P, ..., P)$.

Assumption ND. There is no probability dictator i such that $f(P^1, ..., P^n) = P^i$ for all $P^1, ..., P^n$.

While all of these conditions seem quite plausible it is impossible to find aggregation functions f and g which satisfy them all.

Theorem 15.2. There is no group decision procedure which satisfies assumptions U, AP, AU, BGD, P, UnB, and ND.

Proof. Suppose that $P^i \neq \bar{P}^i$, for all $i \in N$. It must be true that

$$f(P^1, ..., P^n) \neq f(\bar{P}^1, ..., \bar{P}^n). \tag{15.6}$$

If this was not true the following contradiction would occur. Since $P^i \neq \bar{P}^i$ there is a hyperplane with normal X^i which separates P^i and $\bar{P}^i$:

$$P^i X^i < 0 \quad \text{and} \quad \bar{P}^i X^i > 0$$

Let

$$U^i(a, s) = \begin{cases} X^i_s, & s \in S,\ a = a_1, \\ \\ 0, & s \in S,\ a \neq a_1. \end{cases}$$

When only probability distributions change the above inequalities indicate that

$$\sum_s U^i(a_1, s) P^i_s < \sum_s U^i(a, s) P^i_s, \quad \text{for all } i \text{ and all } a \neq a_1.$$

By assumption P, action a_1 cannot be chosen. If the probabilities are $\bar{P}^i$, then the above inequality implies

$$\sum_s U^i(a_1, s) \bar{P}^i_s > \sum_s U^i(a, s) \bar{P}^i_s, \quad \text{for all } i \text{ and all } a \neq a_1.$$

By assumption P no action different from a_1 will be chosen. If $f(P^1, ..., P^n) = f(\bar{P}^1, ..., \bar{P}^n)$ the BGD assumption implies that the decision with either profile must be identical. But then the choice set is empty, contradicting assumption U.

Conclusion (15.6), together with UnB, imply that the group must use the probability distribution of its members:

$$f(P^1, ..., P^n) = P^i, \quad \text{for some } i. \tag{15.7}$$

This must be true since the converse is that $f(P^1, ..., P^n) \neq P^i$ for all i and from (15.6) we have

$$f(f(P^1, ..., P^n), ..., f(P^1, ..., P^n)) \neq f(P^1, ..., P^n),$$

but this is a direct contradiction of UnB.

Conclusion (15.7) implies that someone is decisive for a particular profile. It will be shown that the same individual is decisive no matter what the profile. Let this individual be member 1 without loss of generality. From eq. (15.7) it is clear that

$$f(P^1, P, ..., P) \in \{P^1, P\}.$$

Suppose $f(P^1, P, ..., P) = P$; by eq. (15.6) $f(P, P^1, ..., P^1) \neq f(P^1, P, ..., P) = P$. Hence, $f(P, P^1, ..., P^1) = P^1$.

If $P \neq P^1$, $P^1 \neq P^2$, ..., $P^1 \neq P^n$, then eq. (15.6) implies

$$f(P, P^1, ..., P^1) \neq f(P^1, ..., P^n),$$

but this contradicts the decisiveness of individual 1 in situation $P^1, ..., P^n$. Hence, $f(P^1, P, ..., P) = P^1$. That is to say, if all others agree, no matter what they agree upon, only individual 1's probability will be used. Suppose that member 1 is not decisive when the profile is $\bar{P}^1, ..., \bar{P}^n$, that is,

$$f(\bar{P}^1, ..., \bar{P}^n) \neq \bar{P}^1.$$

The profiles $(f(\bar{P}^1, ..., \bar{P}^n), P, ..., P)$ and $(\bar{P}^1, ..., \bar{P}^n)$ are different in all components for some P and hence

$$f(f(\bar{P}^1, ..., \bar{P}^n), P, ..., P) \neq f(\bar{P}^1, ..., \bar{P}^n).$$

But this contradicts the previous result. The first person is a probability dictator. ■

One way to interpret the result is to say that it implies that the group should not be restricted to act in a Bayesian fashion with separate probabilities and utilities. Alternatively, it might be pointed out that the contradiction occurs because the individuals have failed to reach a consensus on probabilities. The dialogue developed by DeGroot (1974), is based on the assumption that the individuals try to modify their beliefs by exchanging information. If differences occur because of variations in historical perspectives rather than innate disagreements, then perhaps the assumption U is too stringent.

CHAPTER 16

ALTERNATIVE REQUIREMENTS OF FORMAL ORGANIZATION

The impossibility theorems of the previous chapter show the difficulty in reconciling simple design criteria for formal organizational decision-making. In this chapter we explore the robustness of these negative results to variations in the specific requirements. The formal organization should be decisive and perhaps the impossibilities can be avoided by a weaker version of condition O. Non-dictatorship might be prevented by delegating authority to individuals, but this leads to conflicts with the efficiency criteria of Pareto's principle. The universal applicability of the decision mechanism may be too much to ask, especially if there are preconceived ideas about the types of opinions which must be reconciled. Finally, the independence from irrelevant alternatives prevents the use of information about the intensity of opinion in the formal decision process.

An organization ought to be able to make a choice in most simple situations. When the alternatives are unbounded the agenda may be too large to admit a best selection; for *i* the group has a sequence of projects, each slightly more profitable than the next, and a best project simply may not exist. However, it would not be too much to expect of any decision-maker that he be able to select a best activity from a finite collection of potential activities. We will say that a decision-making agent is *decisive* if for any finite set of alternatives, $A = \{a_1, ..., a_\ell\}$, the choice set $C(A, \succsim)$ is not empty.

If the organization has preferences, $\succsim_O$, defined on the set of all alternatives, $\mathscr{A}$, what does the assumption of decisiveness imply about these preferences? First, his preferences must be a reflexive ordering over $\mathscr{A}$. If it is not true that $a \succsim_O a$ for some $a \in \mathscr{A}$, then $a \notin C(\{a\}, \succsim_O)$ since it is not true that a is at least as preferable as all elements of $\{a\}$. Second, the preferences must be complete. If there are two distinct elements, $a, b \in \mathscr{A}$, such that neither $a \succsim_O b$ nor $b \succsim_O a$, then $C(\{a, b\}, \succsim_O)$ is empty. Clearly $a \notin C(\{a, b\}, \succsim_O)$ since $b \in \{a, b\}$ and it is not true that $a \succsim_O b$. Similarly, $b \notin C(\{a, b\}, \succsim_O)$. Third, it *cannot* be said that decisiveness implies transitivity, or even quasi-transitivity of $\succsim_O$. The preference relation over $\{a, b, c\}$, given by $a \succ_O b$, $b \succ_O c$, and $a \sim_O c$, is an example of a non-quasi-transitive (and hence non-transitive) ordering. Yet the choice set is always non-empty. We need only check that $a \in C(\{a, b, c\}, \succsim_O)$ (since $a \succ_O b$ implies $a \succsim_O b$ and $a \sim_O c$ implies $a \succsim_O c$, it is clear that a is a best element of $\{a, b, c\}$). Hence, decisiveness does not imply complete transitivity or quasi-transitivity of $\succsim_O$. It is true, however, that either of these two assumptions guarantee decisiveness in combination with completeness and reflexivity.

Theorem 16.1. If $\succsim_O$ is a complete, reflexive, quasi-transitive relation on $\mathscr{A}$, then the organization is decisive.

Proof. By reflexivity $C(\{a_1\},, \succsim_O) \neq \varnothing$. Assume that the theorem is true for ℓ alternatives and show that it must be true for $\ell + 1$ alternatives. By assumption there is an $a \in \{a_1, ..., a_\ell\}$ such that $a \succsim_O a_i$, $i = 1, ..., \ell$. Assume that $a_{\ell+1}$ is added to this set of alternatives and that the theorem is false. That is, there is no $a' \in \{a_1, ..., a_\ell, a_{\ell+1}\}$ such that $a' \succsim_O a_i$, $i = 1, ..., \ell + 1$. By completeness either $a \succsim_O a_{\ell+1}$ or $a_{\ell+1} \succsim_O a$; $a \succsim_O a_{\ell+1}$ is impossible since then $a' = a$ violates assumption. Therefore $a_{\ell+1} \succ_O a$. Reflexivity implies $a_{\ell+1} \succsim_O a_{\ell+1}$. It cannot be that $a_i \succ_O a_{\ell+1}$, for any $i = 1, ..., \ell$, since by quasi-transitivity this would imply $a_i \succ_O a$, contradicting the definition of a. Hence, $a_{\ell+1} \succsim_O a_i$, $i = 1, ..., \ell + 1$, contradicting the non-existence of a'. Hence, there must exist a best choice from any set of $\ell + 1$ alternatives which by the principle of induction proves the theorem. ∎

Corollary 16.1. If $\succsim_O$ is a complete, reflexive, transitive relation on $\mathscr{A}$, then the organization is decisive.

This follows immediately from the fact that transitivity implies quasi-transitivity.

What exactly is implied by decisiveness? A necessary and sufficient condition of decisiveness, given reflexivity and completeness, is acyclicity.

Definition (Acyclicity). The relation $\succsim_O$ is acyclical over $\mathscr{A}$ if and only if for all $a_1, ..., a_k \in \mathscr{A}$:

$$a_1 \succ_O a_2 \succ_O ... \succ_O a_k \text{ implies } a_1 \succsim_O a_k.$$

Theorem 16.2. If $\succsim_O$ is reflexive and complete, then a necessary and sufficient condition for organizational decisiveness is that $\succsim_O$ be acyclical over $\mathscr{A}$.

Proof. If $\succsim_O$ is not acyclical then there exists a finite number of alternatives such that $a_1 \succ_O a_2 \succ_O ... \succ_O a_k$ and $a_k \succ_O a_1$. This implies that

$C(\{a_1, ..., a_k\}, \succsim_O)$ is empty since $a_i \notin C(\{a_1 ..., a_k\}, \succsim_O)$ for any $i = 1, ..., k$ by the fact that $(i \geqslant 2)\, a_{i-1} \succ_O a_i$ and $(i = 1)\, a_k \succ_O a_1$. Suppose the decision-maker is decisive and let $a_1 \in C(\{a_1 ..., a_k\}, \succsim_O)$ by reindexing alternatives. If it is also true that $a_1 \succ_O a_2 \succ_O a_2 \succ_O a_3 \succ_O ... \succ_O a_k$, it cannot be that $a_k \succ_O a_1$ since a_1 is best. Hence $a_1 \succsim_O a_k$, which was to be shown. ■

Acyclicity, in conjunction with completeness and reflexivity is therefore the exact analog of decisiveness with respect to preference relations.

Transitivity implies quasi-transitivity implies acyclicity but not conversely. Therefore, if we want the organization always to have the capability of making a choice from a finite set of alternatives it is only necessary to assume that the underlying relation is acyclical, although quasi-transitivity or transitivity would be nice additional properties. Are there any reasons for thinking that such additional restrictions on the preferences are not only nice by also appealing? Decisiveness does not (by the above) provide such an argument. However, suppose that we want a decisive decision-maker to satisfy the following property (see Sen, 1970a, 1977):

Property β. If $a, b \in C(A_1)$ and $A_2 \supset A_1$, then $a \in C(A_2)$ if and only if $b \in C(A_2)$.

This property might have the following interpretation. If a thirsty man thinks a glass of lemonade and a glass of orange juice are the best citrus drinks he can select, then when we give him the choice of not only citrus drinks but soft drinks and he thinks lemonade is still best, he should also think that orange juice is best in this expanded set of alternatives. If this property is appealing, then transitivity must be appealing according to the following result (see Sen, 1970a).

Theorem 16.3. If an organization is decisive and satisfies property β then its preferences must be transitive.

Proof. Assume $C(A, \succsim_O)$ is non-empty for all A, and β holds but $\succsim_O$ is not transitive; the following contradiction occurs. Suppose that the violation of transitivity is

$$a \succsim_O b, \qquad b \succsim_O c, \qquad c \succ_O a.$$

Suppose first that $a \succ_O b$. Since $c \succ_O a$ it must be that $c \succsim_O b$, otherwise $C(\{a, b, c\}, \succsim_O)$ is empty. By assumption, $b \succsim_O c$ so $b \sim_O c$, and $C(\{b, c\}, \succsim_O) = \{b, c\}$. Also, $c \in C(\{a, b, c\}, \succsim_O)$ since $c \succsim_O c$, $c \succ_O a$, and $c \sim_O b$. However, $b \notin C(\{a, b, c\}, \succsim_O)$ since $a \succ_O b$, and β is contradicted. Hence, it must be that $a \sim_O b$, so that $C(\{a, b\}, \succsim_O) = \{a, b\}$ and $b \in C(\{a, b, c\}, \succsim_O)$ since $b \succsim_O b$, $b \sim_O a$, and $b \succsim_O c$. However, $a \notin C(\{a, b, c\}, \succsim_O)$ since $c \succ_O a$ and this contradicts β. Since neither $a \succ_O b$ nor $a \sim_O b$, the assumed violation of transitivity cannot occur.

The organization has a collective choice rule which generates an organizational preference relation from a profile of preference orderings. The impossibility theorem 1 of chapter 15 shows that any CCR which satisfies U, IIA, P, and ND must generate a non-transitive or non-reflexive or non-complete organizational preference relation. If the organization is to be a decisive decision-maker, then the organizational preferences must complete, reflexive, and acyclical. It is hard to construct a cogent argument against reflexivity. When reflexivity is violated, the organization may be unable to make a decision even when there is but one alternative. We should not confuse this with the situation where only one alternative is "explicitly" considered but a *status quo* alternative is "implicitly" hiding in the background. In that case "no decision" is actually a choice of the *status quo* as the best alternative.

Only a slightly stronger case might be made that the completeness component of organizational rationality is too stringent. The Pareto rule for determining organizational preferences ($a \succsim_O b$ if and only if $a \succsim_i b$ for all $i \in N$) has a long history in welfare economics. If the members of the organization are decisive, then $\succsim_O$ will be reflexive and transitive but not necessarily complete using only the Pareto rule.

Suppose there are three alternatives, a, b, and c, with the following interpretations: a represents a situation where workers have high wages and management has few perquisites; b represents a situation where workers have low wages and managers have many perquisites; and c represents a situation where workers are without jobs and managers are without perquisites. The Pareto rule would clearly rank $a \succsim_O c$ and $b \succsim_O c$, but a and b are not comparable by this rule. If workers and managers face the agenda $[a, b, c]$ using only the Pareto rule, no decision can be made. While it may seem reasonable to make decisions only when unanimity occurs, this example indicates that the rule may leave the organization helplessly deadlocked in even simple situations. Completeness is a very attractive assumption.

Formally, the organization could permit a certain amount of ambiguity by declaring that all Pareto-efficient alternatives will be viewed indifferently. This approach, called the Pareto-extension rule, defines organizational preferences by $a \succsim_O b$ if and only if either $a \succsim_i b$, $= 1, \ldots, n$, or there exist $j, k \in N$ such that $a \succsim_j b$ and $b \succsim_k a$.

It has been shown by Sen (1970a) that the Pareto-extension rule is the unique collective choice rule which satisfies reflexivity, quasi-transitivity and completeness of organizational preferences, anonymity (labelling of members is inconsequential), and assumptions U, IIA, and P*.

Organizational decisiveness also requires that the collective choice rule produce an acyclical organizational preference relation. It is clear from the above that this is less stringent than full transitivity. As a result the impossibility theorem 1 does not deny that an organizationally decisive collective choice rule does not exist. In fact, the Pareto-extension rule satisfies all the conditions of that theorem. However, it is not clear that by itself acyclicity is perfectly satisfactory. If the organization also wants its decision process to satisfy reasonable properties like β, then nothing short of full transitivity will do. If one wants to split the difference and guarantee only quasi-transitivity, then conditions like positive responsiveness (PR) cannot be satisfied.

In conclusion, the requirement of decisiveness of organizational decision-making is weaker than the requirement of complete, reflexive, transitive organizational preferences. This permits the existence of non-dictatorial collective choice rules which satisfy unrestricted domain, independence of irrelevant alternatives, the Pareto principle, and organizational decisiveness. However, organizational decisiveness by itself is a rather weak requirement. If other additional properties are desired, like property β or condition PR, we cannot escape the negative results of the impossibility theorems.

One argument for complete transitivity is that it guarantees that choice from any agenda is not influenced by the order in which the items are taken up. This last condition has been called *path independence* and defined by

$$C(A_1 \cup A_2, \succsim_O) = C(C(A_1, \succsim_O) \cup C(A_2, \succsim_O), \succsim_O).$$

While transitivity is strong enough to guarantee path independence, it is not equivalent. If $a \sim_O b$, $b \sim_O c$, and $a \succ_O c$, transitivity is violated, yet decisions are independent of paths:

$$C(C(\{a, b\}, \succsim_O) \cup C(\{b, c\}, \succsim_O), \succsim_O)$$
$$= C(\{a, b\} \cup \{b, c\}, \succsim_O) = \{a\}.$$

However, replacing transitivity by the weaker path independence does not eliminate the problems summarized in the impossibility theorems. In particular, the only place transitivity of $\succsim_O$ was used in lemma 1 was to guarantee that $a \succ_O b$ and $b \succ_O c$ imply that $a \succ_O c$. This is also guaranteed by path independence as follows. From path independence and $a \succ_O b$, $b \succ_O c$, it is true that

$$C(C(\{a, b\}, \succsim_O) \cup C(\{b, c\}, \succsim_O), \succsim_O) = C(\{a\} \cup \{b\}, \succsim_O)$$
$$= \{a\} = C(\{a, b, c\}, \succsim_O).$$

Hence, $a \succsim_O c$. If $a \sim_O c$, then by path independence it must hold that

$$C(C(\{a, c\}, \succsim_O) \cup C(\{a, b\}, \succsim_O), \succsim_O) = C(\{a, c\} \cup \{a\}, \succsim_O)$$
$$= \{a, c\} = C(\{a, b, c\}, \succsim_O),$$

but this contradicts the previous equation. Hence, $a \succ_O c$, and the basic lemma of the impossibility is true when path independence replaces transitivity.

The indecisiveness of "committee" decision-making provides a rationale for centralizing all decision-making power in the hands of one individual or establishing formal areas of responsibility so that authority may be easily delegated. Why should the non-dictatorship criteria be applied to private organizations which cannot compel individuals to become members? If the alternatives include the enlistment of members, then the conclusion of lemma 2 implies a dictator must exist if the other criteria are to be satisfied. An individual who can unilaterally determine the activities within the organization will also be determinant on enlistment issues as well.

Might not zones of responsibilities be delegated to individuals, thus providing some degree of autonomy for each member of the organization? Gibbard (1974) points out that the delegation of authority must be done with care in order to prevent internal inconsistencies. For example, suppose the alternatives in $\mathscr{A}$ consist of the specification of outcomes on distinct issues; the element a is a vector

$$a = (a_1, ..., a_\ell),$$

whose hth component determines the choice on issue h from a set $\mathscr{A}_h$. The set of alternatives is the Cartesian product $\mathscr{A} = \mathscr{A}_1 \times ... \times \mathscr{A}_\ell$. One can delegate authority by allowing each member to hold precedence in deciding an issue.

Condition D1. For each individual $i \in N$ there is an issue j such that when a and $\bar{a}$ differ only on issue j ($a_h = \bar{a}_h$ for $h \neq j$), then the CCR makes individual i's preferences determinant ($a \succ_i \bar{a}$ implies $a \succ_O \bar{a}$).

The problem with such a delegation of authority is that the organization may be indecisive if there are no restrictions on the domain of the CCR. Specifically, let individual i be delegated the authority to decide issue i, and let

$$\mathscr{A}_i = \{a_{i1}, a_{i2}\}.$$

Since any individual preference orderings are permitted, assume the preferences of the first two members are

$$(a_{11}, a_{22}) \succ_1 (a_{12}, a_{21}) \succ_1 (a_{11}, a_{21}) \succ_1 (a_{12}, a_{22})$$

and

$$(a_{12}, a_{22}) \succ_2 (a_{11}, a_{21}) \succ_2 (a_{12}, a_{21}) \succ_2 (a_{11}, a_{22}).$$

By the delegation condition D1, and preferences of the members, the organizational ranking must satisfy

$$(a_{11}, a_{22}) \succ_O (a_{12}, a_{22}), \qquad i = 1\text{'s authority};$$
$$(a_{12}, a_{22}) \succ_O (a_{12}, a_{21}), \qquad i = 2\text{'s authority};$$
$$(a_{12}, a_{21}) \succ_O (a_{11}, a_{21}), \qquad i = 1\text{'s authority};$$
$$(a_{11}, a_{21}) \succ_O (a_{11}, a_{22}), \qquad i = 2\text{'s authority};$$

which contradicts acyclicity and implies that the organization is indecisive.

In this example person 2's ranking of a_{21} and a_{22} depends crucially on the outcome chosen on issue 1. When member 1 chooses a_{11}, the second member would like to choose a_{21}, but when member 1 chooses a_{12}, the second member desires a_{22}. Gibbard (1974) shows that if the ranking by the members of their issues are unconditional (person 1 unconditionally prefers a_{11} to a_{12}), then the delegation of authority is internally consistent.

However, Sen (1970b) has shown that internally consistent delegation of authority may still create problems if the Pareto principle is also imposed. Suppose that at least two alternatives are delegated to each member and that member is the determining factor in the organizational ranking of those alternatives.

Condition D2. For each member $i \in N$, there exists a pair of alternatives, $a_i, \bar{a}_i$, so that i is determinant over $\{a_i, \bar{a}_i\}$ (if $a_i \succ_i \bar{a}_i$, then $a_i \succ_O \bar{a}_i$).

For example, let $a_1, \bar{a}_1, a_2$, and $\bar{a}_2$ be four distinct alternatives delegated to members 1 and 2, as in condition D2, and suppose the preferences are

$$\bar{a}_2 \succ_1 a_1 \succ_1 \bar{a}_1 \succ_1 a_2$$

and

$$\bar{a}_1 \succ_2 a_2 \succ_2 \bar{a}_2 \succ_2 a_1.$$

Using the delegation of authority we can conclude that the organizational ranking must satisfy

$$a_1 \succ_O \bar{a}_1 \quad \text{and} \quad a_2 \succ_O \bar{a}_2 .$$

This produces no inconsistency, but the Pareto principle and unanimous desire for $\bar{a}_2$ over a_1 and $\bar{a}_1$ over a_2 implies that the organizational ranking must also satisfy

$$\bar{a}_2 \succ_O a_1 \quad \text{and} \quad \bar{a}_1 \succ_O a_2 .$$

This gives the cycle $a_1 \succ_O \bar{a}_1 \succ_O a_2 \succ_O \bar{a}_2 \succ_O a_1$ and the organization is indecisive.

Gibbard (1974) points out that an individual who is delegated the authority to choose between two alternatives may not want to enforce his ranking if he anticipates that the Pareto principle and authority of others would lead to a final outcome which is unacceptable. In the above illustration, member 1 might reason as follows: "Were I to exert my authority to eliminate $\bar{a}_1$ as a possible choice, then since we both agree that $\bar{a}_2$ is preferable to a_1 the final choice would fall into the realm of member 2's authority and he would choose a_2, the alternative that I dislike the most." If delegated authority is alienable, the first member might consider revoking his power to choose from the set $\{a_1, \bar{a}_1\}$. Gibbard goes on to show that there exist delegations of authority combined with revocation rules which provide some autonomy for each member without conflicting with the Pareto principle. Kelly (1976) has pointed out that the reasoning used by member 1 requires not only information about the preferences of others, but also beliefs about the use of authority by others. If person 1 is considering renouncing his authority, is not person 2 facing a similar dilemma? This interdependence makes the Gibbard system less practicable than even the heavy informational requirements would seem to imply.

Sen (1976) argues forcefully that the line of reasoning which Gibbard uses does not necessarily lead to the renunciation of authority. For example, suppose that we interpret the four alternatives as follows:

a_1 = {buy machine; no advertisements},

$\bar{a}_1$ = {lease machine; no advertisements},

a_2 = {no machine; newspaper advertisements},

$\bar{a}_2$ = {no machine; television advertisements}.

The delegation of authority given above might be because member 1 is the purchasing agent while member 2 is the marketing agent. The conflict between delegated authority and the Pareto principle is because the purchasing agent has stronger preferences for the form of advertisement than for alternative financial arrangements for capital expenditure which are naturally in the purchasing agent's sphere of authority. Rather than renounce authority in the sphere of authority, the purchasing agent may choose not to insist that his preferences *vis-à-vis* advertisement count toward a Pareto improvement. Sen defines a conditional version of the Pareto principle where only a subrelation of the individual preferences are used in judging unanimity. In this example, the purchasing and marketing agent may choose to use the preferences

$$\bar{a}_2 \sim_1 a_1 \succ_1 \bar{a}_1 \sim_1 a_2$$

and

$$a_1 \sim_2 a_2 \succ_2 a_2 \sim_2 a_1$$

when considering the Pareto principle.

Problems of coherent organizational decision-making are the partial result of the wide range of opinions that must be reconciled. If the group had preferences that exhibited harmony, then the difficulties are not insurmountable. Consider the following modification of the unrestricted domain assumption.

Assumption I. The domain of the collective choice rule is the set of all logically possible preference ordering profiles such that at least $n/2 + 1$ of the members have identical preferences (Identical majority preferences).

Clearly, the majority voting rule is a CCR which satisfies assumptions I, O, P, IIA, and ND of chapter 15. The majority of members are unanimous in their beliefs and their rationality translates into the group's decisiveness. An assumption such as I is very strong since it requires the membership of the organization to have great similarity. While it may be unacceptable it does suggest that some weaker form of similarity might eliminate the conflicts between the other conditions in the impossibility theorems.

Black (1958) suggested that rather than require that a majority of the membership hold identical beliefs, it might be more reasonable to assume that all members have roughly similar preferences defined by a condition called "single peaked utilities". A collection of utility functions $U_1, ..., U_m$ (with domains equal to the real numbers) are single-peaked if the graph of each U_i is unimodal. Fig. 16.1 shows three single-peaked functions. There is no presumption that the location

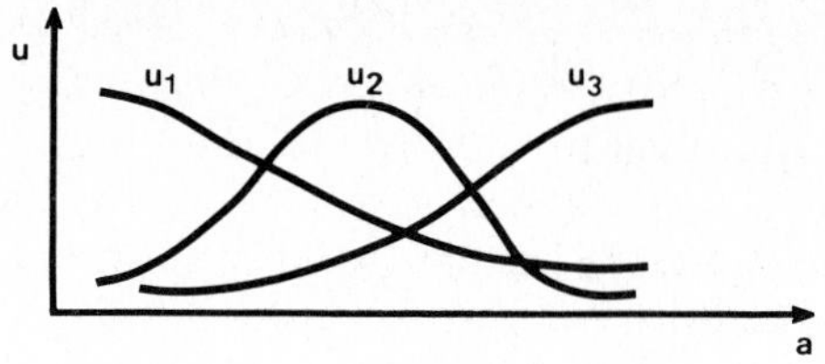

Figure 16.1

or height of the peaks of the utility function are in any way related. Arrow (1951a) uses Black's idea to define single-peaked preference orderings (as opposed to utility functions). Sen (1970a) provides a more general analysis of the concept of similarity of preferences.

Single peakedness basically assumes that individuals agree that some particular alternative is not the worst in the comparison of any triple (a, b, c). Alternative formulations of similarity of preferences would have the members agreeing that one alternative is not medium or not best. An individual i is concerned about alternatives $A \subseteq \mathscr{A}$ if he is not indifferent between every pair of elements in A.

Definition (Value restriction). In any triple (a, b, c) there is some alternative, say a, such that all the concerned individuals agree that a is not worst or agree that a is not best or agree that a is not medium.

If it is assumed that the membership is value restricted but otherwise holds general preferences, then it can be shown that majority voting is a CDF which satisfies quasi-transitive $\succsim_{\mathrm{OC}}$, IIA, P, and ND. Value restriction does not require that all triples lead to the same restricted preference; some triples may be single-peaked, others not medium or none worst.

Theorem 16.4. If individual preferences satisfy value restriction but are otherwise unrestricted, then the method of majority decision on a finite set of alternatives produces a quasi-transitive $\succsim_{\mathrm{OC}}$ and satisfies P, IIA, and ND.

Proof. It is easy to see that majority voting satisfies assumptions P, IIA, and ND. It must be shown that value restriction of preferences leads to quasi-transitive choice. To simplify the exposition it will be assumed that all individuals agree that a is not worst. Other cases follow the same logic. Assume that quasi-transitivity is violated: $b \succ_{\mathrm{O}} c$, $c \succ_{\mathrm{O}} a$, and $a \succ_{\mathrm{O}} b$. This will lead to a contradiction. Since everyone agrees that a is not worst

$$b \succsim_i c \succsim_i a \Rightarrow b \sim_i c \sim_i a, \quad \text{for all } i \in N,$$

and this is exactly equivalent to

(1) not $[b \sim_i c \sim_i a] \Rightarrow [b \succsim_i c \succsim_i a]$, for all $i \in N$.
The following must hold:
(2) not $[b \succsim_i c \succsim_i a] \Rightarrow [b \succsim_i c \Rightarrow a \succ_i c]$ and $[c \succsim_i a \Rightarrow c \succ_i b]$.
Since a is not worst we can conclude that:
(3) $[b \succ_i c \Rightarrow a \succ_i c]$, using (1) and (2);
(4) $[b \sim_i c \Rightarrow a \succsim_i c]$, since $c \succ_i a$ implies not $[b \sim_i c \sim_i a]$ and this leads to a contradiction in (1) and (2);
(5) $[c \succ_i a \Rightarrow c \succ_i b]$, using (1) and (2);
(6) $[c \sim_i a \Rightarrow c \succsim_i b]$, since $b \succ_i c$ implies not $[b \sim_i c \sim_i a]$ and a contradiction of (1) and (2).

Since the number of people who prefer b to c is at most the number of people who prefer a to c, using (3) and (4):

(7) $b \succsim_O c \Rightarrow a \succsim_O c$.
By similar reasoning, (5) and (6) imply:
(8) $c \succsim_O a \Rightarrow c \succsim_O b$.
If $b \succsim_O c$ and $c \succsim_O a$, then by (7) $c \sim_O a$, and by (8) $c \sim_O b$. Therefore,
(9) $[b \succsim_O c, c \succsim_O a, a \succsim_O b] \Rightarrow [b \sim_O c \sim_O a]$.

But by assumption $[b \succ_O c$, $c \succ_O a$, and $a \succ_O b]$ and this implies (by (9)) a contradiction. ■

Actually, it has been shown by Sen (1970a) that value restriction is a significant enough weakening of the domain restriction so that a whole class of collective choice rules will produce quasi-transitive organizational preferences; majority voting is just one example.

Theorem 16.5. If individual preferences are value restricted over a triple of alternatives but otherwise unrestricted, then any CCR which satisfies assumptions P, IIA, ND, and PR does not depend on the labelling of alternatives (neutrality) and which produces a complete ordering $\succsim_O$ is quasi-transitive over the triple.

As a result of this theorem, two-thirds majority voting, representative democracy, and many other CCR will produce organizational orderings if preferences are value restricted.

These conclusions are only partially satisfactory since organizational preferences are transitive only over strict preferences (quasi-transitive). To get full transitivity of majority voting with value restricted preferences it seems to be necessary to assume that the organization has an odd number of members. For example, suppose there are three alternatives, a, b, and c, and two members. Suppose the preferences are $a \succ_1 b \succ_1 c$ and $b \succ_2 c \succ_2 a$. Since both individuals agree that b is not worst, these preferences are similar according to value restriction. Majority voting gives organizational preferences $a \sim_O b$, $b \succ_O c$, and $a \sim_O c$, which contradicts complete (but not quasi-) transitivity. If n is made odd by dropping a member from the decision-making group or perhaps by allowing a member to vote twice when the number of voters is even, then transitivity will be guaranteed. However, the resulting organizational preferences will depend on who is dropped or double counted and therefore such a procedure may be unacceptable.

Sen and Pattanaik (1969) have proposed another restriction of preferences which does not correspond in general to the concept of similarity.

Definition (Extremal restriction). If for any ordered triple (a, b, c) there is some member $i \in N$ with preferences $a \succ_i b \succ_i c$, then another individual $j \in N$ regards c as uniquely best if and only if he regards a as uniquely worst ($c \succ_j a$ implies $c \succ_j b \succ_j a$).

Extremal restriction of preference profiles covers many cases. For example, if there is someone with preferences $a \succ_i b \succ_i c$ and no other member strictly prefers c to a, then extremal restrictions are satisfied. Suppose that if i has the preferences $a \succ_i b \succ_i c$, and everyone else either agrees with this ordering or holds the opposite opinion ($c \succ_j b \succ_j a$), this, too, satisfies extremal restriction. This restriction therefore permits highly similar or highly dissimilar preferences.

There are preference profiles which satisfy value restriction but not extremal restriction, and conversely. For example, take the following two profiles of a three-member organization:

$$\succsim \; = (a \succ_1 b \succ_1 c, c \succ_2 b \succ_2 a, b \succ_3 c \succ_3 a)$$

and

$$\succsim^* = (a \succ_1^* b \succ_1^* c, b \succ_2^* c \sim_2^* a, c \sim_3^* a \succ_3^* b).$$

Profile $\succsim$ satisfies value restriction since everyone agrees that b is not worst, but it does not satisfy extremal restriction since member 1 ranks $a \succ_1 b \succ_1 c$ and member 3 thinks a is worst without thinking c is best. Profile $\succsim^*$ satisfies extremal restriction since no member thinks that a is uniquely worst or c uniquely best, but it does not satisfy value restriction since members do not agree that any element is not worst or not best or not medium.

Extremal restriction of preference profiles is sufficient to guarantee that majority preferences are fully transitive.

Theorem 16.6. If preference profiles are extremal restricted but otherwise unrestricted, then the majority method is a CCR which satisfies assumptions O, IIA, P, and ND.

Proof. If every individual is indifferent between at least one pair of alternatives, then ER holds trivially. This case implies that individuals have one of seven possible preference orderings.

(1) $a \succ_i b \sim_i c$,
(2) $a \sim_i b \succ_i c$,
(3) $b \succ_i c \sim_i a$,
(4) $b \sim_i c \succ_i a$,
(5) $c \succ_i a \sim_i b$,
(6) $c \sim_i a \succ_i b$,
(7) $a \sim_i b \sim_i c$.

Suppose that majority voting leads to a violation of transitivity $a \succsim_O b, b \succsim_O c$, and $c \succ_O a$. If $N(1)$ denotes the number of people who have preferences (1) above, etc., then this non-transitivity implies

$$N(1)+N(6) \geqslant N(3)+N(4),$$
$$N(2)+N(3) \geqslant N(5)+N(6),$$

and

$$N(4)+N(5) \succ N(1)+N(2).$$

The first two inequalities imply that

$$N(1)+N(2) \geqslant N(4)+N(5),$$

which contradicts the third. Hence, if everyone has some indifference majority, voting is transitive.

Next, suppose that for some individual $a \succ_i b \succ_i c$ and ER holds but $a \succsim_O b$, $b \succsim_O c$, and $c \succ_O a$. Since $c \succ_O a$, it must be that

$$N(c \succ a) \succ N(a \succ c).$$

But $N(a \succ c) \geqslant 1$ since person i holds that opinion and hence there exists at least one individual who strictly prefers c to a. By ER that person j must have $c \succ_j b \succ_j a$. Applying ER to person j implies that all individuals have preferences that are one of four orderings:

$$(8)\quad a \succ_i b \succ_i c,$$

$$(9)\quad c \succ_i b \succ_i a,$$

$$(10)\quad b \succ_i c \sim_i a,$$

$$(11)\quad a \sim_i c \succ_i b.$$

The violation of transitivity implies that

$$N(8) + N(11) \geqslant N(9) + N(10),$$

$$N(8) + N(10) \geqslant N(9) + N(11),$$

and

$$N(9) \succ N(8).$$

However, the first two inequalities imply that $N(8) \geqslant N(9)$, a contradiction. Hence non-transitive majority voting is impossible when preferences are extremal restricted. ∎

In summary, the organization which is confident that the membership will hold similar views about the relative rankings of group activities can find collective choice rules which are non-dictatorial, satisfy the Pareto principle, have independence of irrelevant alternatives, and which produce rational organizational decisions. In particular, various voting procedures like majority rule will satisfy these criteria. If the organization does not want to treat every member on an equal basis, some members can be given multiple votes, allowing them to exert proportionately more influence on the outcome.

Does the assumption of similar tastes, even in the form of value or extremal restrictions, seem to be realistic? This depends on the manner in which membership positions are filled from the general population of natural agents. If there is no realistic way that the organization can restrict membership, it may appear that even the weak similarity assumptions may be unrealistic (see, however, Arrow, 1951a, pp. 81–86, for a discussion of this issue). For example, a local government consists of members who live within prescribed geographical boundaries and there may be no way the government can restrict free mobility into the area. On the other hand, many production and consumption organizations (such as a corporation, law partnership, or country club) are able to screen potential members and attempt to accept only those individuals whose preferences lie in prescribed realms.

The concept of screening has received a great deal of attention recently by economists interested in the problems of information (see Arrow, 1973; Stiglitz, 1975; Spence, 1974; and Riley, 1979). The basic problem facing the organization is as follows. A potential member of the decision-making body has preferences which may or may not be similar to those of current members. Because of strategic misrepresentations, it is difficult to be certain that any characteristic of the individual is actually a good indicator of similarity. Some individual characteristics are unalterable – age, performance on tests of ability, criminal records, etc. – but many characteristics may be modified by the individual – education, past occupation, style of dress, etc. The organization will make inferences about preference patterns based on all observed characteristics, but since some characteristics are alterable, it would be expected that individuals will modify these, given the costs of modification, to suit their desires. The organization is in an informational equilibrium when the empirically observed relationship between characteristics and preferences just matches the inferred relationship of the organization. It is easy to show that some potentially useful characteristics may not contribute to the prediction of preferences because the manipulative behavior of individuals makes all individuals indistinguishable. That is to say, screening may be a most difficult job due to the ability of individuals to disguise their true preferences.

Example. Let p be an index of a law student's congruence of preferences with those of the members of a law firm. Suppose that the personal cost of obtaining a high score on the bar exam is related to the score and the parameter p according to the function

$$c = s\, p^{\gamma},$$

where γ is a constant and s is the score on the bar exam. The law firm finds that by varying its salary offer according to the bar exam score it will attract different types of lawyers. Let us suppose that a lawyer's effectiveness depends on how he fits into the decision-making system of the firm. A large congruence parameter means that valuable time is saved in reaching decisions. Assume that the savings in profits from efficient decision-making is

$$\pi = \beta\, p,$$

where β is a positive constant. The competitive pressure of other law firms forces the firm to pay a salary bonus which just matches the profit savings. Since only s is observable directly, the bonus depends only on the bar exam score, $b(s)$. The law students realize that bonuses are obtained from high performance on the exam. They maximize the net benefits of performing well on the bar exam, $b(s) - c$, by choosing s (assuming that s can be increased by exertion and study). The optimal choice of s is characterized by

$$b'(s) = p^{\gamma}, \tag{16.1}$$

and

$$b''(s) \leqslant 0. \tag{16.2}$$

The market will reach an equilibrium if these conditions hold for all p along with the condition that

$$b(s) = \beta p. \tag{16.3}$$

The solution of (16.1) and (16.3) is

$$b(s) = (k + s\,\beta^{-\gamma}\,(1 - \alpha))^{1/(1-\gamma)},$$

where k is an arbitrary constant of integration. However, this will not satisfy the second-order condition (16.2) if $\gamma \geqslant 0$. That is, if a larger degree of congruence implies that the cost of scoring well on the bar exam is larger, the students will not study for the exam. The score on the exam will not serve as a proxy for preference congruence and the firm will not offer a bonus to the high-scoring law students. Notice that the bonus schedule is not unique because of the arbitrary constant k. The firm is indifferent to changes in k because it is forced by competitive pressure to pay each lawyer his marginal profitability irrespective of the bonus level. On the other hand, all the lawyers are made better off by a decrease in k. This follows from the assumption that the bonuses given by (16.3) are independent of k, but the optimal response to a lower k is to cut back on s and save personal costs of preparing to score well on the bar exam. ■

Independence of irrelevant alternatives simultaneously removes all collective choice rules which rank two alternatives by comparing them to bench-mark (but irrelevant) alternatives, and prevents numerical aggregation of utility indicators. The first point is clear but the second is not so obvious. Suppose that there are two alternatives, a and b, and two members. If each member i has a utility function U_i, then one method of ranking alternatives is based on the Benthamite sum of individual utilities:

$$a \succsim_O b, \quad \text{if and only if } U_1(a) + U_2(a) \geqslant U_1(b) + U_2(b),$$
$$b \succsim_O a, \quad \text{if and only if } U_1(a) + U_2(a) \leqslant U_1(b) + U_2(b).$$

Suppose the members have utility functions which satisfy the following inequalities:

$$0 \leqslant U_1(b) - U_1(a) \leqslant U_2(a) - U_2(b).$$

The organization will then find a at least as preferable as b using the Benthamite rule. Now suppose that member 1 changes his utility indicator by multiplying both $U_1(a)$ and $U_1(b)$ by a large positive number. This does not change the ranking of a and b for member 1 and independence of irrelevant alternatives would imply no change in the organization's choice between a and b. However, the second inequality above may be violated by this multiplicative change in utility indicator and the organizational choice would be from a to b. Although no irrelevant alternative has been considered, the Benthamite rule violates condition IIA. Similar constructions could be made for any utility aggregating rule.

Most economists take the position that interpersonal comparisons of utility indicators are not meaningful. Two reasons are given. First, the measurability of individual well-being by a unique numerical indicator does not follow from acceptable axioms. Even under the axiomatic approach to preference under risk developed by Von Neumann and Morgenstern (1944), the utility indicator has arbitrary zero point and unit scale. In more general situations any monotonic increasing transformation of the indicator is an equally good representation of tastes. Second, even if individuals have unique cardinal utility functions, it requires unacceptable value judgements to suppose that personal capacities for satisfaction can be compared.

More cogent arguments have been given for collective choice rules which violate IIA without presuming cardinal utility. Borda (see Black, 1958) proposed a rank-order method of collective choice which is used frequently in clubs. If there are a finite number of alternatives, the members give their most desirable alternative a preassigned weight w_1, their next most desirable alternative a weight w_2, $w_2 < w_1$, etc. After adding the weights assigned to each alternative by the members, the alternative with the highest total weighting is chosen. This collective choice rule satisfies assumptions U, R, P, and ND but not assumption IIA. To see this suppose there are four alternatives, a, b, c, and d, and three members with the preferences

$$a \succ_1 b \succ_1 c \succ_1 d,$$
$$a \succ_2 b \succ_2 c \succ_2 d,$$
$$c \succ_3 d \succ_3 a \succ_3 b.$$

If the preassigned weights are $w_1 = 4$, $w_2 = 3$, $w_3 = 2$, and $w_4 = 1$, then the Borda rank-order rule produces total weights as follows: *a* has 10, *b* has 7, *c* has 8, and *d* has 5. Given these alternatives and rankings the organizational choice would be alternative *a*. Now suppose alternative *b* is infeasible so that it is dropped from the list and rank-ordering is done for the three alternatives, *a*, *c*, and *d*, with weights $w_1 = 3$, $w_2 = 2$, and $w_3 = 1$. The total weights are: *a* has 7, *c* has 7, and *d* has 4. By dropping alternative *b*, alternative *a* is no longer the most desired organizational activity; alternative *c* is equally good. Assumption IIA has been violated. This seems to be a highly undesirable result. In the above example, dropping alternative *b*, which is uniformly inferior to alternative *a*, could lead to the organization switching its choice from *a* to *c*. Any collective choice rule which violates independence of irrelevant alternatives will on occasion produce perverse decisions, as illustrated above. Without IIA, the agenda of the organization plays an important role in actual decision-making.

CHAPTER 17

EXPEDIENCE AND INCENTIVES

An organizational decision-making system which is designed to work well when individuals act in an honest, ethical fashion may be highly susceptible to manipulation by knowledgeable, self-interested individuals. In fact, it will be shown below that *all* systems are open to possible manipulation. To motivate this result we will show examples of how rank-order voting, majority voting, market exchange of private property, determination of quantities of public goods, and the determination of optimal output of a two-division firm with cost interdependence can be influenced by the participants to their advantage.

Vickery (1960) objected to collective choice rules which violate assumption IIA because such CCRs permit a certain amount of non-ordinal intensity of preference to influence the organization's choice. Since intensity is a purely subjective concept, an individual may find it in his self-interest to misrepresent his preferences in a strategic attempt to manipulate the organization. As an example, suppose that the organization has four possible alternatives, a, b, c and d, and three members with preferences

$$a \succ_1 b \succ_1 c \succ_1 d,$$
$$a \succ_2 b \succ_2 c \succ_2 d,$$
$$b \succ_3 a \succ_3 c \succ_3 d.$$

Using rank-ordering with weights 4, 3, 2, and 1, the alternatives a, b, c, and d total weights 11, 10, 6, and 3, respectively. However, member 3 might notice that by misrepresenting his preferences (by announcing that alternative a is the worst rather than second best) he may manipulate the organizational decision. Suppose member 3 announces the strategically misrepresented preference ordering

$$b \overset{*}{\succ}_3 c \overset{*}{\succ}_3 d \overset{*}{\succ}_3 a.$$

The rank-ordering rule with preferences $(\succsim_1, \succsim_2, \overset{*}{\succsim}_3)$ results in total weights for alternatives *a*, *b*, *c*, and *d* of 9, 10, 7, and 4. The organization would choose alternative *b* if member 3 misrepresents his tastes as above. Chapter 15 above shows formally that any collective choice rule which produces unique decisions and violates assumption IIA will be susceptible to such strategic misrepresentations. Moreover, assumptions U, P, and IIA seem to be sufficient to guarantee that a collective choice rule is immune to strategic manipulation by individuals.

Just because a collective decision rule is susceptible theoretically to strategic manipulation does not imply that it can always be manipulated. In the above example, player 3 had to know the preferences of the other members over all alternatives in order to successfully manipulate the organizational decisions. If in fact member 3 thought the preferences were as above but in fact they were

$$a \succ_1 c \succ_1 b \succ_1 d,$$
$$a \succ_2 c \succ_2 b \succ_2 d,$$

then the misrepresented preferences $\overset{*}{\succ}_3$ might lead to an organizational choice of alternative *c* which is not only less desirable than *b* but also less desirable than *a* which would have been chosen if member 3 was honest. Loosely speaking, if the number of alternatives is large or if the number of members is large and have unknown preferences, it will be difficult for any individual to effect a desirable manipulation of the decision rule by strategically misrepresenting his tastes.

Suppose that an organization consisting of 3 members, $i = 1,2,3$, must choose the color of the walls, white, blue, or green, using majority rule with the following agenda. First determine whether white or blue should be eliminated and second determine whether green is superior to the first choice. Suppose that the members rank the colors in the following fashion:

$$\text{green} \succ_1 \text{blue} \succ_1 \text{white},$$
$$\text{white} \succ_2 \text{blue} \succ_2 \text{green},$$
$$\text{blue} \succ_3 \text{green} \succ_3 \text{white}.$$

The decision procedure will eliminate white in the first vote and in the second stage will select blue over green.

The first member desires green walls more than he desires blue walls but can do nothing to effect this, once the choice is down to these two alternatives. However, if member 1 knows the preferences of $i = 2, 3$, he will be able to calculate that green is more popular than white. Is there any way he can manipulate the decision procedure so that the final choice is between green and white? If he is willing to deceive his colleagues, yes. Suppose that member 1 votes according to the preferences

$$\text{green} \succ_1^* \text{white} \succ_1^* \text{blue}.$$

The change in ranking of white and blue makes just enough difference to switch the decision at the first stage, eliminating blue. At the second stage green is selected over white, improving member 1's position.

Hurwicz (1972) has given the following example to show that even markets for exchange of private property are susceptible to undetectable manipulation. Suppose there are two private goods, x and y, which are desired by two individuals, 1 and 2. The first individual begins with 1 unit of x and 0 units of y and desires x and y according to the utility function

$$U_1(x, y) = x^{1/2} y^{1/2}.$$

Similarly, the second individual begins with 0 units of x and 1 unit of y and desires x and y according to the utility function

$$U_2(x, y) = x^{1/2} y^{1/2}.$$

The competitive equilibrium is a pair of prices (P_x, P_y) and an allocation $\{(x_1, y_1), (x_2, y_2)\}$ such that

$$\begin{aligned}
&x_1, y_1 \text{ maximizes } U_1(x_1, y_1) \\
&\text{subject to } P_{x1} + P_{y1} \leqslant P_x \cdot 1, \\
&x_2 y_2 \text{ maximizes } U_2(x_2, y_1) \\
&\text{subject to } P_x x_2 + P_y y_2 \leqslant P_y \cdot 1,
\end{aligned}$$

and $x_1 + x_2 = 1, y_1 + y_2 = 1$

The extreme symmetry of this problem leads to a simple determination of equilibrium: $P_x = P_y$, $x_1 = 1/2 = x_2$, $y_1 = 1/2 = y_2$. The equilibrium allocation is the exact center of the Edgeworth box in fig. 17.1.

Suppose that the first individual knows the preferences of the second individual, and can calculate that for positive prices the demands for x_2 and y_2 as a function of prices are

$$x_2 = 1/2(P_y/P_x),\ y_2 = 1/2.$$

If individual i can manipulate the relative price P_y/P_x below 1, then he will be able to obtain a larger share of x than the 1/2 unit he gets from the competitive equilibrium above. One way of doing this is to exaggerate his desires for x and drive P_x up by pretending that this preferences are

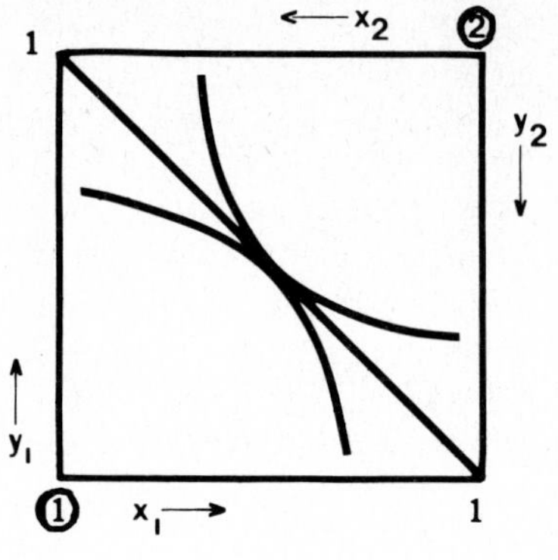

Figure 17.1

$$U_1^*(x, y) = x^\alpha y^{1-\alpha}, \ 1/2 < \alpha < 1.$$

When these are the preferences, the demand for x and y by individual 1 would be

$$x_1 = \alpha, \ y_1 = (1 - \alpha)(P_x/P_y).$$

The market clears at relative prices

$$(P_y/P_x) = 2(1 - \alpha) < 1, \ \text{if } \alpha > 1/2.$$

The first individual's final consumption is

$$x_1 = \alpha > 1/2, \ y_1 = 1/2,$$

which is more desirable than the honest equilibrium consumption $x_1 = 1/2$, $y_1 = 1/2$. This improvement comes about without changing the form of the utility function but merely by adjusting the parameters.

Ledyard and Roberts (1974) have modified Hurwicz's argument to show that economies with public goods are also open to deception, even when full "free riding" is not optimal. Suppose there is a private good x and a public good z and two consumers, 1 and 2, who each have 1 unit of the private good. The private good may be transformed into public good according to the production relation $x + z \leqslant 0$. The preferences of both consumers are identical and given by

$$U_i(x, z) = \begin{cases} x + z, & \text{if } x \geqslant z, \\ \frac{1}{2}(3x + z), & \text{if } x \leqslant z. \end{cases}$$

An allocation specifies values for x_1, x_2, and z. The collection of allocations which are efficient and which improve upon the endowment is the union of the two sets:

$$E_1 = \{(x_1, x_2, z) \geqslant 0 \mid x_1 + x_2 + z = 2,\ x_1 = z, \tfrac{4}{10} \leqslant x_2 \leqslant \tfrac{2}{3}\},$$

$$E_2 = \{(x_1, x_2, z) \geqslant 0 \mid x_1 + x_2 + z = 2,\ x_2 = z, \tfrac{4}{10} \geqslant x_1 \leqslant \tfrac{2}{3}\}.$$

If the procedure for allocating resources selects an allocation in $E_1 \cup E_2$, then the procedure can be manipulated by one of the individuals. For example, suppose that the allocation procedure would lead to the allocation $(x_1\ x_2, z) = (\frac{2}{3}, \frac{2}{3}, \frac{2}{3})$ which belongs to both E_1 and E_2. If individual 1 were to misstate his preferences as

$$U_1^*(x, z) = \tfrac{1}{2}(3x + z), \qquad \text{for all } x, z,$$

then the set of efficient allocations which improves upon the endowment is

$$E_3 = \{(x_1, x_2, z) \mid x_1 + x_2 + z = 2, x_2 = z, \tfrac{4}{5} \leqslant x_1 \leqslant 1\}.$$

The worst situation in E_3 for individual 1 would be $(x_1, x_2, z) = (\frac{4}{5}, \frac{3}{5}, \frac{3}{5})$. However, the true evaluation,

$$U_1(\tfrac{2}{3}, \tfrac{2}{3}) = \tfrac{4}{3} \leqslant U_1(\tfrac{4}{5}, \tfrac{3}{5}) = \tfrac{7}{5},$$

implies the first individual is better-off by claiming his preferences are U_1^* rather than U_1. Individual 1 only has to give up $\frac{1}{5}$ (rather than $\frac{1}{3}$) of his private good in order to get $\frac{3}{5}$ units public goods (rather than $\frac{2}{3}$) because the other individual has a strong preference for public goods.

Groves (1976) has shown that when an enterprise consists of several autonomous divisions whose activities are interdependent, explicit mechanisms for achieving coordination may be manipulated to the advantage of the divisional decision-makers. The following example illustrates his point. Suppose a firm consists of two divisions, 1 and 2. The output and input of division i are denoted y_i and x_i. In addition z is a variable representing a productive activity of division 1 which damages the second division. Let us assume that the relationship between outputs, inputs, and externality is:

$$y_i = \sqrt{x_i}\, z^{\beta_i},\ 0 < \beta_1 < 1 \text{ and } -1 < \beta_2 < 0.$$

All other things being equal, division 1 would like a large z and division 2 would like a small z. Let us assume that the price of output is 1 and the price of input i is w_i. The organization would like to maximize total profits by selection of y_1, y_2, x_1, x_2, z. One way to accomplish that is for each division to specify how its profits are related to the external variable, z, and then maximize the sum of these profits by choice of z. Define the divisional profit function by

$$\pi_i(z) \equiv \max_{y_i, x_i} y_i - w_i x_i \text{ s.t. } y_i = \sqrt{x_i} z^{\beta_i}.$$

For the above technology these are

$$\pi_i(z) = z^{2\beta_i}/4w_i,\ i = 1,2.$$

The optimal level of externality is therefore,

$$z^* = \left(\frac{-\beta_2}{\beta_1}\ \frac{w_1}{w_2}\right)^{1/[2(\beta_1 - \beta_2)]}.$$

If the divisional decision-makers are paid higher salaries for higher divisional profits, there is every reason to suspect that the first divisional manager will overstate β_1 because this will increase z^*. Similarly, the second divisional manager will understate β_2 to try to lower z^*. Moreover, without detailed knowledge about w_i, the owner would not be able to ascertain whether the large profits came from deception about β_i or just unusually low factor prices.

The above examples of decision-making and deception were first put into a general form by Gibbard (1973) and Satterthwaite (1975). A game form specifies precisely one outcome for each possible selection of strategies by the members of the organization. To each individual, $i = 1, 2, ..., n$, let A_i denote a set of possible strategies which can be selected. The set of all consequences which influence individual well-being is denoted R. A *game form* is a function which assigns to each n-tuple of strategies, $a = (a_1, a_2, ... a_n)$, a unique outcome $g(a_1, a_2, ..., a_n)$ in R. It will be assumed that R is defined so that the range of g equals R. If one also specifies the preferences individuals have for the outcomes in R, then a *game* has been defined in normal form.

There are several solution concepts available from game theory. Two are of importance here. For given preferences for outcomes, $\succsim_i$, the strategy a_i^* is $\succsim_i$-*dominant* for the game form g if for all $i \in N$

$$g(a) \precsim_i g(a\, i/a_i^*), \qquad \text{for all } a \in A_1 \times \ldots \times A_n,$$

where

$$a\, i/a_i^* = (a_1, \ldots, a_{i-1}, a_i^*, a_{i+1}, \ldots, a_n).$$

For given preference profiles, the n-tuple of strategies $a^* = (a_1^*, \ldots, a_n^*)$ is a *Nash equilibrium* when for all $i \in N$

$$g(a^* i/a_i) \precsim_i g(a^*), \qquad \text{for all } a_i \in A_i.$$

Clearly, if a_i^* is $\succsim_i$-dominant, $i \in N$, then a^* is a Nash equilibrium. However, not all Nash equilibria are dominant since dominancy requires a_i^* to be attractive even when a_j^* is changed. Only some game forms have a Nash equilibrium and even then only for some given preferences and not others. A counter-example is where there are two outcomes, $R = \{0,1\}$, two individuals with two strategies each, $A_i = \{a_{i2}, a_{i2}\}$, preferences $1 \succsim_1 0$, $0 \succsim_2 1$, and game form

$$g(a_1, a_2) = \begin{cases} 1, & \text{if } (a_1 = a_{11} \text{ and } a_2 = a_{21}) \text{ or} \\ & \quad (a_1 = a_{12} \text{ and } a_2 = a_{22}), \\ 0, & \text{if } (a_1 = a_{11} \text{ and } a_2 = a_{22}) \text{ or} \\ & \quad (a_1 = a_{12} \text{ and } a_2 = a_{21}). \end{cases}$$

As a zero-sum game this would be represented by the payoff matrix

$$\begin{bmatrix} 1 & 0 \\ 0 & 1 \end{bmatrix}.$$

A game form is *straightforward* when there is a dominant strategy for each individual, no matter what the preference profile. If there was a straightforward game form, then it would be a bench-mark toward which we could look for reasonable decision systems. However, Gibbard (1973) and Satterthwaite (1975) have shown that the only game forms which are straightforward for $|R| \geqslant 3$ are dictatorial. Individual i is a dictator for game form g if for every outcome r in the range there is a strategy $a_i(r)$ for i such that $g(a) = r$ when $a_i = a_i(r)$. To every non-dictatorial game form there is a preference profile such that the strategy selected by individual i depends on the strategy used by individual j; hence, individual i is made susceptible to manipulation by person j. Further interpretation is given following a formal statement.

Theorem 17.1. (Gibbard–Satterthwaite). Every straightforward game form with at least three possible outcomes is dictatorial.

Proof. The technique of proof is to assume that g is straightforward, and construct a collective choice rule which satisfies assumptions U, O, P, and IIA. By the fundamental impossibility result, this collective choice rule must be dictatorial which implies that the game form is dictatorial.

Since g is straightforward by assumption let $\sigma_i(\succsim_i)$ be $\succsim_i$-dominant and let $\sigma(\succsim) = (\sigma_1(\succsim_1), \ldots, \sigma_n(\succsim_n))$ be the straightforward strategy for preference profile $\succsim$. For any given subset $W \subseteq R$, let us construct a new preference profile which is a strict ordering on R by raising all elements of W to the most preferred position and ranking other elements according to an arbitrary but fixed (strict) ordering $\overset{+}{\succ}$:

$$x \succsim_i^W y \text{ if } \begin{cases} x, y \in W \text{ and } x \succ_i y \text{ or} \\ \qquad x \sim_i y \text{ and } x \overset{+}{\succ} y, \\ \\ \text{or } x \in W, y \notin W, \\ \text{or } x \notin W, y \notin W, \text{ and } x \overset{+}{\succ} y. \end{cases}$$

Notice that $(\succsim_i^W)^U = \succsim_i^U$ if $U \subseteq W$.

Let us define a collective choice rule by the binary relation $x \succsim_O y$, if and only if $x = y$ or $y \neq g(\sigma(\succsim^{\{x,y\}}))$. That is, x is at least as desirable as y if $x = y$ or if y is not the outcome of the game form when the dominant strategy is used for preferences which have x and y pushed to the top. It remains to be shown that this collective choice rule satisfies transitivity of $\succsim_O$, independence of irrelevant alternatives, and the Pareto principle.

Assertion 1. The collective choice rule satisfies the Pareto principle.

Assume that $x \succ_i y$ for all i and show $x \succ_O y$. Suppose $y \succsim_O x$. There must be some strategy $a' = (a'_1, \ldots, a'_n)$ such that $x = g(a')$. Let

$$a(i) = (a'_1, \ldots, a'_i, \sigma_{i+1}(\succsim^{\{x,y\}}), \ldots, \sigma_n(\succsim^{\{x,y\}})).$$

Let j be the smallest i such that $x = g(a(i))$. Clearly, $j \leqslant n$, by the definition of a'. It must be that $g(a(j-1)) \neq x$ and $g(a(j)) = x$. But $a(j-1)$ and $a(j)$ differ only the change in the jth individual's strategy. This contradicts the assumption that $\sigma_i(\succsim^{\{x,y\}})$ is a dominant strategy. Hence $x \succ_O y$.

Assertion 2. The collective choice rule satisfies independence of irrelevant alternatives.

Let $\succsim$ and $\succsim^*$ be identical on $\bar{R} \subseteq R$. We wish to show that $\succsim_O$ and $\succsim_O^*$ are identical on $\bar{R}$. Suppose not: $x, y \in \bar{R}, x \neq y$, and $x \succsim_O y, y \succsim_O^* x$. By the definition $\succsim^{\{x,y\}}$ and the fact that $\succsim, \succsim^*$ agree on $\{x, y\} \subseteq \bar{R}$, it must be that

$$\succsim^{\{x,y\}} \equiv \succsim^{*\{x,y\}}.$$

By the property of dominant strategy it must be that

$$x = g(\sigma(\succsim^{\{x,y\}})) = g(\sigma(\succsim^{*\{x,y\}})) = y,$$

but this contradicts the assumption that x and y are distinct.

Assertion 3. The collective choice rule produces transitive organizational preferences.

The transitivity assumption, $x \succsim_O y$ and $y \succsim_O z$ implies $x \succsim_O z$, can be stated in contrapositive form as $z \succ_O x$ implies $y \succ_O x$ or $z \succ_O y$. Let us define $\succsim'$ by bringing $\{x, y, z\}$ to the top: $\succsim' = \succsim^{\{x,y,z\}}$. By a property of $\succsim^W$,

$$\succsim'^{\{x,z\}} \equiv \succsim^{\{x,z\}}.$$

It is then clear that $\succsim_O$ and $\succsim_O'$ agree with each other on $\{x, z\}$. By similar arguments they agree on $\{x, y\}$ and $\{y, z\}$. Therefore we must show that

$$z \succ_O' x \text{ implies } y \succ_O' x \text{ or } z \succ_O' y.$$

Since $z \succ_O' x$ we know that $x \neq z$. If $y = x$, then clearly $z \succ_O' y = x$, so we only need worry if $y \neq x$. Suppose $z = g(\sigma(\succsim'))$, but then $z \succ_O' y$. Suppose $z \neq g(\sigma(\succsim'))$. Since $z \succ_O' x, x \neq g(\sigma(\succsim'))$ because $z \succ_O' x$. If $w \notin \{x, y, z\}$, then $z \succ_i' w$ for all i by definition of $\succ_i'$, hence $w \neq g(\sigma(\succsim'))$. By elimination, $y = g(\sigma(\succsim'))$. But then $y \succ_O' x$, and therefore the ordering $\succsim_O$ is transitive.

The impossibility theorems of collective choice imply that $\succsim_O$ must have a dictator: there is a k such that $x \succ_k y$ implies $x \succ_O y$. We must show that k is able to dictate the outcome of the game form g. Without loss of generality, it will be assumed that the dictator is $k = 1$. If 1 is not a dictator for g, then there exists a strategy, a, such that $x \neq g(a)$ even though $x \succ_1 g(a), g(a) \succ_i x, i = 2, ..., n$, and $a_1 = \sigma_1(\succsim_1)$. However, since 1 is a dictator for $\succsim_O$,

$$x \succsim_O g(a).$$

Let $\succsim' \equiv \succsim^{\{x, g(a)\}}$. Define strategy $a(i)$ by

$$a(i) = (\sigma_1(\succsim_1'), ..., \sigma_i(\succsim_i'), a_{i+1}, ... a_n).$$

Since $g(\sigma(\succsim')) = g(a(n)) = x$ and $g(a(1)) = g(a)$, there exists a $1 \leqslant j \leqslant n$ such that

$$g(a(j)) = g(a),$$

$$g(a(j+1)) \neq g(a).$$

If $g(a(j+1)) = x, g(a) \succ_{j+1} x$ implies $g(a) \succ_{j+1}' x$. But thus contradicts the dominance of the strategy $\sigma_{j+1}(\succsim_{j+1}')$. If $g(a(j+1)) \in \{x, g(a)\}$, then by construction of $\succ_{j+1}' g(a) \succ_{j+1} g(a(j+1))$ but this implies that $\sigma_{j+1}(\succsim_{j+1}')$ does not dominate a_{j+1}. Hence it cannot be that $x \neq g(a)$. ■

The concept of a game form can be specialized to situations where strategies consists of orderings of the set of alternatives. A voting scheme is a game form v such that the set A_i of strategies for individual i is the set of all complete, reflexive, transitive orderings of a set $Z \subseteq R$. A non-dictatorial voting scheme cannot, by the above result, be straightforward. This leads to the idea that the true preferences, $\succsim_i$, may not be the preferences strategically selected by the individual i from A_i. A voting scheme v is *manipulable* if there is a preference profile which, if held by the individuals, would not be a Nash equilibrium in the voting scheme. That is, there exists $\succsim'$ such that for some k there is a $\succsim_k^*$ such that

$$v(\succsim k/\succsim_k^*) \succ_k v(\succsim).$$

Theorem 17.2. (Gibbard–Satterthwaite). Every voting scheme with at least three outcomes is either dictatorial or manipulable.

Proof. From theorem 17.1, if v is non-dictatorial, then it cannot be straightforward. If it is not straightforward then, there must exist a profile $\succsim$ such that some individual, say 1, has no $\succsim_1$-dominant strategy. In particular the strategy $a_1 = \succsim_1$, honesty, cannot be $\succsim_1$-dominant. This simply states that there is another profile $\succsim'$ such that

$$v(\succsim_1', \succsim_2', \ldots, \succsim_n') \succ_1 v(\succsim_1, \succsim_2', \ldots \succsim_n').$$

If the other agents honestly held the preferences $\succsim_2', \ldots, \succsim_n'$, then v would be susceptible to manipulation by 1 since $\succsim_1, \succsim_2', \ldots, \succsim_n'$ is not a Nash equilibrium because of $\succsim_1'$. ■

The above result does not say that all non-dictatorial voting schemes will be manipulated. It simply states that in some circumstances all such voting schemes could be manipulated. Even if the preferences were such that v is manipulable by individual k, that does not imply that k has the required knowledge to compute the strategic misrepresentation which he should make. Moreover, even if preferences were not truly such that manipulation is desirable for individual k, this does not say that he will not try to manipulate. He may have inaccurate beliefs about the other elements of the preference profile.

Blin and Satterthwaite (1977) have shown how the previous results imply that the *beliefs*, accurate or inaccurate, about the preferences profile can sometimes influence voting. Let $\succsim^B(i) = (\succsim_1^B, \ldots, \succsim_{i-1}^B, \succsim_{i+1}^B, \ldots, \succsim_n^B)$ be a profile of preferences for all members but i, which individual i believes to be the honest preferences of his colleagues. The true preferences are given by a profile $\succsim\ = (\succsim_1, \ldots, \succsim_n)$. A decision function is a mapping σ_i which for each $(\succsim_i, \succsim^B(k))$ selects a strategy from A_i. The strategy selected is denoted $a_i = \sigma_i(\succsim_i, \succsim^B(i))$. A completely described voting procedure (CDVP) is a game form g together with a decision pattern $\sigma = (\sigma_1(\succsim_1, \succsim^B(1)), \ldots, \sigma_n(\succsim_n, \succsim^B(n))$. A CDVP is *independent of beliefs* if for all $\succsim$ and all $\succsim^B(i), \succsim^{B^*}(i), i = 1, \ldots, n$,

$$\sigma_i(\succsim_i, \succsim^B(i)) = \sigma_i(\succsim_i, \succsim^{B^*}(i)).$$

That is, the choice of strategy is independent of his beliefs about the preferences held by other individuals.

The assumption of belief independence cannot be held for decision functions σ_i of a rational individual because of the previous result on straightforward game forms. If a CDVP is independent of beliefs, then

$$g(\sigma(\succsim, \succsim^B)) = g(\sigma(\succsim)) \equiv f(\succsim).$$

The previous results imply that there is a profile $\succsim$ and an individual k with $\succsim_k'$ such that

$$f(\succsim k/\succsim_k') \succ_k f(\succsim).$$

No matter what the beliefs, the individuals will calculate the strategies

$$a = \sigma(\succsim).$$

but if k were well-informed and knew $\gtrsim$, then he would know that $\sigma_k(\gtrsim_k)$ is not optimal and would prefer strategy $a_k' = \sigma_k(\gtrsim_k')$ since it improves the outcome from his vantage. Hence, rationality of k implies that he would not like a decision function which is independent of beliefs.

If results more positive than those above are to be obtained, then either the assumptions must be strengthened or the conclusions must be weakened. The work of Groves (1973), Clarke (1971), and Green and Laffont (1977) have looked at what can be obtained if the preferences of individuals are limited to the class of separable, freely transferable utilities. Hurwicz and Schmeidler (1978), Peleg (1978), and Dutta and Pattanaik (1978) have studied alternatives to the dominance requirement of straightforward game forms.

Suppose that the organization must select a project, r, from a set R. Members of the organization derive benefits from the alternative selected and from money which they receive, t_i. Rather than using binary relations to represent preferences, suppose that each individual has a separable transferable utility function

$$u_i(r, t_i) = v_i(r) + t_i.$$

The function v_i is called the valuation function of individual i and represents the individual's tastes for projects in R. Because the utility is separable the valuation of the organizational alternatives is independent of money and thus money can be used to coax honest behavior without disturbing the relative desirability of projects.

A game form in this situation is an $n + 1$-tuple of functions $(\alpha, \tau_1, ..., \tau_n)$ where $\alpha(a)$ is the alternative chosen when the strategy vector $a = (a_1, ..., a_n) \in \times_{i=1} A_i$ has been selected by the individuals and where $\tau_i(a)$ is the monetary transfer to individual i when strategy a is selected. If the strategy set A_i consists of all allowable valuation functions, then the game form is a *revelation mechanism*. If the revelation mechanism has a decision rule α which selects the project with the highest total valuation,

$$\alpha(v_1, ..., v_n) \in \left\{ r \in R \mid r \text{ maximizes } \sum_{i=1}^{n} v_i(r) \right\},$$

then we say it is a *direct revelation* mechanism.

Let $\mathscr{D}_i(v_i) \subseteq A_i$ be the set of all dominant strategies of individual i for a game form when his true valuation function is v_i. That is,

$$a_i \in \mathscr{D}_i(v_i), \text{ if and only if}$$

$$v_i(\alpha(\bar{a})) + \tau_i(\bar{a}) \leqslant v_i(\bar{a}i/a_i)) + \tau_i(\bar{a}i/a_i),$$

$$\text{for all } \bar{a} \in \mathop{\mathrm{X}}_{i=1}^{n} A_i.$$

A game form is *decisive* if and only if all individuals have a dominant strategy no matter what their true valuation function:

$$\mathscr{D}_i(v_i) \neq \varnothing, \quad \text{for all } v_i, \quad i = 1, ..., n.$$

If a revelation mechanism always has the true valuations as a dominant strategy, then it is *strongly individual incentive compatible*:

$$v_i(\alpha(w)) + \tau_i(w) \leqslant v_i(\alpha(wi/v_i)) + \tau_i(wi/v_i), \quad \text{for all } w.$$

This characteristic is essentially the same as being straightforward, only here we are dealing with revelation mechanisms which are more specific than game forms. A game form is *successful* if all dominant strategies lead to the alternative which maximizes the total organizational valuation:

$$\text{If } a_i \in \mathscr{D}_i(v_i), \ i = 1, ..., n, \text{ then}$$

$$\text{then } \alpha(a) \text{ maximizes } \sum_{i=1}^{n} v_i(x) \text{ on } X.$$

A decisive game form which is successful will be called *satisfactory*.

While there are no straightforward game forms which are non-dictatorial, it can be shown that there is an entire class of strongly individually incentive compatible relevation mechanisms. The reason the outcome has improved is that we have restricted perferences to be separable and tranferable. Without this additional assumption it would make no sense to have individuals evaluate alternatives without knowing how monetary benefits will be allocated. The class of mechanisms will be called Groves mechanisms although Clarke (1971) has independently proposed one member of this family as an attractive mechanism.

A *Groves mechanism* is a direct revelation mechanism where for valuation profile $w = (w_1, ..., w_n)$ the alternative selected is

$$\alpha^*(w) \text{ maximizes } \sum_{i=1}^{n} w_i(r) \text{ on } R,$$

and the transfer of money are given by rules of the form

$$\tau_i^*(w) = \sum_{j \neq i} w_j(\alpha^*(w)) + h_i[w_1, ..., w_{i-1}, w_{i+1}, ..., w_n].$$

The transfer consists of the reported value to all other individuals of the alternative which maximizes total valuation plus an arbitrary functional which depends on the evaluation functions of all other individuals. The idea behind the Groves mechanisms is to make impossible for individuals to increase their transfer by misstating their valuation. This mechanism is strongly individually incentive compatible, and since it is a direct revelation mechanism it is also satisfactory.

Theorem 17.3. A Groves mechanism is strongly individually incentive compatible and satisfactory.

Proof. For any allowable valuation profile w

$$v_i(\alpha^*(wi/v_i)) + \sum_{j\neq i} w_j(\alpha^*(wi/v_i)) + h_i[w_{)i(}]$$

$$- \left\{v_i(\alpha^*(w)) + \sum_{j\neq i} w_j(\alpha^*(w)) + h_i[w_{)i(}]\right\}$$

$$= v_i(\alpha^*(wi/v_i)) + \sum_{j\neq i} w_j(\alpha^*(wi/v_i)) - \left\{v_i(\alpha^*(w)) + \sum_{j\neq i} w_j(\alpha^*(w))\right\}$$

$$= \max_{r\in R} \left[v_i(r) + \sum_{j\neq i} w_j(r)\right] - \left\{v_i(\alpha^*(w)) + \sum_{j\neq i} w_j(\alpha^*(w))\right\}.$$

However, the definition of maximization implies that the first term is at least as large as the second. Therefore,

$$v_i(\alpha^*(wi/v_i)) + \tau_i^*(wi/v_i) \geqslant v_i(\alpha^*(w)) + \tau_i^*(w),$$

for all allowable w, and v_i is dominant. v_i is not the only dominant strategy since v_i + constant will also work. However, all dominant strategies lead to maximization of $\Sigma_{i=1}^n v_i(r)$ + constant which also maximizes $\Sigma_{i=1}^n v_i(r)$ and therefore a Groves mechanism is satisfactory. ■

Green and Laffont (1977) have been able to show that Groves mechanisms are the only strongly individually incentive compatible mechanisms and (up to an isomorphism) the only satisfactory mechanisms. They also show by counter-example that if separability of utility is dropped, then there does not always exist a strongly individually incentive compatible mechanism. See also Dasgupta et al. (1979) and Green and Laffont (1979).

The Groves mechanisms have the unattractive feature that there is no guarantee of balancing monetary transfers within the organization. In particular it is not true that

$$\sum_{i=1}^{n} \tau_i^* (v) = \text{constant}, \quad \text{for all } h \text{ and all } v.$$

While the Groves mechanism is successful it does not necessarily produce efficiency since some money may have to be disposed of or acquired to run the mechanism. In certain special circumstances Groves and Loeb (1975) were able to "balance the budget", but in general this is impossible. Clarke (1971) suggested selecting the functionals h_i so that

$$h_i[w_{)i(}] = -\sum_{j \neq i} w_j(r_i),$$

where r_i maximizes $\Sigma_{j \neq i} w_j(r)$ on R.

This clearly implies that $\tau_i^* (w) \leqslant 0$, so that money will be supplied by the individual to run the Groves mechanism. Groves and Ledyard (1977) have placed the entire question in a general equilibrium framework and displayed a Groves mechanism which does balance the budget, but weakens the incentive characteristic; truth is a Nash equilibrium is not a dominant strategy. Green, Kohlberg and Laffont (1976) have studied a special case of the Groves mechanisms, called pivotal Groves mechanisms, and have shown that in a stochastic sense the budget will be balanced.

To demand that a game form be straightforward is to restrict the possibilities significantly. Hurwicz and Schmeidler (1978) have defined a game form as being *acceptable* if for every preference profile there is a Nash equilibrium and every Nash equilibrium produces an outcome which is efficient. They show that for organizations with just two members only dictatorial game forms are acceptable. However, it can be shown that for $n \geqslant 3$ there do exist game forms which are acceptable if preferences are strict and weakly acceptable and if indifference is allowed.

To demonstrate the first result let us assume that $R = \{a, b\}$ and that each of the two individuals has but two strategies. There are a total of sixteen possible game forms in this situation, but if we ignore the labelling permutations of individuals, outcomes, and strategies, these can be summarized by just four matrices (person 1 selects rows and person two selects columns):

a	b
a	b

g_1

a	a
a	a

g_2

a	a
a	b

g_3

a	b
b	a

g_4

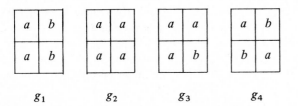

Game form g_1 gives individual 2 dictatorial power; game form g_2 would not produce efficiency if both individuals preferred b to a. For game g_3, if $b \succ_1 a$ and $b \succ_2 a$, then the top left-hand corner is a Nash equilibrium but is not efficient. Finally, if $a \succ_1 b$ and $b \succ_2 a$, then there is no Nash equilibrium in g_4.

When there are three or more individuals, acceptable game forms *do* exist for strict preference orderings. Again let us assume that there are two alternatives and two strategies for each of the three individuals. There are $2^8 = 256$ game forms possible. A game form can be represented here by two 2 x 2 matrices: player 1 controls rows, player 2 controls columns, and player 3 controls which matrix is used. Consider the following game form:

a	a
b	b

a	b
a	b

This game form is called "the kingmaker" since individual 3 can give either of the other two individuals the power to select the outcome: if he takes the left strategy, individual 1 is "king", and if he takes the right strategy, individual 2 is "king". The game form is not dictatorial since neither 1 nor 2 can have power without member 3 approving, and once the power is granted member 3 has no control. Moreover, every Nash equilibrium is efficient. Suppose the equilibrium strategy is (top, left, left). Clearly $a \succ_1 b$ or this would not be an equilibrium for individual 1 (who is the king). Hence, there is no element in R which is at least as preferable as a to all, and strictly more preferable than a for one individual. Clearly, for each strict preference profile a Nash equilibrium exists since the kingmaker can select the individual $i = 1, 2$ who has his preferences; or if neither do, then either will lead to an equilibrium. These results can be easily extended to more than 3 individuals if preferences are strict.

The kingmaker game form is not symmetric across individuals. One individual gets to be the kingmaker. Hurwicz and Schmeidler (1978) show that there are game forms which are acceptable and symmetric across individuals. In fact, there are essentially two:

b	a
a	a

a	a
a	b

and

a	b
b	b

b	b
b	a

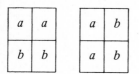

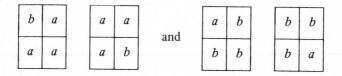

This result shows that majority voting is not acceptable since its game form is

a	*a*
a	*b*

a	*b*
b	*b*

The problem with majority voting is that if everyone preferred *a* to *b* but voted for *b*, this strategy would be a Nash equilibrium since individual vote switching cannot be critical.

REFERENCES

Akbari, A., Hess, J., Kagiwada, H. and Kalaba, R. (1980) "The Equivalence of Team Theory's Integral Equations and a Cauchy System: Sensitivity Analysis of a Variational Problem", *Applied Mathematics and Computation*, 6, 21–36.

Akerlof, G. (1970) "The Market for Lemons", *Quarterly Journal of Economics*, 84, 488–500.

Alchian, A. and Demsetz, H. (1972) "Production, Information Costs and Economic Organization", *American Economic Review*, LXII, no. 5, 777–795.

Allais, M. (1953) "Le Comportement de l'homme Rationel Devant la Risque: Critique des Postulats de l'Ecole Americaine", *Econometrica*, 21, 503–546.

Arrow, K. (1951a) *Social Choice and Individual Values* (Yale University Press, New Haven).

Arrow, K. (1951b) "An Extension of the Basic Theorems of Classical Welfare Economics", in: J. Neyman (ed.), *Proceedings of the Second Berkeley Symposium on Mathematical Statistics and Probability* (University of California Press, Berkeley).

Arrow, K.J. (1951c) "Alternative Approaches to the Theory of Choice in Risk Taking Situations", *Econometrica*, 19, 404–437.

Arrow, K.J. (1970) "The Organization of Economic Activity: Issues Pertinent to the Choice of Market versus Non-Market Allocation", in: R. Havemen and J. Margolis (eds.), *Public Expenditures and Policy Analysis* (Markham, Chicago).

Arrow, K. (1971a) "The Role of Securities in the Optimal Allocation of Risk Bearing", in: K. Arrow (ed.), *Essays in the Theory of Risk-Bearing* (Markham, Chicago).

Arrow, K.J. (1971b) "Theory of Risk Aversion", in: K. Arrow, *Essays in the Theory of Risk-Bearing* (Markham, Chicago).

Arrow, K.J. (1973) "Higher Education as a Filter", *Journal of Public Economics*, 2, 193–216.

Arrow, K. and Hahn, F. (1972) *General Competitive Analysis* (North-Holland, Amsterdam).

Aumann, R.J. (1964) "Markets with a Continuum of Traders", *Econometrica*, 32, 39–50.

Beckmann, M. (1960) "Returns to Scale in Business Administration", *Quarterly Journal of Economics*.

Beckmann, M. (1977) "Management Production Functions and the Theory of the Firm", *Journal of Economic Theory*, 14, 1–18.

Benders, J.F. (1962) "Partitioning Procedures for Solving Mixed-Variables Programming Problems", *Nemerische Mathematik*, 4.

Bernoulli, Daniel (1730) "Exposition of a New Theory on the Measurement of Risk", reprinted in: *Econometrica*, 22 (1954), 23–26.

Black, D. (1958) *The Theory of Committees and Elections* (Cambridge University Press).

Blackwell, D. (1950) "Comparison of Experiments", in: *Proceedings of the Second Berkeley Symposium on Mathematical Statistics and Probability* (University of California Press, Berkeley).

Blin, J. and Satterthwaite, M. (1977) "On Preferences, Beliefs, and Manipulation within Voting Situations", *Econometrica*, 45, 881–887.

Calvo, G. and Wellisz, S. (1978) "Supervison, Loss of Control and the Optimum Size of the Firm", *Journal of Political Economy*, 943–952.

Clarke, E.H. (1971) "Multipart Pricing of Public Goods", *Public Choice*, 11, 17–33.

Coase, R. (1937) "The Nature of the Firm", *Economica*.

Cremer, J. (1980) "A Partial Theory of the Optimal Organization of a Bureaucracy", *Bell Journal of Economics*, 11, no. 2, 683–693.
Dantzig, G. and Wolfe, P. (1960) "Decomposition Principles for Linear Programs", *Operations Research*, 8.
Dasgupta, P.S., Hammond, P.J. and Maskin, E.S. (1979) "The Implementation of Social Choice Rules: Some General Results on Incentive Compatibility", *Review of Economic Studies*, XLVI, no. 143, 185–216.
Debreu, G. (1959) *Theory of Value* (Yale University Press, New Haven).
Debreu, G. and Scarf, H. (1963) "A Limit Theorem on the Core of an Economy", *International Economic Review*, 4, 235–246.
De Finetti, B. (1964) "Foresight: Its Logical Laws, Its Subjective Sources", in: H. Kyburg and H. Smokler (eds.), *Studies in Subjective Probability*. (John Wiley, New York).
DeGroot, M. (1970) *Optimal Statistical Decisions* (McGraw-Hill, New York).
DeGroot, M. (1974) "Reaching a Consensus", *Journal of the American Statistical Association*, 69, no. 345, 118–121.
Drèze, J.H. (1974) "Axiomatic Theories of Choice, Cardinal Utility, and Subjective Probability: A Review", in: J. Drèze (ed.), *Allocation under Uncertainty: Equilibrium and Optimality* (John Wiley, New York).
Dutta, B. and Pattanaik, P.K. (1978) "On Nicely Consistent Voting Systems", *Econometrica*, 46, 163–170.
Edgeworth, F.Y. (1881) *Mathematical Psychics*, (Kegan Paul, London).
Edwards, W. (1961) "Behavioral Decision Theory", *Annual Review of Psychology*, 12, 473–498.
Ellsberg, D. (1961) "Risk, Ambiguity and the Savage Axioms", *Quarterly Journal of Economics*, 75, 644–661.
Farrell, M.J. (1959) "The Convexity Assumption in the Theory of Competitive Markets", *Journal of Political Economy*, 377—391.
Fishburn, P.C. (1973) *The Theory of Social Choice* (Princeton University Press).
Foley, D. (1970) "Economic Equilibria with Costly Marketing", *Journal of Economic Theory*, 2, 276–291.
Geoffrion, A.M. (1972) "Generalized Benders Decomposition", *Journal of Optimization Theory and Applications*, 10, no. 4, 232–260.
Gibbard, A. (1973) "Manipulation of Voting Schemes: A General Result", *Econometrica*, 41, no. 1, 587–601.
Gibbard, A. (1974) "A Pareto Consistent Libertarian Claim", *Journal of Economic Theory*, 7, no. 4, 388–410.
Good, I.J. (1950) *Probability and the Weighing of Evidence* (Hafner, New York).
Green, J. and Laffont, J. (1977) "Characterization of Satisfactory Mechanisms for the Revelation of Preferences for Public Goods", *Econometrica*, 45, no. 2, 427–430.
Green, J. and Laffont, J. (1979) *Incentives in Public Decision-Making* (North-Holland, Amsterdam).
Green, J., Kohlberg, E. and Laffont, J. (1976) "Partial Equilibrium Approach to the Free-Rider Problem", *Journal of Public Economics*, 6, 375–394.
Groves, T. (1973) "Incentives in Teams", *Econometrica*, 41, 617–633.
Groves, T. (1976) "Information, Incentives, and the Internalization of Production Externalities", in: S. Lin (ed.), *Theory and Measurement of Economic Externalities*, (Academic Press, New York).
Groves, T. and Ledyard, J. (1977) "Optimal Allocation of Public Goods: A Solution to the Free Rider Problem", *Econometrica*, 45, 783–819.
Groves, T. and Loeb, M. (1975) "Incentives and Public Inputs", *Journal of Public Economics*, 4, 211–226.
Harris, M. and Raviv, A. (1978) "Some Results on Incentive Contracts", *American Economic Review*, 68, no. 1, 20–30.

Hart, O. (1975) "On the Optimality of Equilibrium when the Market Structure is Incomplete", *Journal of Economic Theory*, 11, 418–443.

Heal, G.M. (1973) *The Theory of Economic Planning* (North-Holland, Amsterdam).

Heller, W.P. (1972) "Transactions with Set-Up Costs", *Journal of Economic Theory*, 4, 465–478.

Hess, J. and Kalaba, R. (1978) "Direct Transformation of Variational Problems into Cauchy Systems. I. Scalar-Quadratic Case", *Journal of Optimization Theory and Applications*, 25, no. 1, 41–55.

Hildenbrand, W. (1974) *Core and Equilibria of a Large Economy* (Princeton University Press).

Hirshleifer, J. (1971) "The Private and Social Value of Information and the Reward to Inventive Activity", *American Economic Review*, 61, 561–574.

Hirschman, A.O. (1970) *Exit, Voice, and Loyalty* (Harvard University Press, Cambridge, Mass).

Holmstrom, B. (1979) "Moral Harzard and Observability", *Bell Journal of Economics*, 10, no. 1, 74–91.

Hurwicz, L. (1960) "Optimality and Informational Efficiency in Resource Allocation Processes", in: K. Arrow et al. (eds.), *Mathematical Methods in the Social Sciences* (Stanford University Press, Stanford).

Hurwicz, L. (1972) "On Informationally Decentralized Systems" in: McGuire and Radner (eds.), *Decision and Organization* (North-Holland, New York).

Hurwicz, L. (1973) "The Design of Mechanisms for Resource Allocation", *American Economic Review*, 63, no. 2, 1–30.

Hurwicz, L. and Schmeidler, D. (1978) "Construction of Outcome Functions Guaranteeing Existence and Pareto Optimality of Nash Equilibrium", *Econometrica*, 46, no. 6, 1447–1474.

Hylland, A. and Zeckhauser, R. (1979) "The Impossibility of Bayesian Group Decision Making with Separate Aggregation of Beliefs and Values", *Econometrica*, 47, no. 6, 1321–1336.

Ireland, N.J. (1977) "Ideal Prices vs. Prices vs. Quantities", *Review of Economic Studies*, XLIV (1), no. 136, 183–186.

Jensen, M.C. and Meckling, W. (1976) "Theory of the Firm: Managerial Behavior, Agency Costs and Ownership Structure", *Journal of Financial Economics*, 3, 304–360.

Johnson, N. and Kotz, S. (1972) *Distributions in Statistics: Multivariate Distributions* (John Wiley, New York).

Kahneman, D. and Tversky, A. (1979) "Prospect Theory: An Analysis of Decision Under Risk", *Econometrica*, 47, no. 2, 263–292.

Kaldor, N. (1934) "The Equilibrium of the Firm", *Economic Journal*, XLIV, 70–71.

Kelly, J. (1976) "Rights-Exercising and a Pareto Consistent Libertarian Claim", *Journal of Economic Theory*, 13, No. 1, 138–153.

Koopman, B.O. (1940) "The Axioms and Algebra of Intuitibe Probability", *Annals of Mathematics*, 41, 269–292.

Koopmans, T. (1957) *Three Essays on the State of Economic Science* (McGraw-Hill, New York).

Kurz, M. (1974) "Equilibrium with Transaction Cost and Money in a Single Market Exchange Economy", *Journal of Economic Theory*, 7, 418–452.

Laffont, J. (1975) "Optimisim and Experts against Adverse Selection in a Competitive Economy", *Journal of Economic Theory*, 10, 284–308.

Laffont, J.J. (1977) "More on Prices vs Quantities", *Review of Economic Studies*, XLIV (1), no. 136, 177–182.

Ledyard, J.O. (1971) "The Relation of Optima and Market Equilibria with Externalities", *Journal of Economic Theory*, 3, 54–65.

Ledyard, J. and Roberts, D.J. (1974) "On the Incentive Problem with Public Goods", Centre for Mathematical Studies in Economics and Management Science, D.P. no. 116, Northwestern University.

Malcomson, J.M. (1978) "Prices vs. Quantities: A Critical Note on the Use of Approximations", *Review of Economic Studies*, 45, no. 139, 203–207.
Malinvaud, E. (1967) "Decentralized Procedures for Planning", in E. Malinvaud and M.O.L. Bacharach (eds.), *Activity Analysis in the Theory of Growth and Planning* (Macmillian, New York).
Mardia, K.V. (1970) *Families of Bivariate Distributions* (Hafner Publishing, Darien, Conn.).
Marglin, S. (1974) "What do Bosses Do?", *Review of Radical Political Economy*, 6, no. 2.
Marschak, J. and Miyasawa, K. (1968) "Economic Comparability of Information Systems", *International Economic Review*, 9, 137–174.
Marschak, J. and Radner, R. (1972) *Economic Theory of Teams* (Yale University Press, New Haven).
Mas-Colell, A. and Sonnenschein, H. (1972) "General Possibility Theorem for Group Decisions", *Review of Economic Studies*, 39, 185–192.
McKenzie, L. (1981) "The Classical Theorem on Existence of Competitive Equilibrium", *Econometrica*, 49, no. 4, 819–843.
Milleron, J. (1972) "Theory of Value with Public Goods – A Survey Article", *Journal of Economic Theory*, 5, 419–477.
Mirrlees, J. (1976) "The Optimal Structure of Incentives and Authority Within an Organization", *Bell Journal of Economics*, 7, no. 1, 105–131.
Mood, A. and Graybill, F. (1963) *Introduction to the Theory of Statistics*, 2nd edn. (McGraw-Hill, New York).
Nikaido, H. (1968) *Convex Structures and Economic Theory* (Academic Press, New York).
Oniki, H. (1974) "The Cost of Communication", *Quarterly Journal of Economics*, no. 353, 529–550.
Osana, H. (1972) "Externalities and the Basic Theorems of Welfare Economics", *Journal of Economic Theory*, 4, 401–414.
Parzen, E. (1960) *Modern Probability Theory and its Applications* (John Wiley, New York).
Peleg, B. (1978) "Consistent Voting System", *Econometrica*, 46, 153–162.
Phelps, E.S., et al. (1970) *Microeconomic Foundations of Employment and Inflation Theory* (Norton, New York).
Postlewaite, A. and Roberts, D.J. (1976) "The Incentives for Price-Taking Behavior in Large Exchange Economies", *Econometrica*, 44, 115–128.
Pratt, J.W. (1964) "Risk Aversion in the Small and in the Large", *Econometrica*, 32, 122–136.
Radner, R. (1961) "The Evaluation of Information in Organizations", in: J. Neyman (ed.), *Proceedings of the Fourth Berkeley Symposium on Mathematical Statistics and Probability* (University of California Press, Berkeley).
Radner, R. (1962) "Team Decision Problems", *Annals of Mathematical Statistics*, 33, 857–881.
Radner, R. (1968) "Competitive Equilibrium Under Uncertainty", *Econometrica*, 36, 31–58.
Ramsey, F.P. (1950) *The Foundations of Mathematics and Other Logical Essays* (Humanities Press, New York).
Rapoport, A. (1970) *N-Person Game Theory* (University of Michigan Press, Ann Arbor).
Riley, J. (1979) "Informational Equilibrium", *Econometrica*, 47, 331–360.
Robertson, D.H. (1935) *Control of Industry*.
Robinson, E.A.G. (1934) "The Problem of Management and the Size of Firms", *Economic Journal*, XLIV, 240–254.
Ross, S.A. (1974) "On the Economic Theory of Agency and the Principle of Similarity", in: M. Balch, D. McFadden and S. Wu (eds.), *Essays on Economic Behavior under Uncertainty* (North-Holland, Amsterdam).
Satterthwaite, M. (1975) "Strategy-Proofness and Arrow's Conditions", *Journal of Economic Theory*, 10, no. 2, 187–217.
Savage, L.J. (1951) "The Theory of Statistical Decision", *Journal of the Americal Statistical Association*, 46, 55–67.

Savage, L.J. (1954) *The Foundations of Statistics* (John Wiley, New York).
Sen, A. (1970a) *Collective Choice and Social Welfare*, (Holden-Day, San Francisco).
Sen, A. (1970b) "The Impossibility of a Paretain Liberal", *Journal of Political Economy*, 78, no. 1, 152–157.
Sen, A. (1976) "Liberty, Unanimity and Rights", *Economica*, 43, no. 171, 217–245.
Sen, A. (1977) "Social Choice Theory: A Re-Examination", *Econometrica*, 45, no. 1, 53–89.
Sen, A.K. and Pattanaik, P.K. (1969) "Necessary and Sufficient Conditions for Rational Choice under Majority Decision", *Journal of Economic Theory*, 1, 178–202.
Shavell, S. (1979) "Risk Sharing and Incentive in the Principal and Agent Relationship", *Bell Journal of Economics*, 10, no. 1, 55–73.
Shavell, S. (1981) "On The Design of Contracts and Remedies for Breach", National Bureau of Economic Research, Working Paper no. 727; to Appear in *Quarterly Journal of Economics*.
Shavell, S. (1982) "Suit and Settlement vs. Trial: A Theoretical Analysis Under Alternative Methods for the Allocation of Legal Costs", *Journal of Legal Studies*, 11, no. 1, 55–81.
Simon, H. (1951) "A Formal Theory of the Employment Contract", *Econometrica*.
Slovic, P. and Lichtenstein, S. (1971) "Comparison of Bayesian and Regression Approaches to the Study of Information Processing in Judgement", *Organizational Behavior and Human Preference*, 6, 649–744.
Smith, A. (1776) *The Wealth of Nations*.
Spence, A.M. (1974) *Market Signalling: Informational Transfer in Hiring and Related Processes* (Harvard Univesity Press).
Speyer, J., Marcus, S. and Kranaic, J. (1980) "A Decentralized Team Decision Problem with an Exponential Cost Criterion", *IEEE Transactions on Automatic Control*, AC-25, no. 5, 919–924.
Srinivasan, V. (1981) "The Equal Commission Rate Policy for a Multi-Product Salesforce", *Management Science*, 27, no. 7, 731–756.
Starr, R. (1969) "Quasi-Equilibria in Markets with Nonconvex Preferences", *Econometrica*, 37, 25–38.
Starrett, D.A. (1972) "Fundamental Nonconconvexities in the Theory of Externalities", *Journal of Economic Theory*, 4, 180–199.
Stiglitz, J.E. (1975) "The Theory of Screening, Education and the Distribution of Income", *American Economic Review*, 65, 283–300.
Vickery, W. (1960) "Utility, Strategy, and Social Decision Rules", *Quarterly Journal of Economics*, LXXIV, 507–535.
Von Neumann, J. and Morgenstern, O. (1944) *Theory of Games and Economic Behavior* (John Wiley, New York).
Wald, A. (1945) "Statistical Decision Functions which Minimize the Maxamum Risk", *Annals of Mathematics*, 46, 265–280.
Watanabe, S. (1969) *Knowing and Guessing* (John Wiley, New York).
Weitzman, M. (1970) "Iterative Multi-Level Planning with Production Targets", *Econometrica*, 38, no. 1, 50–65.
Weitzman, M. (1974) "Prices Versus Quantities", *Review of Economic Studies*, 41, 477–491.
Williamson, O. (1967) "Hierarchical Control and Optimum Firm and Size", *Journal of Political Economy*, 75, no. 2, 123–138.
Williamson, O. (1975) *Markets and Hierarchies* (The Free Press, New York).
Williamson, O. (1980) "The Organization of Work: A Comparative Institutional Assessment", *Journal of Economic Behavior and Organization*, 1, no. 1, 5–38.
Wilson, R. (1968) "The Theory of Syndicates", *Econometrica*, 36, no. 1, 119–132.
Wilson, R. (1975) "Informational Economies of Scale", *Bell Journal of Economics*, 6, no. 1, 184–195.
Yohe, G. (1978) "Towards a General Comparison of Price Controls and Quantity Controls Under Uncertainty", *Review of Economic Studies*, XLV (2), No. 140, 229–238.

AUTHOR INDEX

SUBJECT INDEX